CW01369669

Buffy the Vampire Slayer
20 years of slaying

The Official Companions to the Show

The Watcher's Guide, Volume 1
The Watcher's Guide, Volume 2
The Watcher's Guide, Volume 3
The Monster Book
Sunnydale High Yearbook

Buffy
the Vampire Slayer
20 years of slaying

THE
WATCHER'S GUIDE
AUTHORIZED

Christopher Golden

With Jessica Smith, Nancy Holder, Jeff Mariotte, Maryelizabeth Hart, and Paul Ruditis

Simon Pulse
New York   London   Toronto   Sydney   New Delhi

First published in Great Britain in 2017 by Simon and Schuster UK Ltd
A CBS COMPANY

First published in the USA in 2017 by Simon Pulse an imprint of
Simon & Schuster Children's Publishing Division

Interior: TM & © 1998, 2000, 2004, 2017 by Twentieth Century Fox Film Corporation.
All rights reserved.

Portions of this material were previously published in *The Watcher's Guide Volumes 1-3* Cover: Buffy the Vampire Slayer TM & © 2017 by Twentieth Century Fox Film Corporation. All rights reserved. Cover illustrations by Neal Williams

Cover designed by Regina Flath
Interior designed by John Candell
The text of this book was set in Avenir, MrsEaves, and Rockwell.

This book is copyright under the Berne Convention.
No reproduction without permission.
All rights reserved.

The right of Twentieth Century Fox Film Corporation to be identified as the copyright holder of this work has been asserted by them in accordance with sections 77 and 78 of the Copyright, Design and Patents Act, 1988.

The opinions in the essays and interviews included are those of their respective authors, and not those of Twentieth Century Fox or of Simon & Schuster.

1 3 5 7 9 10 8 6 4 2

Simon & Schuster UK Ltd
1st Floor, 222 Gray's Inn Road
London
WC1X 8HB

www.simonandschuster.co.uk

Simon & Schuster Australia, Sydney
Simon & Schuster India, New Delhi

A CIP catalogue record for this book is available from the British Library.

HB ISBN: 978-1-4711-6916-8
eBook ISBN 978-1-4711-6917-5

Printed in the United States of America

CONTENTS

Foreword by Jessica Smith.. ix
Introduction: Life After *Buffy* by Christopher Golden................... xi

SEASON 1
Welcome to the Hellmouth/The Harvest (Episodes 1.1 and 1.2)............... 2
Angel (Episode 1.7)... 5
Prophecy Girl (Episode 1.12).. 7
CATCHING UP WITH THE CAST AND CREW
    Anthony Stewart Head.. 10
    Julie Benz.. 16
    Erika Amato... 19

SEASON 2
Lie to Me (Episode 2.7).. 24
What's My Line? Part One (Episode 2.9)................................... 26
What's My Line? Part Two (Episode 2.10).................................. 28
Innocence (Episode 2.14)... 30
Passion (Episode 2.17)... 32
Becoming, Part One (Episode 2.21).. 35
Becoming, Part Two (Episode 2.22).. 37
CATCHING UP WITH THE CAST AND CREW
    James Marsters.. 39
    Juliet Landau... 47
    Cynthia Bergstrom... 52

SEASON 3
Lovers Walk (Episode 3.8).. 56
The Wish (Episode 3.9)... 60
Amends (Episode 3.10).. 63
The Zeppo (Episode 3.13)... 66
The Prom (Episode 3.20).. 69

    Graduation Day, Part One (Episode 3.21) 72
    Graduation Day, Part Two (Episode 3.22) 75
    CATCHING UP WITH THE CAST AND CREW
        Harry Groener. 78
        Jane Espenson 82
        Douglas Petrie 86

SEASON 4
    Hush (Episode 4.10) 90
    This Year's Girl (Episode 4.15) 94
    Who Are You (Episode 4.16) 97
    Superstar (Episode 4.17) 100
    Primeval (Episode 4.21) 103
    Restless (Episode 4.22) 106
    CATCHING UP WITH THE CAST AND CREW
        George Hertzberg. 110
        Marc Blucas. 112
        James C. Leary. 114
        Todd McIntosh 117
    LOOKING BACK: INTERVIEWS OVER THE YEARS
        Alyson Hannigan 121
        Nicholas Brendon. 122
        Charisma Carpenter 122
        David Boreanaz 124
        Seth Green 125
        Robia LaMorte. 126
        Armin Shimerman 127
        Kristine Sutherland 128
        Emma Caulfield. 131
        Alexis Denisof 133
        Elizabeth Anne Allen 135
        Marcia Shulman 137
        Joss Whedon 139

SEASON 5
    No Place Like Home (Episode 5.5) 144
    Family (Episode 5.6) 148

Fool for Love (Episode 5.7) 151
The Body (Episode 5.16) 154
The Weight of the World (Episode 5.21) 158
The Gift (Episode 5.22) 161

CATCHING UP WITH THE CAST AND CREW

    Clare Kramer 167
    Amber Benson 170
    David Fury 174

SEASON 6

Bargaining, Part One (Episode 6.1) 180
Bargaining, Part Two (Episode 6.2) 184
Once More, with Feeling (Episode 6.7) 187
Tabula Rasa (Episode 6.8) 192
Normal Again (Episode 6.17) 196
Villains (Episode 6.20) 199
Grave (Episode 6.22) 202

CATCHING UP WITH THE CAST AND CREW

    Tom Lenk 205
    Adam Busch 207
    Danny Strong 210
    Drew Z. Greenberg 213

SEASON 7

Help (Episode 7.4) 218
Selfless (Episode 7.5) 222
Conversations with Dead People (Episode 7.7) 226
Showtime (Episode 7.11) 230
Storyteller (Episode 7.16) 234
Chosen (Episode 7.22) 238

It Didn't End in Sunnydale: The Official Post-TV Seasons 243
Where Are They Now? 249
In Memoriam 252
Final Thoughts from the Creator of *Buffy*: Joss Whedon 254
"Restless": A Path to Premonitions, Teleplay Written and Directed by
    Joss Whedon, Additional Commentary by Paul Ruditis 257

FOREWORD

By Jessica Smith

Into every generation new *Buffy the Vampire Slayer* fans are born.

It's 2017, and we've found ourselves in a world full of endless hours of television. Thanks to the Internet, with its streaming sites and instantly downloadable content, we're overwhelmed with options for how to spend our time consuming media. It's amazing that any show is able to hold the spotlight for long. And yet *Buffy the Vampire Slayer* has accomplished this very feat for twenty years. *Twenty years!*

If you check your social media sites, chances are someone you follow is talking about *Buffy*, whether reminiscing about it or watching it for the first time. For seasoned fans, it's gratifying to see *Buffy* enjoy such longevity. And for the people just discovering the show, it's exciting to enter into such a large group of passionate people. It makes you wonder: How has *Buffy* captured our imaginations for so long?

Multiple reasons come to mind, many of which *Buffy* has been hailed for since the first season. *Buffy* was one of the first series to portray a main female character as a powerful action hero who has to save the day—a role that was typically reserved for men. The show mastered the structure of having individual plots within an episode while following a larger arc throughout the season. It made the struggles of its characters relatable and heartbreakingly real, despite being set in a world filled with the supernatural.

One of the best parts of *Buffy* is its range. Ask me about the funniest episode I've ever seen, and I might say "Tabula Rasa" or "Superstar." The saddest? "The Body," or "Becoming, Part Two." Buffy displays this on a smaller scale as well, bringing the laughs and tears all in one episode, such as in "Once More, with Feeling." (Will I ever be able to forget the look on Willow's face when she realizes she wrenched Buffy out of Heaven? Probably not.)

In an interview for the first Watcher's Guide, Joss calls *Buffy* "the most personal work I've ever done." For a lot of people, it's the most personal thing they've ever watched. Getting to the bottom of *Buffy*'s popularity isn't brains, children. It's emotion. It's the feeling you get when you hear the theme song. It's cheering the characters on when they succeed and crying along with them when they fall (which is a lot of season six, let's be honest). It's watching an unlikely hero slaying real-world problems in the form of terrifying (and ridiculous) monsters and knowing that while Buffy is saving lives in Sunnydale, she's saving some of us, too.

In this twentieth-anniversary collector's edition Watcher's Guide, you'll find the series episode highlights, from fan favorites and pivotal plot points to episodes that challenged the genre itself, such as "Hush" and "The Body." Interspersed between the seasons are exclusive, never-before-seen interviews with some of your favorite cast and crew as they look back at their time on *Buffy*. In the middle of the guide we've included an "intermission" of interviews collected from the original Watcher's Guides, in which actors discuss auditioning for *Buffy*, favorite moments on set, and more. (Keep an eye out for fun facts in there too, and find out if Elizabeth Anne Allen [Amy Madison, part-time witch, part-time rat] likes cheese.) Wrapping up the collector's edition is a special bonus from the third Watcher's Guide—the complete teleplay to the episode "Restless," with comments from Paul Ruditis, who uncovers how this one episode foreshadows the seasons to come.

In putting this Watcher's Guide together as an ode to our beloved *Buffy*, we hope to have given you a reason to revisit this amazing show. Thanks for reading!

INTRODUCTION: LIFE AFTER *BUFFY*

By Christopher Golden

It's difficult to remember with any real clarity what the pop cultural landscape was like before the arrival and the popularity of *Buffy the Vampire Slayer*. One can point to the landmark television series *Hill Street Blues* and note that the multilayered, interwoven-POV ensemble drama did not really exist before that Steven Bochco cop show came along. It's simple work to examine Shawn Ryan's post-*Buffy* FX cable series *The Shield* and examine the way in which it inspired other cable networks to invest massively in the leap of faith necessary for a story arc that spans the entire run of a series. But to really appreciate the influence of *Buffy the Vampire Slayer* requires a first step many are unwilling to take: brushing aside their assumptions.

Before *Buffy* even made its debut, millions of potential viewers and loads of critics had already dismissed the series based on topic and title alone. A television series about a high school girl named—of all things—Buffy, who happened to hunt and kill vampires . . . there's a fundamental absurdity to the idea that was part of the plan all along. At his best, Joss Whedon's genius is about subverting the expectations of his audience. But even Whedon never could have anticipated how profoundly his cult hit on the fledgling WB network would impact pop culture and the basic building blocks of the global television market.

Of course, Buffy Summers did not leave her mark only on television. Her influence has extended to feature films, comic books, and book publishing in general, including the massive worldwide phenomenon of *Twilight*.

On television, however, *Buffy* effectively erased the line—really, the wall—that had previously existed between genre material and the presumption of quality. There had been series before that were embraced by critics, various *Star Trek* series as the best examples, but *Buffy* shattered preconceptions in large part because it broke so many rules. Was the show a drama or comedic fluff? Was it a high school soap or a horror series? Most fundamentally, were we supposed to take this strange chimera of a show seriously?

The answer to that last question was a resounding yes. Viewers, critics, and even (in huge numbers) academics took *Buffy the Vampire Slayer* very seriously indeed. People named their children after the characters. The slang popularized in the series—even the cadence of the characters' vocal patterns—infiltrated modern language. At universities around the world, scholars began to write papers and teach classes about the philosophy, structure, and impact of the series. Hundreds of scholarly books and articles have been written about the show—and that's just from the academic side. There are many thousands of articles out there dissecting every bit of minutiae from the show's history, not to mention the lives of its cast and crew.

When *Buffy* took off, fans gathered in dedicated online forums and at conventions around the world in a community that redefined modern fandom for generations. That fandom centralized in a posting board called *The Bronze*—after the Sunnydale club where the characters hung out. In the virtual Bronze, fans would gather to discuss the series, often with the creators and cast themselves. Joss Whedon dropped by frequently, and most of the writers and cast members showed up from time to time to interact directly with the fans. In the days before social media, this pure and direct contact was unlike anything fans had experienced before. The people on *The Bronze* were from all over the world, and they didn't just talk to one another about *Buffy*. They built a community that spawned lifelong friendships, weddings, cross-country moves, and an annual Posting Board Party in Los Angeles that was routinely attended by the people who were creating their favorite show week after week.

Ask a hundred *Buffy* fans what it was, precisely, that inspired such adoration for the series, and you're likely to get a hundred different answers. Yet many of those answers will be threads in a single philosophical fabric woven with purpose and intent by Joss Whedon and his staff. From its opening moments, the series embraced people who had felt isolated or misunderstood. It presented a powerful female role model who was confused, reluctant, and full of doubt, yet courageous and determined and fiercely loyal. Perhaps most importantly, it presented a decisive young woman who became a leader alongside male characters who never doubted her strength, intelligence, or ability to lead (or, if they did, their hesitations were not gender based).

Pop culture had presented us with empowered female protagonists before—Ellen Ripley and Sarah Connor come immediately to mind—but the entire mythology of the Slayer revealed feminist roots. Millions of girls saw in Buffy evidence that they were capable of finding their own paths, making their own choices, and making a difference. Authors, screenwriters, producers, directors, and studio executives were inspired to follow *Buffy*'s lead for a variety of reasons, ranging from artistic to social justice to mercenary motivations. The series' acceptance of characters who would normally have been ignored or presented as outsiders resonated broadly.

When sweet and shy Willow Rosenberg, Buffy's closest friend and a major player from the very beginning of the series, begins to realize she is gay, falls in love, and eventually comes out to her friends, the character was not only bending the norms of prime-time television at the time—she was breaking them. There had been gay characters before, of course, but never a long-established character going through such a personal epiphany in a real and human way. When Willow finally kissed her girlfriend, Tara Maclay, on camera—in a moment of shared grief and compassion—it seemed to many viewers that the promise of the series had been fulfilled. In a show filled with monsters and magic and fantastical creatures, the love and pain of human beings was presented with more openness and sincerity than on many shows that prided themselves on their "gritty" reality.

The series that so many had been unwilling to take seriously when it debuted—that so many would still be unwilling to take seriously today—changed the face of television. It inspired people and changed lives. In many cases, as reported to so many members of the cast and crew, it saved the lives of people who considered taking their own.

In a broader sense, *Buffy the Vampire Slayer* changed modern television in its entirety. Scan through the offerings of the past decade and you will see the show's influence everywhere, even if you don't notice it at first. The "new" version of *Doctor Who* would likely not exist if not for the success of *Buffy*. Rose Tyler and the Christopher Eccleston Doctor would fit very comfortably in the world of Buffy, Angel, and Spike. The list of television series owing a massive debt to *Buffy the Vampire Slayer* is exhaustive, far beyond the actual spinoff series, *Angel*. Series like *Charmed*, *Supernatural*, *Grimm*, and *The Vampire Diaries* might never have been greenlit had *Buffy* not come first, but monsters are not a necessary ingredient to have benefited. It's impossible to watch *Veronica Mars*, *Alias*, *Pretty Little Liars*, or *Heroes* without seeing the DNA of *Buffy*. The same could be said of series from foreign shores, like the UK's *Being Human* and *Misfits*. There are so many more.

The creation of season-long arcs and the use of "Big Bads"—central villains around which those season arcs revolved—came to prominence thanks to *Buffy the Vampire Slayer*. But one of the strongest and most lasting influences of *Buffy* is the use of the "found family" or "chosen family." Buffy had Giles, Willow, Xander, Cordelia—and more as the series progressed. Angel had Cordelia, Wesley, Gunn, Fred—and, again, more. Taking a group of people who are close friends or allies and giving them a shared enemy, building a web of relationships around the hub of a crusade or mission, has become the basis of many successful TV series, including *Agents of S.H.I.E.L.D.*, *The Flash*, *Arrow*, *Supergirl*, *Quantico*, and Whedon's own *Dollhouse* and *Firefly*.

Twenty years after it debuted, as the new Golden Age of Television has produced one extraordinary narrative after another, it would be easy to forget just how groundbreaking a series *Buffy the Vampire Slayer* really was, but its global influence and success are impossible to deny.

Not bad for a former cheerleader who burned down her high school gymnasium.

SEASON 1

Welcome to the Hellmouth/The Harvest
Episodes 1.1 and 1.2

WRITTEN BY: Joss Whedon
DIRECTED BY: Charles Martin Smith (Ep. 1.1) and John T. Kertchmer (Ep. 1.2)
GUEST STARS: Mark Metcalf as the Master, Brian Thompson as Luke, David Boreanaz as Angel, Ken Lerner as Principal Flutie, Kristine Sutherland as Joyce Summers, Julie Benz as Darla
WITH: Mercedes McNab as Harmony

THE PLOT THICKENS:
Buffy Summers and her mother, Joyce, have moved from Los Angeles to the suburb of Sunnydale, California, and Joyce drives Buffy to her first day at the prosaically named Sunnydale High School. On that first day, Buffy meets a new world of people who will have a profound effect on her life. Principal Bob Flutie says that he believes in clean slates and won't hold the fact that she burned down her previous school's gymnasium against her. Cordelia, popular girl on campus, gives Buffy a test for her "coolness factor" and extends the hand of friendship—until Buffy starts to hang out with Willow, a horribly shy computer nerd, and her friends Xander and Jesse. Giles, the school librarian, not only knows that Buffy is the Slayer but has been assigned to be her Watcher.

Later that night, Buffy meets the mysterious Angel, who informs her that Sunnydale is located on the Hellmouth, a focal point of demonic activity of all sorts that attracts vampires like moths to a flame, and that she needs to be ready for the Harvest. Buffy ignores both Giles and Angel, hoping to return to some semblance of a normal life after her experience with vampires in LA.

In the catacombs underneath the town, the vampiric Luke awakens the Master so he will be ready for the Harvest. The Master, a very old, very powerful vampire, has been trapped underneath Sunnydale for sixty years, ever since his attempt to open the Hellmouth was foiled by an untimely earthquake. The time is right for the Harvest, which will give him the power to break free.

Luke sends vampires out for food, and Jesse is captured, although Buffy saves Willow and Xander—and also realizes that she must fulfill her duties as Slayer, or people will die. She goes to rescue Jesse, with some unwanted help from Xander, only to find that Jesse has been turned into a vampire. Xander and Buffy escape and then must stop Luke, who serves as the Master's vessel and is attacking the Bronze. With assistance from Giles, Willow, and Xander, Buffy kills Luke and several other vampires (Xander winds up inadvertently staking his old friend Jesse), though Darla survives.

QUOTE OF THE WEEK:
   CORDELIA: "It's in the bad side of town."
   BUFFY: "Where's that?"
   CORDELIA: "It's about half a block from the good side of town. We don't have a whole lot of town here."

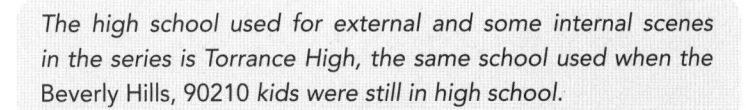

> The high school used for external and some internal scenes in the series is Torrance High, the same school used when the Beverly Hills, 90210 kids were still in high school.

LOVE, SLAYER STYLE:
Xander's first sight of Buffy causes him to crash into a railing while skateboarding, and he gamely attempts to flirt with her. Angel and Buffy meet and are immediately at odds, thanks to his being overwhelmingly cryptic.

> According to Joss Whedon's script, the Master's real name is Heinrich Joseph Nest.

BUFFY'S BAG OF TRICKS:
Buffy carries a stake and uses several random items (tree branches, pool cues, and the like) as substitute stakes. She beheads one vampire with a drum cymbal. At the climax, she unpacks her supplies from a trunk with a false bottom, which include several stakes, vials of holy water, garlic, and crosses.

> Brian Thompson, who plays Luke, also later appeared in both "Surprise" and "Innocence" as the Judge.

CONTINUITY:
Viewers of the movie *Buffy the Vampire Slayer* might be confused at the repeated references to Buffy burning the gym down, since that didn't happen in the movie. The solution is simple: Joss Whedon has spun this series off of his *original* movie script for *Buffy*, which did indeed have Buffy performing a touch of necessary arson on the gym. Two previous Slayers—Lucy Hanover in

1866 Virginia and an unidentified woman in 1927 Chicago—are mentioned in an opening montage, thereby extending the Slayer lore, although neither reference is to be found as such in Whedon's screenplay, nor in any other episode.

Buffy has the first of many prophetic dreams ("Prophecy Girl," "Surprise," "Innocence"). Joyce's parting words to Buffy as she drops her off are to extract a promise not to get kicked out of this school, a promise she will wind up breaking a year and a half later ("Becoming, Part Two"). Angel acts as if he's never seen Buffy before, which belies the flashback in "Becoming, Part One." The Master's first attempt to open the Hellmouth was in 1937; his next will be in "Prophecy Girl."

FROM THE ORIGINAL TELEPLAY:

The following exchange was cut from the "Welcome to the Hellmouth" script because of the length:

MR. FLUTIE: "Oh! Buffy! Uh, what do you want?"
BUFFY: "Um, is there a guy in there that's dead?"
MR. FLUTIE: "Where did you hear that? Okay. Yes. But he's not a student! Not currently."
BUFFY: "Do you know how he died?"
MR. FLUTIE: "What?"
BUFFY: "I mean—how could this have happened?"
MR. FLUTIE: "Well, that's for the police to determine when they get here. But this structure is safe, we have inspectors, and I think there's no grounds for a lawsuit."
BUFFY: "Was there a lot of blood? Was there any blood?"
MR. FLUTIE: "I would think you wouldn't want to involve yourself in this kind of thing."
BUFFY: "I don't. Could I just take a peek?"
MR. FLUTIE: "Unless you already are involved . . ."
BUFFY: "Never mind."
MR. FLUTIE: "Buffy, I understand this is confusing. You're probably feeling a lot right now. You should share those feelings. With someone else."

Angel
Episode 1.7

WRITTEN BY: David Greenwalt
DIRECTED BY: Scott Brazil
GUEST STARS: Mark Metcalf as the Master, David Boreanaz as Angel, Kristine Sutherland as Joyce Summers, Julie Benz as Darla
WITH: Andrew J. Ferchland as the Anointed One, Charles Wesley as Meanest Vamp

THE PLOT THICKENS:
After hovering on the periphery for several episodes, Angel's secret is finally revealed: he's a vampire. This realization does not come until he and Buffy admit their feelings for each other and share their first kiss. At first this leads Buffy to think that Angel's past actions are part of a plot to set her up for a fall, especially after she finds her mother in Angel's arms with bite marks on her neck. (In light of Angel's actions in the later half of the second season, this is an even more reasonable assumption.)

Soon enough, Buffy learns the whole truth. Angel was "sired" (vampire language for turning a human into a vampire) by Darla 240 years before. Eighty years ago, he tortured and killed a Romany woman, and her clan put a curse on him: they restored his soul. He became a vampire with a conscience, a unique creature among the undead. Darla's attempts to bring him back to the Master's fold fail, and she winds up on the wrong end of a stake wielded by Angel.

QUOTE OF THE WEEK:
Xander, laying it out for Buffy after Angel's vampirism is revealed:
"Angel's a vampire. You're a Slayer. I think it's obvious what you have to do."

> *It took an hour and a half to apply Angel's vamp face to David. One of his favorite parts of being a vampire was the weird yellow contact lenses.*

LOVE, SLAYER STYLE:
The Angel/Buffy relationship goes into full bloom here, starting with his spending the night in her bedroom (though he is, as she says, a perfect gentleman), continuing to their first kiss, and ending with another kiss that, thanks to Buffy's crucifix necklace, leaves a burning impression on Angel's chest. Their continued insistence that "This can't ever be anything" rings hollow even as they say it, more so in light of where the relationship does actually go.

Meanwhile, a hint of the future with Cordelia and Xander comes in an early scene on the dance floor ("Boy, that Cordelia's a breath of vile air"), and Willow continues to moon for Xander to Buffy, though Buffy's repeated urges for Willow to actually say something are met with vehement refusal ("No, no, no, no. No speaking up. That way leads to madness and sweaty palms").

BUFFY'S BAG OF TRICKS:
Giles trains Buffy in both quarterstaffs and a crossbow. She uses the latter on Darla (piercing her in the stomach rather than the heart), and tries but fails to use it on Angel (the impression being that her shot went wild on purpose).

CONTINUITY:
The Master has begun training the Anointed One ("Never Kill a Boy on the First Date"). Buffy invites Angel into her home for the first time ("Passion"). Angel describes Darla making him and his cursing at the hands of the Romany, both later dramatized in "Becoming, Part One."

Angel's duster was from Hugo Boss and cost $1,000.

Prophecy Girl
Episode 1.12

The first season finale, "Prophecy Girl," is the payoff to the promise of the early episodes. Throughout a season made up of mostly excellent monster-of-the-week stories—complete with teen-angst metaphors and life lessons—the Master lurks in the background as the show's first Big Bad. As we learn to love these characters and their relationships, the Master's presence in Sunnydale makes him Buffy's personal bogeyman. When he escapes from his subterranean prison . . . well, we all saw that coming, but nobody figured he'd actually manage to murder Buffy in the process. Xander proves his mettle by seeking her out and resuscitating her, Cordelia actually joins forces with the classmates she's despised for so long, the Hellmouth opens underneath the Sunnydale High library, Buffy beats her bogeyman—killing the Master—and nothing is ever the same again. More than anything, that last bit is the true hallmark of the series. Joss and his team allowed their characters to be forever altered by the things they experienced, keeping the series in a constant state of evolution.

WRITTEN AND DIRECTED BY: Joss Whedon
GUEST STARS: Mark Metcalf as the Master, David Boreanaz as Angel, Kristine Sutherland as Joyce Summers, Robia LaMorte as Jenny Calendar, Andrew J. Ferchland as the Anointed One

THE PLOT THICKENS:
On the eve of the prom, Giles translates a rather devastating prophecy in *The Pergamum Codex*: "The Master shall rise and the Slayer shall die." Several portents—noticed by Giles, Jenny Calendar, and Buffy—point to the Master finally freeing himself from his imprisonment. Giles tries to keep the prophecy from Buffy, but she overhears him discussing it with Angel. Though at first she rejects both the prophecy and her continuing as the Slayer ("Giles, I'm sixteen years old—I don't want to die"), the news

of two students' deaths at the hands of vampires on school grounds makes her realize her duty, and she goes after the Master. Angel and Xander follow her, arriving in time to find Buffy drowned and the Master free. Use of CPR revives Buffy, and she, Angel, and Xander return to Sunnydale High to find that the Hellmouth is opening—right under the library—despite the best efforts of Giles, Jenny, Willow, and Cordelia. Buffy confronts the Master once again, and this time he is the one who dies. "We saved the world," says Buffy at the end of it all. "I say we party."

QUOTE OF THE WEEK:
This is said by Willow, the Master, and Angel to Buffy at various times; Buffy's mother bought her the dress to wear to the prom:
"By the way, I like your dress."

LOVE, SLAYER STYLE:
Xander finally comes out and expresses his feelings for Buffy in the form of a labored attempt to ask her to go to the prom with him. Buffy turns the offer down, not feeling that way about Xander, prompting a snide comment about how one has to be undead to get her attention. ("I don't handle rejection well. Funny, considering all the practice I've had.") Later on, Xander recruits Angel to follow Buffy in going after the Master ("You're in love with her," Angel says, to which Xander replies frankly, "Aren't you?").
Xander practices his pickup line to Buffy on Willow, which is some comfort for her, though not enough for her to accept his post-Buffy's-rejection offer of the two of them going to the prom.

> The moment Willow discovers the corpses of Kevin and his friends in the audio/visual room is a major turning point for the character. From that point on, Willow becomes more proactive about her involvement with the Slayer. In that moment, she grows up.

> Both Willow and the Master compliment Buffy on her dress, but the final exchange (Angel: "I really like your . . ." Buffy: "Yeah, yeah. It was a big hit with everyone.") was added during production and was not in the original script.

POP-CULTURE IQ:
Xander, upset by Giles's maddening reserve, referring to the emotionless cyborg characters on *Star Trek*:
"Calm may work for Locutus of Borg here, but I'm freaked and I intend to stay that way."

CONTINUITY:
The Master's imprisonment finally comes to an end, with the help of the Anointed One, and he makes his second attempt to open the Hellmouth ("Welcome to the Hellmouth"). For the second time, but not the last, Buffy has a prophetic dream ("Welcome to the Hellmouth," "Surprise," "Innocence"). Buffy and the Slayerettes finally realize that the vampire they killed in "Never Kill a Boy on the First Date" *wasn't* the Anointed One. Jenny reminds Giles of her help in destroying Moloch ("I Robot, You Jane") when she tries to pry some solid information out of him. Since "Witch," Cordelia has passed driver's ed and obtained a car. Unlike other vampires, the Master's bones remain intact upon his death, which proves important in "When She Was Bad."

> *The massive demon coming up out of the Hellmouth at the end of "Prophecy Girl" had to be frightening, but the budget didn't allow for computer-generated images. The masterminds at Optic Nerve ended up making tentacle "costumes." Each of the tentacles has a human being inside, manipulating it from within.*

FROM THE ORIGINAL TELEPLAY:
The following scene, right after Buffy has turned down Xander's request that she go to the prom with him, was cut from this episode's script because of length:

Xander bails, wandering off under the archway. Buffy sits by herself on the bench, bummed.

Which is when the hail of pebbles starts.

The first few get Buffy's attention, tiny hard pellets hitting the ground around her. She stands as more start coming down.

People—including Buffy—all run for cover as the real shower starts. Buffy stands under the archway, watching the hail come down.

ANGLE: XANDER

Walking away, not near Buffy. He hears:

STUDENT (O.S.): "Check it out! It's raining stone!"

Xander looks back over his shoulder.

XANDER: "Figures."

ANTHONY STEWART HEAD (RUPERT GILES)

You'd been a working actor for many years before *Buffy* came along, and you've appeared in many roles in the years since. In between was this thing, *Buffy*, that made you instantly recognizable to millions of people around the world. Personally and professionally, was that a blessing or a curse?

ANTHONY: "A huge blessing. One of the weird things about my career is that I have a number of shows that have that kind of strange mystique about them. What I find remarkable is when young kids come up to me and they say it's *Buffy* that they know me from. I think, *How? You weren't even alive.* But of course the show has just gone round and round and round; it's been cyclical the way it's been on Netflix, it's been on FX, it's been on a number of channels. And young people keep picking up on it because it's so relevant to growing up and to finding your place in the world. But there's also *Merlin*, and there's *Manchild* to a certain extent, then there's *Little Britain*. There's a number of appearances I've made—even the one appearance on *Doctor Who* has been resonant.

"Before *Buffy*, I was known on both sides of the Atlantic for the [Taster's Choice] coffee ad. And it sort of—it didn't close things down here, but it did sort of limit what I was being seen for in terms of TV and film, because it was sort of the young romantic hero, and it was a sixty-second commercial. What *Buffy* gave me the opportunity to do was nothing I'd ever done before, which was to actually play a character role. And I saw it immediately. When I saw it on the page, I thought, *This is perfect. It's exactly what I want*, because at the time I wasn't particularly character actor stuff. I am now, strangely—but I was sort of the young romantic lead, and that can be limiting, and the whole thing that *Buffy* gave me was this complete new trajectory in my career.

"In terms of being a blessing or a curse, there was a moment when the BBC were making noises [of interest in *Buffy*]. I asked the [Fox] television international sales department how we were doing selling it to England, because one English actor long ago said, 'The worst thing about doing an American show that doesn't get shown in your home country is that you basically disappear.' This particular actor was in something that ran for seven or eight seasons, so when he went home, nobody knew him at all. That doesn't happen so much now. Things have changed, and most shows are seen internationally. But back in the day, when I first started on *Buffy*, if a show wasn't successful on American TV, if it hadn't made at least two seasons, it wasn't seen in England."

As I understand it, and please correct me if I'm wrong, during your tenure as a regular on *Buffy*, you lived a transatlantic life, working in LA but still calling the UK home. Was it a relief—and how much of an adjustment was it—when you no longer had to split your time like that?

ANTHONY: "It was a double-edged sword. *Buffy* was the best job; it was just perfect. But at the same time, I was away from my family, as you point out. And my kids were very young when I started and basically because of the [Taster's Choice] commercial limiting things that I was available for, that was when Sarah, my partner, said, 'Look, you've always wanted to work in America; this is your opportunity, because the commercial is just as successful in the States as it is in England, and they have a much freer kind of attitude about commercials.'

"These days it doesn't matter at all, but at the time I had such a high profile in the commercial that it was a bit limiting here. So she said she would be a single mum and that I should go out and see what I could find. And bless her heart, I didn't really think about what that meant and she really was a single mum; she was basically looking after the two girls from four and six or maybe even younger, three and five. Every time I got six days clear . . . nothing shorter because [. . .] they would just be getting into the groove of me being back home and then I'd have to go again. So six days we found was the minimum, and the production side of *Buffy* was very, very generous. If I looked at the episode and saw that I was only in two or three days out of the eight, I'd sort of add up the week and go, 'Look, is there any way of shooting that end so that, you know . . .' And they'd look at it and they'd try, and sometimes it didn't work, but more often than not Gareth, the producer, was brilliant.

"We also made use of holidays—we'd turn up in the States for three weeks. For two weeks we'd just be hanging out on the beach and doing our stuff, and then the third week I'd start work and the girls would join me. The crew and the cast were just lovely, so welcoming. It was really a family affair. Such a lovely crew. That largely came from Joss, because Joss was very welcoming, and when the girls sort of came on set, they were allowed to sit and watch the monitors. I think [my daughter] Daisy was allowed to say 'Action' at one point. And they used to hang out with me in my trailer, and Alyson was like a big sister, Sarah Michelle was like a big sister to them. They loved the girls. The girls were so easy to have around the set, extremely polite, you know, they didn't run around making noise. They were cool, really cool. It's no surprise that they are such brilliant actresses as they are, because they've been around it for so long that it's sort of in their bones.

"In terms of adjusting when I got back, no it wasn't a huge adjustment at all. I basically said to Joss at the end of the fifth season—because I'd thought I had a five-season, five-year contract, and it was a seven-year contract. Oops!—and I said, 'Look, dude, I don't know if I can do another two years as a regular. What's the chances of me leaving and going home?' Bless him—he said, 'I'd rather not lose you completely, but would you consider being a recurring rather than a regular?' So in season six I did something like eight episodes, and in season seven I did more—I did about fourteen. But just having that wiggle room, as they say, meant that I wasn't sort of going from the American way of life straight back into England. It was a perfect way of shoehorning my way back into life here. And also I did *Manchild*—I think that began in season six anyway. But, yeah, it was a relief to be home."

You've had all sorts of roles before and after *Buffy*, including on *Manchild*, *The Invisibles*, *Little Britain*, and the 2017 ShondaLand series *Still Star-Crossed*. Which role would you hope *Buffy* fans would track down and watch, if they haven't seen it?

ANTHONY: "There's one show called *Free Agents* that I did for NBC. They made eight episodes and they only screened four, I think. Nearly worked. It was just getting into its groove when they canceled it, unfortunately, but I think the British version of it—which I did with Sharon Horgan and Steve Mangan—is brilliant. I play a very outrageous character. If you have sensitivities, you probably shouldn't watch it. And oh God—*Manchild*. I love *Manchild*. I think the Americans tried to remake it. The idea was fiftysomethings who have all the boys' toys. The idea basically was, by the time you can actually afford all the stuff that you dream of as a man, you actually are too old to own it. It was very funny, but I think for some reason the Americans thought it was embarrassing, having fiftysomethings doing this, so they made it forty-somethings, which is a completely different ball game.

"The thing that I'm doing now I sincerely hope is a success, the ShondaLand series, is from a book called *Still Star-Crossed*. . . . I play Lord Capulet, and it's basically about what happens after Romeo and Juliet die. It's set in Renaissance Italy, when the political climate was very, very active. There was lots of stabbing in the back and betrayals and all the rest of it. It's about two warring families, the Montagues and the Capulets."

Your middle name has vanished and reappeared in credits over the years. I've always wondered why. Care to elaborate?

ANTHONY: "Basically, that's a union thing. When I first went over to the States, when I joined the Screen Actors Guild, I found out that there was another Tony Head, who at the time was largely a musical actor. And I think he was in *The Wire*. I asked if I could make it Anthony S. Head, but he said no. If the roles were reversed and he was here [in the UK], I would appreciate his need for me to be completely different. Anyway, bottom line is, in America I'm Anthony Stewart Head, and in England I'm Anthony Head. I'm presuming I will be Anthony Stewart Head for [*Still Star-Crossed*]."

You've been recording music almost as long as you've been acting. It's been a couple of years since your latest album, *Staring at the Sun*. What's next for you on the music front?

ANTHONY: "Taking time out to make music is sort of [difficult]. When I'm home, it's relatively full-on. We've got lots of animals, and my partner has put life on hold while I go off to film. So when I come back, I throw myself wholeheartedly into whatever's needed. But I have been working on something while I was in Spain, which I'm still tinkering with—and

I will be tinkering with a lot—which is a version of *Macbeth* with music. It's not a musical. It's something that I started doing when I was in class at the Beverly Hills Playhouse with Milton Katselas. You would get up and do scenes, and there were times when I didn't have time to rehearse with someone else, so I thought, *I know, I'll just do a Shakespeare scene or something.* And I started off with *Richard III*: 'Now is the winter of our discontent.' But I found it was quite interesting to just add little lines of contemporary music to offset the verse. Not all the way through, good God, but just occasionally point up a line by finding something which was relevant in some way. And there was a point when I was doing *Richard II* and someone said, 'Oh, are you gonna put music to it?' and I thought, *Oh, I wasn't going to, but actually now you mention it, all right.* There was a song, which made me very emotional, which I used to put on in my car, called 'Highway Highway' by Stephen Allen Davis. If you don't know it, you should check it out. It's on the album, I did a cover of it. It's a beautiful, beautiful song, and it's about going off in two different directions, and it used to make me cry. So I thought—I dunno, at one point I was climbing across the audience, and I started singing, and it had an extraordinary emotional resonance.

"Anyway, long story short, I also did a little piece of *Macbeth*, and it's a part that I'd always been interested in. There's an angle on it that I have that I've always wanted to do. And it's set in a period where the music is incredibly creative. So being able to refer to the stuff that was going on, and also have incidental music, and maybe a soliloquy or so being sung. Don't know yet—still playing with it. But I've been in talks with someone who runs a theater in the West End. It's definitely an experimental show, and I'm sure all the purists will say, 'Why, why do you have to mess around with Shakespeare?' Well, you don't. Shakespeare works really well on his own, but I'm sure he would appreciate the occasional little bit of, let's try this, let's see what we can do. And it may end up just that I do all the music and then go, 'No it's not gonna work,' and we'll just do it as a straight piece. But that's what I'm working on."

Your daughters, Emily and Daisy, are both actresses, marking the third generation of Heads to go into the family business. Have they always known they wanted to act?

ANTHONY: "Absolutely. Well, Emily always did. Daisy was always brilliant but wasn't motivated that way necessarily from the beginning. Emily used to write little plays, as kids sometimes do. And they'd sort of go off and rehearse, and then they'd put it on in the front room and we'd all sit and watch. And Daisy would reluctantly be coerced into doing it, and she would insist on everybody turning away, looking in the other direction, when she was on, because she didn't like us all looking at her. Thankfully that no longer exists, because she does really, really well. Both of them are wonderful and completely different. One of the moments that I was most pleased . . . They did a show called *Doc Martin*. I think they both went up because the agent was told they were looking for two sisters. In the end they got there and [learned that] no, these are two completely different characters. And they booked Emily, and then they came back and said they could not get Daisy out of their heads. They would try and make it work. And it did. And a number of people had no idea that they were sisters. It was great, absolutely great, the fact that they could play in a show, not playing sisters—because they'd done a couple of things where they were sisters.

"Basically, [they were] ten and twelve [when] they asked if they could do it professionally, because their ballet school had suddenly started putting some of the students up for things like *Harry Potter* and *The Lion, the Witch and the Wardrobe*, and all those—*Peter Pan*—there were lots of films at the time, suddenly that was the fashion. And they asked if they could do it professionally. I said maybe just do it at school and then go to drama school, and Sarah said, 'Back in your box. You have no clue whether they're gonna want to do it when they're twenty-five, but you can be sure that when they're forty and they didn't do it, you were the one that got in their way.' And I have actually met someone who that happened to, that their mother basically stopped them.

"Not that I would have stopped the girls from acting, but Sarah's point was also that it's a real test of fire. You find out a lot about yourself and about presenting yourself, and it would pay off somewhere down the line if they chose to do another career. But I think it was the second, or maybe even the first interview that Daisy went to, she booked a really great TV show with a dear friend of ours, Aaron Taylor-Johnson. A great show, and she was great in it. [Emily and Daisy] know how it is. It's not like one has to say it's a hard business, because they've seen me have to deal with rejection, have to deal with getting a job and then literally just before the job's about to go, it gets canceled for lack of funds or something, and you have to deal with the disappointment. So they know what the gig is. But they're both doing really, really well, I have to say. I'm very, very proud of them."

You and your partner, Sarah Fisher, have been deeply involved in animal-welfare issues. What are the charities and organizations you're focused on now, and what message would you like to give your fans about animal welfare?

ANTHONY: "The one thing I would say to people about animals is, don't assume that we know what an animal is thinking. For some strange reason, we always latch on to animals being stubborn, [animals being] deliberately cantankerous. Sarah's just written a book about donkeys. Donkeys have a tendency to suddenly stop, and that's nothing to do with being naughty or being stubborn. That's because, in that moment, they are overfazed. There's just too much information, and the only way they can deal with it is to stop still until they're ready to deal with it. And part of what Sarah does . . . all of her work is about observing and then working with the animal. I think she's called an animal behavioral consultant. But by and large, a lot of animals have some sort of tension patterns going on in their body because of either fear or the memory of fear, or pain—pain is a huge one. We always think that animals can just ride through pain, and actually quite often they do, but it can affect the way they respond to what we're asking them to do.

"But, what charities? Loads. Loads and loads and loads. From big organizations like Battersea Dogs & Cats Home and Dogs Trust to very small organizations like Dogstar in Sri Lanka. We have a thing called 'Cool to Be Kind,' which Sarah brilliantly invented. It's cool to be kind to animals. Basically we offer animal welfare organizations and shelters the opportunity to sell some wristbands, which have 'Cool to Be Kind' and four little animal prints on them. Most of them don't have the finances to be able to initiate merchandise, because it costs money to actually supply merchandise, and if they have a very small area that they cover, it's just not cost-effective. So we send them a starter pack of wristbands, which they sell for three euros or so. Of course, that may change now after Brexit. But they then can choose to do what they want with the profits. Sometimes they just keep it, and that's the end of that, but more often than not they reinvest it, they buy more bands at cost and sell them again at the retail price, and therefore they make a profit, again and again. It's perfect. When I'm working with people with a high profile, I ask them if they'd like a band, and then I photograph them with it on. For instance I did a radio show with Benedict Cumberbatch and the day after we put that up on the Facebook page, we didn't have enough bands to go around. It's the power of profile. It's very simple and very effective."

So much time has passed. What are your favorite behind-the-scenes memories of your time on the series?

ANTHONY: "So many. There was one moment that I will always remember, which I think was on 'Passion.' There was a phone call between Giles and Willow, where he tells her that Jenny Calendar is dead. Michael Gershman, our director of photography, who directed that episode, asked them to put a landline, a telephone connection, between us so that I was really talking to her. I was watching the monitor, and it was heartbreaking. Alyson was spot on, and it was so emotional.

"On the more humorous side, there was the episode—I can't remember what it was called—when I'm a Fyarl demon, driving around in the Giles mobile with Spike—with James. It was great stuff, with him slagging me off. There was a scene where I have to chase someone down the street. They originally had me in slippers, and I said no, surely, can't we do something that's sort of like cloven feet? And I ended up designing them, and I think props made them in the end. Basically they were a pair of high heels, with a hoof at the front part and you couldn't really see the heel part, and I think you only actually see them once, when I tread on some kid's toy in a back garden. But there was a moment when I was walking across the car park and Nicky [Brendon] said, 'Show me a bit of Frank-N-Furter,' because I played Frank in *Rocky Horror*. So I did, and suddenly the Fyarl demon was swinging his hips. Because I'm, I don't know, bizarrely comfortable with a pair of heels."

Everyone says that working on a long-running TV series is a lot like high school, with circles of friends and then those people you wish you'd hung out with more. Who do you wish you'd hung out with more?

ANTHONY: "I hung out with everyone, pretty much. I spent a lot of time with Nicky, and Alyson, and Emma. Couldn't really spend much time with Sarah Michelle—I've spent a lot of time since, whenever I visit—but, because she was working all the time. Hung out with David, hung out with James. Hung out with Seth a bit—I mean the bottom line is we all stayed really friendly. I always look them up when I go [to LA]. And Joss.

"Joss used to do these Shakespeare readings on Sundays. It started off when Kai, his wife, went off to do a sabbatical in Japan to do an architecture course, and he just thought, *What should I do? All right, let's do some Shakespeare readings*. And they turned into musicals. He'd get his music books out, and then James brought a guitar, and so the musical was born. We used to hang out a lot, and I have really fond memories. I have some really, really good friends because of it, and I will always look on them with great fondness."

What are you working on now, and what does the future hold for Anthony Head?

ANTHONY: "I'm waiting to see if the Shonda show gets picked up. [Ed. note: It did!] I'm fascinated—we've watched an edit of the pilot, which is changing because we shot some more stuff. And we watched rough assemblies of the second and third episodes. Quite astonishing, quite astonishing stuff. Beautiful. It's all on location. We're shooting in Spain for Renaissance Italy, because there's an enormous amount of extraordinary architecture in Spain. It's a beautiful country and there are large, vast untouched plains and forests and all sorts of stuff. Watching the three episodes I now have, I'm absolutely blown away. It's absolutely stunning.

"And, as I said, I'm working on this play idea. I've also got three or four things that I've written that I finally decided to see if I can get some interest in, just because it would be nice to be in control of something, to have written something that I'm in."

JULIE BENZ (DARLA)

Many of the actors who appeared on *Buffy* and *Angel* had their real breakout roles with either show, but you'd already had several recurring roles and numerous guest spots before you appeared as Darla in the pilot of *Buffy*. Do you still feel the role was a breakout for you?

JULIE: "Yes, definitely! I had been kicking around in Hollywood for a bit, working mostly on sitcoms. Darla was my first dramatic, multidimensional, complex character."

You've had a very successful career post-Whedonverse, including significant roles on series like *Dexter*, *Hawaii Five-0*, *Desperate Housewives*, *Defiance*, and *No Ordinary*

Family, and appearances in films and many other series. What role are you most proud of? Which would you point *Buffy* fans to if they wanted so see something very different from Darla?

JULIE: "Rita from *Dexter* is the complete opposite of Darla and a role I am very proud of. Also Robin from *Desperate Housewives*—she was pure joy to play!"

You started ice-skating at the age of two and competed in the 1988 junior ice dancing US Championships. An injury at age fourteen kept you off the ice. Do you look back on that now as a blessing in disguise, or would you rather have been skating all along?

JULIE: "It was definitely a blessing, which I actually recognized at the time. I started skating before I could even fully speak. It was just something we did in our family. I knew in my heart I wasn't going to ice-skate forever, but I didn't know what else I was going to do. I knew I loved performing. My injury forced me to explore other outlets for performing, and that's how I discovered acting. It was really a confluence of circumstances. I got injured and then met my manager, Vincent Cirrincione (who is still my manager thirty-one years later), within the same year. Had I not gotten injured, I doubt I would be where I am today!"

You speak the first words in the *Buffy* pilot, and yet Darla was originally intended to die in that episode. Looking back now, what stands out to you about the process of being cast as Darla—about the audition or your first look at the script, or both?

JULIE: "I was a big fan of the movie, so when I was offered the role of Vampire Girl #1 in the pilot presentation, I took it even though I knew I was gonna die right away. I was still a struggling actress at the time, so I was just hungry to work. And Joss's passion and energy for the project was infectious! I remember once the show went to series and we reshot the pilot, Vampire Girl #1 was given a name . . . but I was still supposed to die. We were filming my death scene on set when Joss came up to me and said, 'We decided not to kill you. You're gonna be back next episode. And then we're gonna kill you.' This went on for a few episodes. It was exciting and fun for me as an actress, but I never thought Darla would develop and become such a pivotal part of the story line."

For a character who only appears in five episodes of *Buffy*, Darla looms large. Even when she appears on *Angel*—for twenty episodes—her history with him casts a long shadow over both series. And yet the writers killed your character over and over again. Do you think they knew each time they'd be bringing you back, or is Darla just that irresistible?

JULIE: "Joss and the writers wrote a great character. . . . She was irresistible! And the great thing about the show was that you could die and come back over and over and over again. Except I never expected it. Every time I was killed, I thought it was final and that I would never be back again. I remember being sad on set one day when we were shooting one of my many deaths and everyone (cast and crew) were like, 'You'll be back next week!' And they were right! Darla was always brought back—to my surprise!"

How often do you get recognized in public? Do you enjoy it, or do you want to hide?

JULIE: "I'm often impressed when someone recognizes me, because I never recognize anyone! I've always had great fan experiences and I appreciate them. I remember when I was ten years old I asked a famous ice-skater for an autograph and she refused. It devastated me. It took so much courage on my part to ask her. I was crushed. I don't ever want to make anyone feel that way."

So much time has passed. What are your favorite behind-the-scenes memories of your time on the two series, particularly *Buffy*?

JULIE: "My favorite moments were with David [Boreanaz]. We had a natural chemistry and mutual respect from the very beginning. Working with him was easy and fun. We would be shooting these very intense, emotional scenes, and as soon as the director yelled cut we would start laughing. He was my rock throughout Darla's journey. I always felt safe with him."

Everyone says that working on a long-running TV series is a lot like high school, with circles of friends and then those people you wish you'd hung out with more. You were only on five episodes of *Buffy*, but twenty of *Angel*. Who do you wish you'd hung out with more?

JULIE: "Everyone! My first few episodes of *Buffy* were tough because I was dealing with the contact lenses and the prosthetic makeup. They created the vampire makeup on my face. At that time, the process was long, tedious, and uncomfortable. I became allergic to the chemicals that were being used, and the removal process was very painful. Add in the fact that I could barely see because of the contact lenses . . . needless to say, I didn't get to spend a lot of time bonding with the rest of the cast. Plus, I mostly only worked with Sarah and David."

Overall how would you characterize the influence of your time on *Buffy* and *Angel* on your life?

JULIE: "For me, working on *Buffy* and *Angel* was like attending the most amazing graduate school for acting. Every week I was challenged emotionally and physically. I was buried alive, had to ride a horse through fire, had to sing (and I'm *not* a singer!). The writers pushed the boundaries, and I loved every minute of it! We were encouraged to make strong choices with our characters, and we were always supported by amazing writing. Darla was a once-in-a-lifetime role, and I am filled with gratitude that I was chosen to bring her to life."

What are you working on now, and what does the future hold for Julie Benz?

JULIE: "I am currently filming *Training Day* for CBS with Katrina Law, Drew Van Acker, and Marianne Jean-Baptiste. And if you think you know what the future holds for me, I'm all ears!"

ERIKA AMATO (LEAD SINGER OF VELVET CHAIN)

You started your career as an actress in an episode of *Quantum Leap*, but all the while, you were performing as a musician, singing and writing songs with your band Velvet Chain, which became something of a big deal in the LA club scene. What was life like pre-*Buffy* for you and the band?

ERIKA: "I was actually on *Quantum Leap* before I even met Jeff Stacy (my husband and co-founder of Velvet Chain). I was doing the typical aspiring actress thing: auditioning, taking classes, doing plays here and there, and booking the occasional TV or indie film role. After about a year of that, I met Jeff through a friend of mine who was singing backup in his band, and we started dating immediately. That old band featured a male lead singer (Jeff wrote all the songs, though), and I joined the band as a backup singer who occasionally sang lead. After only a few months of that configuration, we dissolved that band and started a new one with me as the only singer, and renamed ourselves Velvet Chain. We made a demo, immediately started getting booked in clubs all over LA, and started to develop a really good following."

How did Velvet Chain's appearance (performing onstage at the Bronze) in the episode "Never Kill a Boy on the First Date" come about?

ERIKA: "That came directly from the music supervisor, John King, who had become a fan of ours. He saw us play back in early 1996, really liked us, thought we'd be a good fit for the show, and asked us to come on. Our episode was actually the third one ever shot (although it was the fifth one to air), and nobody knew whether or not the show was even going to be successful, much less become such a phenomenon! At the time, we were told the show was a mid-season replacement. And it was on The WB. I mean, who knew it would be such a hit? We shot the episode something like six months before it ever even got released! But as soon as I tuned in to watch our episode when it aired in 1997, I knew we were a part of something special."

After that episode, your music also appeared on the official soundtrack for the series, a one-two punch that gave Velvet Chain a new level of exposure. What impact did it have?

ERIKA: "It had a huge impact. Just being on the show gave us a ton of exposure. We went from playing the great small clubs in the area to some of the biggest and most famous venues in

LA—like the world-famous Troubadour, the Key Club, and House of Blues. Coincidentally, we'd been signed to an indie label just before our episode of *Buffy* aired, so when we went out on tour in support of our album (*Warm*), we were able to build off that national exposure, which was great. (And it certainly gave us great stuff to talk about in radio interviews at the time!) And then getting selected to be on the official soundtrack album was an even bigger boost. Plus, by that point, the show had been airing internationally, so we were selling albums worldwide. It was all really great stuff. Plus, I was a huge fan of Garbage at the time, so the fact that our tracks were right next to each other on the album was really special to me. We'll always be super grateful to Joss for personally pushing for us to be on that album."

Although Velvet Chain certainly wasn't the only band to have their music get the spotlight on *Buffy*, you and the band seemed to be embraced by the *Buffy* fandom with more enthusiasm than most. Why do you think that happened?

ERIKA: "I think it was probably due to a combination of factors. I'd like to think it was primarily due to the music, but I also know that the fact that the cast really liked us and developed a friendship with us and would come to our gigs in Hollywood didn't hurt! (We were even the official entertainment at the show's season two wrap party. Fun stuff!) I was also very active on all the various incarnations of the posting board and made some really good friends among the fans. Plus, I wore some pretty cool outfits. I think it all contributed!"

What are your favorite memories, all these years later, of your interactions with the *Buffy* fans?

ERIKA: "There are so many! I really loved performing at the PBP (Posting Board Party) at the Hollywood Athletic Club. . . . I got to meet so many people IRL that I only knew from their online handles. And I'm still friends with a bunch of them—they even come to see me in my theater productions! We also participated in a couple of conventions, which were really fun because we got to be 'famous.' You know, signing autographs, posing for pictures, etc. But I think my favorite memory may be when we crowdsourced the fans on the posting board to give us general ideas for our James Bond–style *Buffy* song. That was super fun. (I'm aware that the song seems kind of lame to people who don't get the tongue-in-cheek tone, but the folks who do get it, love it. And for what it's worth, it's got a fantastic bass line!) And side note, to this day, when new people find out that my band was on *Buffy*, they freak out. The show's fans are the *best*."

Were you a fan yourself, and was it strange to appear as—essentially—yourself?

ERIKA: "Well, as I mentioned earlier, we were on the third episode ever shot, so I wasn't a *Buffy* fan beforehand—the show didn't even exist yet! But yes, as soon as I saw our episode, I knew it was a great show, and I started watching it every week. As for it being strange . . . *yes*! Not so much seeing myself onscreen as 'myself' (we'd shot some Velvet Chain videos already, etc.), but the strangest part was having to lip-synch to myself—but wait, it gets weirder—in *silence*! See, during filming, they would start rolling our track so that we could get a sense of the tempo, but then they'd turn it *off* so that they could record the dialogue for the scene. And I'm just up there onstage, lip-synching in a vacuum, hoping that I'm at least somewhat close. That was just bizarre. I was very grateful to see that I actually did a pretty good job!"

9/11 had an enormous impact on you and was directly responsible for your decision to focus on pursuing roles in the theater. How did that shift come about, and how did you put that decision into action?

ERIKA: "Very long story short: my dad worked in the building directly across from the Twin Towers and took the train in to the World Trade Center every day. For about twelve hours on 9/11, I had no idea whether he was alive or dead (thankfully, he was fine), but if he hadn't been running late (not at all typical for him), he would have been one of the victims crushed in the PATH train below the towers. And yeah, he was okay, but what about the over three thousand people who were killed? And what about their families and friends? Anyway, that day served as an epiphany for me, and I realized that life is just too short to not go for your dreams with everything you have. I came to the conclusion that I absolutely didn't want to hold down a day job anymore, and I had a gut feeling that I could make a living in musical theater (something which I'd been resisting for various reasons), so I immediately picked up a copy of *Backstage*, auditioned for something, booked it, and quit my full-time job at Bloomingdale's. And I haven't had a day job since!"

You've won numerous awards for your stage performances Off-Broadway and in regional theater, and you were a part of the national tour of *Flashdance the Musical*. What has been your favorite stage role thus far?

ERIKA: "That's actually a tough question. . . . I've been fortunate enough to have played some of the greatest roles in musical theater, and I've loved so many of them for different reasons. I loved playing The Witch in *Into the Woods* because the songs are amazing, I adore Sondheim, and it's a real diva-style role. I loved doing Velma Von Tussle in *Hairspray* because that's just the most joyous, fun show and that role is hilarious and a real blast to play. I adored being Maria in *The Sound of Music* because it's one of the most iconic roles in musical theater, the songs are all American classics, it was my very first Equity role (i.e., the role with which

I joined Actors' Equity Association, the union for professional stage actors in the United States), and every night a gaggle of little girls would swarm me at the stage door and make me feel like a Disney princess. And there are so many more . . . but I think my most rewarding stage experience was when I voiced the role of the Bad Fairy in the original musical *Sleeping Beauty Wakes*, which was co-produced by Deaf West Theatre and Center Theatre Group in Los Angeles. I spoke and sang for deaf actress Deanne Bray in addition to playing my own supporting role (speaking, singing, and signing ASL for myself). It was the biggest challenge of my career—and I was nominated for an Ovation Award for it, which was cool!"

What are you up to now, and what does the future hold for Erika Amato?

ERIKA: "Well, literally right now [December 2016], I'm performing all over New York and New Jersey as a professional a cappella singer, plus I'm singing in a few Christmas concerts as a soloist. As for the future, I'm waiting to hear about a few projects for which I'm in contention (two regional theater productions and a national tour), but even more importantly, Jeff and I are planning to release a *new* Velvet Chain album sometime in 2018! Keep an eye out for our soon-to-be-launched fund-raising campaign!"

SEASON 2

Lie to Me
Episode 2.7

WRITTEN AND DIRECTED BY: Joss Whedon
GUEST STARS: Robia LaMorte as Jenny Calendar, James Marsters as Spike, Jason Behr as Billy Fordham, Jarrad Paul as Diego, Juliet Landau as Drusilla
WITH: Julia Lee as Chanterelle, Will Rothhaar as James

THE PLOT THICKENS:
After observing Angel talking to a strange, attractive woman, Buffy starts moping—right until the arrival of Billy Fordham, "Ford" to his friends. Buffy's former crush and best friend for many years back at her old high school, Ford says he's transferred to Sunnydale High. In due course, Ford reveals that he knows that Buffy is the Slayer. A suspicious Angel has Willow check up on him, and they discover that he hasn't actually transferred and that he's part of a club that worships vampires and wishes to become like them. Ford's plan is to give Spike the Slayer in exchange for becoming a vampire—a preferred alternative to dying of a brain tumor, which is his expected fate. Buffy, however, manages to turn the tables on him and prevent the club members from being massacred by Spike and Drusilla.

The entire episode continues to turn on the theme of lies, and the title becomes particularly valid in the poignant conversation at the episode's end between Buffy and Giles, as she asks him to lie to her, to tell her that everything will be all right.

QUOTE OF THE WEEK:
Angel, describing to Willow how Buffy has changed his life:
> "Things used to be pretty simple. A hundred years, just hanging out, feeling guilty. I really honed my brooding skills. Then *she* comes along."

LOVE, SLAYER STYLE:
Buffy is jealous when she sees Angel with Drusilla and latches on to Ford as soon as he arrives, even hanging around with him to the exclusion of Angel at the Bronze. Later, though, she finally comes out and admits that she loves Angel.

Jenny and Giles go on their second date, which Jenny keeps a surprise; it turns out to be a monster truck rally.

CONTINUITY:
Spike has one of his vampires steal the du Lac manuscript from the library (later used in "What's My Line?"). Buffy learns of Drusilla's existence; Giles had believed her killed in Prague ("School Hard"). Willow points out to Angel that he's acted jealous in the past ("Some Assembly Required"). Willow has also upgraded from a desktop to a laptop since "I Robot, You Jane" ("Passion"). Angel details how he tortured Drusilla and made her insane before he finally changed her into a vampire ("Becoming, Part One").

FROM THE ORIGINAL TELEPLAY:
The following line of Angel's was cut from this episode for length:
> "Yeah, I eat too. Not for nutritional value—it just kind of passes the time."

What's My Line? Part One
Episode 2.9

WRITTEN BY: Howard Gordon and Marti Noxon
DIRECTED BY: David Solomon
GUEST STARS: Seth Green as Oz, James Marsters as Spike, Eric Saiet as Dalton, Kelly Connell as Mr. Pfister, Bianca Lawson as Kendra, Saverio Guerra as Willy, Juliet Landau as Drusilla, Armin Shimerman as Principal Snyder
WITH: Michael Rothhaar as Suitman, P. B. Hutton as Mrs. Kalish

THE PLOT THICKENS:
It's Career Week at Sunnydale High School, which just drives home to Buffy that she can't possibly have a normal life. She proceeds to mope for some time, leading Angel to invite her to a skating rink. It cheers her up—right until she is attacked by a huge biker-dude type who is wearing a ring that identifies him as part of the Order of Taraka, a group of supernatural assassins. Three have been sent after Buffy by Spike, who doesn't want any distractions from curing Drusilla. The method for doing so is in the du Lac manuscript that had been stolen from the Sunnydale High library, which Spike eventually translates. Angel's attempt to find out what is going on is interrupted by a woman who attacks him and locks him in a cage until sunup. The same woman then attacks Buffy, who has taken refuge from the assassins in Angel's empty apartment, and identifies herself as "Kendra, the Vampire Slayer."

> The hold of the plane in which Kendra arrives was constructed on the set and later turned upside down and redesigned as a sewer tunnel.
>
> The ice rink where Angel and Buffy skate in this episode is, in real life, a place called Iceland, which is located at 8041 Jackson Street, in Paramount, California, about twenty-five miles from the actual set of the show.

QUOTE OF THE WEEK:
Xander:
  "It's a statistical impossibility for a sixteen-year-old to unplug a telephone."

LOVE, SLAYER STYLE:
Angel is waiting in Buffy's bedroom when she returns from slaying, saying he's worried; she tells him, "You're the one freaky thing in my freaky world that still makes sense to me." They also make out at the skating rink (observed by Kendra, leading to the new Slayer attacking the old one at the episode's climax).

POP-CULTURE IQ:
Xander, to Cordelia, referring to the crime-busting kids who hung around with that famous cartoon Great Dane, Scooby-Doo:
  "You wanna be a member of the Scooby Gang, you gotta be willing to be inconvenienced now and then."

CONTINUITY:
The truth of the du Lac manuscript stolen from Giles in "Lie to Me" is revealed. Oz and Willow finally meet ("Inca Mummy Girl," "Halloween"), as both are chosen as recruiting fodder for a computer-software megacorporation in Seattle (never identified by name) during Career Week. Willow's fear of frogs is first mentioned ("Killed by Death").

What's My Line? Part Two
Episode 2.10

WRITTEN BY: Marti Noxon
DIRECTED BY: David Semel
GUEST STARS: Seth Green as Oz, James Marsters as Spike, Saverio Guerra as Willy, Bianca Lawson as Kendra, Kelly Connell as Mr. Pfister, Juliet Landau as Drusilla
WITH: Danny Strong as Jonathan Levenson

THE PLOT THICKENS:
Kendra and Buffy call a truce and realize that the former truly is a Slayer. When one Slayer dies, another is activated, and Buffy did die, however briefly. To Buffy's chagrin, Kendra seems more dedicated, more studious, and seems to get along better with Giles—but she also has had no life to speak of, and is long on duty but short on passion.

Meanwhile, Angel has been rescued from his cage by the slimy bartender, Willy, who hands him over to Spike. The two other Tarakan assassins attack, one going after Xander and Cordelia at Buffy's house, the other shooting at Buffy in school.

As the Slayers figure out for themselves, the ritual to restore Drusilla to full health requires the presence of her sire—Angel. Brutal questioning of Willy by Buffy and Kendra reveals the location of the church where the ceremony will be performed, and they attack. Buffy manages to end the ceremony before Angel is drained of all life, then literally drops a church organ on Spike's head while the church burns around them. With the bad guys defeated and Angel saved, Kendra heads back home. But Drusilla has survived the church burning and rescued Spike—and she's stronger than ever. . . .

QUOTE OF THE WEEK:
Buffy, getting her dander up:
  "'Cause I've had it. Spike is going down. You can attack me, you can send assassins after me, that's fine. But *nobody* messes with my boyfriend."

LOVE, SLAYER STYLE:
While trapped in Buffy's basement by one of the assassins, Xander and Cordelia get

into a knock-down, drag-out argument that culminates in a kiss, followed by a heartfelt "We *so* need to get out of here." An attempt to redistance themselves at the climax fails miserably, and they wind up in each other's arms again, following yet another nasty argument, thus setting the tone for their relationship.

Oz and Willow make the first steps toward their eventual relationship, as Oz saves Willow's life from one of the assassins, then proceeds to flirt with her while discussing animal crackers.

> Buffy tells Kendra to watch the movie on her flight home unless it's a "movie with a dog in it and Chevy Chase." This is a reference to Funny Farm, a 1988 movie starring Chase that Gellar had a small, uncredited role in.

POP-CULTURE IQ:
Buffy, admonishing Kendra to not go off half-cocked, referring to one of the title characters in *Mighty Morphin Power Rangers*:
  "Back off, Pink Ranger!"
Buffy, once again admonishing Kendra, referring to the legendary movie hero:
  "It's a little more complicated than that, John Wayne."

> The "Pink Ranger" line has additional significance beyond being a standard Buffy pop-culture reference: Sarah Michelle Gellar's stunt double, Sophia Crawford, used to play the Pink Ranger on Mighty Morphin Power Rangers.

CONTINUITY:
Kendra's activation as the Slayer apparently happened after Buffy died in "Prophecy Girl." Drusilla tortures Angel prior to the ceremony, reminding him of what he did to her ("Lie to Me," "Becoming, Part One"). When Xander reveals that he and Cordelia encountered an assassin that is literally made of maggots, Buffy asks, "You and bug people, Xander—what's up with that?" ("Teacher's Pet"). Spike and Drusilla have their roles reversed at the end of the episode, as Spike is badly injured and Drusilla is at full strength.

FROM THE ORIGINAL TELEPLAY:
The following exchange was cut from the opening of this episode's script for length:
  KENDRA: "Your English is very odd, you know."
  BUFFY: "Yeah—it's something about being woken by an ax. Makes me talk all crazy."

> Willow wears a backpack that has a little lion poking its head out from under a rainbow.

Innocence
Episode 2.14

WRITTEN AND DIRECTED BY: Joss Whedon
GUEST STARS: Seth Green as Oz, Kristine Sutherland as Joyce Summers, Robia LaMorte as Jenny Calendar, Brian Thompson as the Judge
SPECIAL GUEST STARS: Vincent Schiavelli as Uncle Enyos, James Marsters as Spike, Juliet Landau as Drusilla
WITH: James Lurie as Mr. Miller, Carla Madden as Woman, Parry Shen as Student, Ryan Francis as Soldier

THE PLOT THICKENS:
Angel's soul is again lost, and he has reverted to the same old vampire he was prior to the Romany curse. Spike and Drusilla are thrilled to find their sire back in the saddle, and invite him to join them in destroying the world with the Judge. Buffy, meanwhile, knows only that Angel has disappeared, and the Slayerettes are no closer to finding out anything useful about how to stop the Judge.

When Buffy finally finds Angel, he is standoffish and dismissive of her feelings. Then he attacks Willow at the school, though Xander and Buffy manage to drive him off. Jenny, under pressure from Buffy, reveals that she knew about the curse, that it was removed, and that she had been sent to Sunnydale to keep an eye on Angel. She takes Buffy to her uncle, but Angel has gotten there first and killed him. Xander, meanwhile, comes up with a plan: to use a missile launcher, a weapon that is made, not forged, against the Judge. It works, but Buffy finds it impossible to kill Angel when she confronts him.

QUOTE OF THE WEEK:
Willow, insisting, along with Xander, that they go after Angel and Buffy, who have not checked in since their attack on the Factory:
"My God! You people are all— Well, I'm upset, and I can't think of a mean word right now, but that's what you are, and we're going to the Factory!"

LOVE, SLAYER STYLE:
Angel and Buffy obviously are on the outs; indeed, Angel is disgusted with the way he acted around the Slayer and is determined to hurt her in much the same way he hurt Drusilla before he turned her into a vampire. His initial foray is a textbook example of the Insensitive Male After Sex, culminating with, "I'll call you." He also starts his campaign to come between Spike and Drusilla ("Bewitched, Bothered, and Bewildered," etc.).

Xander and Cordelia are caught kissing by a devastated Willow. ("It's against all laws of God and man!") Xander's attempt to explain that it doesn't mean anything falls on deaf ears, as Willow realizes that "You'd rather be with someone you hate than be with me." Later, Willow asks Oz if he wants to make out with her, which he politely declines, knowing that she's only doing it to get back at Xander; the maturity of this response charms Willow.

The Giles and Jenny coupling comes to a screeching halt with the revelation of Jenny's true reason for being in Sunnydale.

> *Often the scripts will contain some wry humor even in the stage directions. In the script for this episode, Joss Whedon wrote, "A couple of soldiers pass. Xander suavely nods to them. They nod back and pass without comment, because they are extras."*

CONTINUITY:
Buffy continues to have prophetic dreams ("Welcome to the Hellmouth," "Prophecy Girl," "Surprise"). Xander's memories of his transformation into a soldier remain intact ("Halloween") and allow him and Cordelia to successfully break into an armory and make off with the missile launcher, and also allow Xander to instruct Buffy in its use.

FROM THE ORIGINAL TELEPLAY:
The following exchange was cut from this episode's script for length:
 GYPSY MAN: "You! Evil one!"
 ANGEL: "Evil one? Oh, man, now I've got hurt feelings."
 GYPSY MAN: "What do you want?"
 ANGEL: "A whole lot. Got a lot of lost time to make up for. Say, I guess that's kind of your fault, isn't it? You Gypsy types, you go and curse people, you really don't care who gets hurt. Of course, you did give me an escape clause, so I gotta thank you for that."
 GYPSY MAN: "You are an abomination. The day you stop suffering for your crimes, you are no longer worthy of a human soul."
 ANGEL: "Well, that pesky little critter's all gone. So we can get down to business. . . . Don't worry, it won't hurt a bit . . . after the first hour."

> *The multiplex/mall set was in a closed Robinsons/May department store on South Grand Avenue in Los Angeles. A moat was built around the set to catch the water from the overhead sprinklers.*

> *Another Whedon stage direction, regarding Xander and Cordelia kissing: "They haben der big smootchen."*

Passion
Episode 2.17

"Passion" will always be the episode in which we learned Joss Whedon was *not* messing around. Prior to the tentative, adorable courtship between Giles and Jenny Calendar, it would have been hard to imagine any new character joining the core group of Scoobies, but Jenny truly seemed to belong. She had her own dark secrets and regrets and was in the process of trying to make up for them—choosing her new friends and her new love over familial loyalty. When Angelus chases her through Sunnydale High School after dark and murders her, the shock wasn't only that a character we'd come to love might die . . . it was that on this series, anything might happen. With Jenny's death, it was clear that nobody was safe. And when Angelus stages Giles's apartment to make it appear that Jenny has prepared a romantic evening for the two of them . . . only to use a trail of rose petals to lead Giles to the discovery of Jenny's corpse, our hearts broke right along with his.

WRITTEN BY: Ty King
DIRECTED BY: Michael E. Gershman
GUEST STARS: Kristine Sutherland as Joyce Summers, Robia LaMorte as Jenny Calendar, James Marsters as Spike, Juliet Landau as Drusilla
WITH: Richard Assad as Shopkeeper

THE PLOT THICKENS:
Buffy wakes up to find a charcoal drawing of herself sleeping left on her bed by Angel, and Willow finds her fish dead in an envelope in her bedroom. At their behest, Giles searches for a spell that will uninvite the vampire from the Summers and Rosenberg residences. The spell comes from Jenny, meant as a reconciliation gesture. Angel, meanwhile, plays the stalking ex-boyfriend role on Joyce, complete with mention of the fact they made love, which leads to a rather difficult conversation between Joyce and her daughter.

    Meanwhile, Jenny is working to try to translate the spell that would return Angel's soul to him. Late one night, she finally does so, saving the file to a disk and printing it out. However, Angel has learned of this project, thanks to a prophetic vision from Drusilla, and destroys Jenny's computer and the printout, and brutally kills Jenny. He then places the body in Giles's bedroom, setting the place up with champagne and flowers, making it all the more devastating when Giles finds the corpse. The move backfires rather spectacularly, as Giles firebombs the Factory and manages to do some serious damage to Angel before the vampire gets the upper hand. Luckily, Buffy shows up and proceeds to pound on Angel, though she is forced to cut it short in order to save Giles from the fire.

> Director Michael Gershman is also the series's director of photography. The first two seasons of Buffy were shot on super 16mm film stock.

QUOTE OF THE WEEK:
Spike, criticizing Angel's methods:
  "You're supposed to kill her, not leave gag gifts in her friends' beds."

LOVE, SLAYER STYLE:
Jenny has a few heartfelt conversations with Giles ("I know you feel betrayed." "Yes, well, that's one of the unpleasant side effects of betrayal"), even admitting she loves him. Despite Buffy's anger at Jenny, the Slayer does encourage Jenny to try to reconcile with Giles, because he misses her, even if he won't admit it. Her death puts Giles in full "Ripper" mode.

The Angel-Drusilla-Spike triangle gets worse. Dru gets Spike a puppy that she names Sunshine, which makes Spike feel like he needs to be fed like a child, and Angel's jokes about Spike's wheelchair-bound condition grow crueler.

POP-CULTURE IQ:
Xander, on Giles's course of action following Jenny's murder, referring to the title of a Russ Meyer movie:
  "If Giles wants to go after the fiend that killed his girlfriend, I say, 'Faster, Pussycat! Kill! Kill!'"

CONTINUITY:
The Slayerettes cast a spell that uninvites Angel from the Summers house ("Angel"), the Rosenberg house ("Lie to Me"), and Cordelia's car ("Some Assembly Required"). When Buffy warns her mother about Angel possibly coming around, Joyce remembers him as "the college boy who's tutoring you in history" ("Angel"). Using a computer program, Jenny manages to re-create the spell that originally cursed Angel ("Angel," "Surprise," "Innocence"), but the

only copy is on a disk that falls between her desk and a cabinet, where it remains until "Becoming, Part One." At the end of the episode, Willow becomes the substitute computer-science teacher, a post she winds up retaining for the balance of the school year ("I Only Have Eyes for You," "Go Fish," "Becoming, Part One"). The Factory, which has been vampire headquarters all season ("When She Was Bad," etc.), is destroyed by Giles, which will lead Angel, Spike, and Drusilla to take up residence in the mansion ("I Only Have Eyes for You").

FROM THE ORIGINAL TELEPLAY:
During the sequence just after Jenny is killed, we hear Angel in voice-over while we watch through the window of Buffy's home as the phone rings and she and Willow learn of Jenny's death. What follows is the dialogue the viewer can't hear:

> WILLOW: "So was it horrible?" (referring to "The Talk" between Buffy and her mom)
> BUFFY: "It wasn't too horrible." [phone rings] "Hello?"
> GILES (ON THE PHONE): "Buffy?"
> BUFFY: "Giles! Hey, we finished the spe—"
> GILES (ON PHONE): "Jenny . . . Ms. Calendar . . . she's been killed."
> BUFFY: "What . . .?"
> GILES (ON PHONE): "It was Angel."
> BUFFY DROPS THE PHONE.
> WILLOW: "Buffy?" [She picks up the phone] "Giles?"
> GILES (ON PHONE): "Willow. Angel's killed Jenny."
> WILLOW: "What? No . . . oh . . . no . . ."
> JOYCE: "Willow! My God, Buffy! What's wrong? Has something happened?"

Becoming, Part One
Episode 2.21

WRITTEN AND DIRECTED BY: Joss Whedon
GUEST STARS: Seth Green as Oz, Kristine Sutherland as Joyce Summers, Max Perlich as Whistler, Bianca Lawson as Kendra, Julie Benz as Darla, James Marsters as Spike, Juliet Landau as Drusilla, Armin Shimerman as Principal Snyder
WITH: Richard Riehle as Merrick, Jack McGee as Doug Perren, Nina Gervitz as Teacher

THE PLOT THICKENS:
The construction of a new housing project has unearthed the sarcophagus of Acathla, a demon that was turned to stone by a knight. Angel makes off with the sarcophagus and wishes to use the demon to bring about Hell on Earth, destroying everything. Meanwhile, Buffy and Willow discover the backup disk that Jenny Calendar had made with the translation of the spell to restore Angel's soul. Though Xander thinks re-cursing Angel is a mistake and Giles thinks Willow isn't ready to channel that kind of magick, Willow prepares to cast the spell.

Kendra reappears with the sword blessed by the knight who imprisoned Acathla, and a warning from her Watcher that something awful is about to happen. Angel's first attempt to make that something awful happen fails, and so he lures Buffy away from the library so Drusilla can lead a raiding party to kidnap Giles. That raid leaves Willow comatose with a nasty head injury, Xander with a broken wrist, Giles kidnapped, and Kendra slaughtered. Buffy returns to the library just in time for Kendra's dying breath—and the arrival of the cops, accusing her of the murder.

QUOTE OF THE WEEK:
Spike, less than impressed with Acathla's sarcophagus:
> "It's a big rock. I can't wait to tell my friends. They don't have a rock this big."

LOVE, SLAYER STYLE:
In one of the episode's many flashbacks, Angel gets his first look at Buffy when Merrick first tells her she is the Chosen One, and it's obviously love at first sight.

BUFFY'S BAG OF TRICKS:
She is given a sword by Kendra to stop the demon, and Kendra also gives Buffy her favorite stake, which she has named "Mr. Pointy."

POP-CULTURE IQ:
Buffy mispronounces Acathla as "Alfalfa" (likely referring to the *Little Rascals* character) and "Al Franken" (referring to the comedian/writer/actor/politician).

CONTINUITY:
This episode is festooned with flashbacks that detail important events in the lives of the characters: Darla turning Angel into a vampire ("Angel"), Angel torturing Drusilla ("Lie to Me"), Angel being cursed by the Romany people ("Angel," "Surprise," "Innocence"), and Buffy's first learning that she is the Slayer ("Welcome to the Hellmouth"). The disk with the spell to restore Angel's soul is rediscovered ("Passion"), though Willow's attempt to cast it is interrupted; her next chance comes in "Becoming, Part Two." Angel's diversion of Buffy to get at the Slayerettes mirrors the similar stunt executed by the Anointed One and Absalom in "When She Was Bad," of which Angel reminds Buffy.

FROM THE ORIGINAL TELEPLAY:
The following line was cut from the script for length:
> **WHISTLER:** "There are three kinds of people that no one understands: geniuses, madmen, and guys that mumble."

Becoming, Part Two
Episode 2.22

WRITTEN AND DIRECTED BY: Joss Whedon
GUEST STARS: Seth Green as Oz, Kristine Sutherland as Joyce Summers, Robia LaMorte as Jenny Calendar, Max Perlich as Whistler, James Marsters as Spike, Juliet Landau as Drusilla, Armin Shimerman as Principal Snyder

THE PLOT THICKENS:
Buffy runs from the cops before they can mistakenly arrest her for Kendra's murder. She later goes to the hospital to learn that Xander's wrist is broken but fine and Willow's still in a coma. Whistler shows up and tells Buffy she has to know how to use the sword, but his importuning falls on frustrated ears. Spike then approaches Buffy with a proposal: a temporary alliance against Angel in exchange for Spike and Drusilla's being allowed to leave Sunnydale. Reluctantly, Buffy agrees. Meanwhile, Willow awakens from her coma and insists on trying to cast the spell again, and Angel is physically torturing Giles for information on how to awaken Acathla, which the librarian is handily resisting. However, Giles breaks when Drusilla creates the illusion of Jenny Calendar in his mind. Angel learns that his blood must be used to open the portal to Hell—and, as Buffy learns from Whistler, only Angel's blood can subsequently close it. She goes to the mansion, determined to free Giles and kill Angel, and unaware—through Xander's omission—that Willow is attempting the ritual again. With Spike's help, she does fairly well, but Angel manages to open the portal anyhow. When the curse takes effect and Angel's soul is restored, Buffy realizes that she has to impale the man she loves and send him to Hell in order to close the gate. She does so, and then departs from Sunnydale on a bus, leaving only a note for her mother.

> Joss Whedon's stage directions this time around included, "Yes, it's sunrise. Sue me." Sunrises and sunsets are almost impossible to film because they are so brief and difficult to schedule, much less capture on film.

> *Exterior shots of the mansion were filmed in a residential neighborhood on a hill. The crew had to get special permission to drive a 6,000-pound crane on the street, and all filming had to be wrapped by 10 a.m. This is called the "taillights at ten" rule.*

QUOTE OF THE WEEK:
Angel, describing Giles's immediate future:
  "I want to torture you. I used to love it, and it's been a long time. I mean, the last time I tortured someone, they didn't even *have* chain saws."

LOVE, SLAYER STYLE:
Xander admits he loves Willow just before she awakens from her coma—so, naturally, the first thing she does upon awakening is call for Oz. Drusilla is able to use Giles's grief over Jenny Calendar's death to her and Angel's benefit. The re-souled Angel and Buffy exchange a passionate kiss and declare their love for each other right before she is forced to stab him.

> *The Factory set was torn down to make room for the mansion set on a* Buffy *soundstage.*

BUFFY'S BAG OF TRICKS:
She uses the sword Kendra brought for her.

CONTINUITY:
The police talk to Joyce regarding Buffy's possible involvement in Kendra's death, referring to her history of violence. After a vampire attacks Joyce, Buffy is forced to finally tell her mother that she is the Slayer—a concept Joyce has understandable problems facing. When Joyce asks Spike if they know each other, Spike reminds her that she hit him with an ax ("School Hard"). Spike's speech on how much he likes the world and doesn't want to destroy it ("Billions of people walking around like Happy Meals with legs") belies his actions with the Judge in "Surprise" and "Innocence." Buffy is expelled by Snyder, making Buffy two-for-two regarding high schools ("Welcome to the Hellmouth"). More hints regarding the apparent conspiracy among the authorities in Sunnydale are dropped via a phone call Snyder makes to the Mayor ("School Hard," "I Only Have Eyes for You"). Spike and Dru leave Sunnydale the way they came in: driving in a fast car ("School Hard"). Again Angel is cursed with a soul ("Angel," "Surprise," "Innocence," "Becoming, Part Two"), but Buffy has to send him to Hell regardless.

> *To put himself in an "agonizing" frame of mind, Tony Head chopped chili peppers into small bits and popped them into his mouth before every take of Giles's torture scene.*

JAMES MARSTERS (SPIKE)

You've got a new Web series called *Vidiots*. What is it, how was it born, and what kind of feedback are you getting?

JAMES: "*Vidiots* is the story of two fools who travel the world, one of whom is named James Marsters. They travel first class, stay in four-star hotels, live the celebrity rock-and-roll lifestyle, have fans, make films and television, and perform rock concerts, but all they really want to do is get back to the hotel and play video games.

"I travel with a man named Mark Devine, who helps me with my table at conventions, and at the end of a long day, we like to go and play video games. Mark is the funniest man I know. He is also really horrible at video games—he just gets slaughtered. He constantly has me in stitches when we play together. He cracks great jokes, but then his reaction to defeat is fabulous. I thought it would be great to film this happening, because there are a lot of Web shows about gaming, where the person is a great gamer—which always makes me feel like less than a great gamer—and they try humor. They may be great gamers, but they fail at comedy.

"So I thought it would be kinda fun to flip that on its head and be terrible at gaming, but really good at comedy. So we started filming this and it was going really well. We were playing *Assassin's Creed: Unity* in Paris and the game is set in Paris. We had the curtains drawn on a beautiful spring day, and we were playing this video game, and I said to Mark, 'We're idiots. We're pretending to be in Paris, but we're actually here. We should turn the video game off and go look at the actual city.'

"Those two ideas made the show, this combination of *An Idiot Abroad* with funny video gaming. I don't know if you know the series *An Idiot Abroad* with Karl Pilkington and Ricky Gervais, but it's a really funny show. *Vidiots* is just two stupid Americans, walking around the world, really a lot going over their heads, and then watching them video game. And then also the 'backstage with the celebrities' element.

"The reaction we have been getting has been outstanding— people are loving it. And the most important one was my wife, who actually said, and I quote, 'I know I have said in the past that you play too many video games. I was wrong.' That makes the whole endeavor worthwhile right there."

Looking back now, what stands out to you about the process of being cast as Spike, your audition or your first look at the script, or both?

JAMES: "I was in a new relationship, and I was feeling very sexy. That part of the relationship was going really well. My confidence level was sky high. I think that played a large part. Also, at that time I was a very proud stage actor who had no respect for film acting whatsoever. Which I think also helped. I remember doing Shakespeare monologues in the audition room in front of the other actors in order to shove in their faces that they were in the presence of a 'real actor,' and I was sure that they would quail in the face of my ability. It took me a couple of years in Hollywood to realize that almost all the tools that I had learned from stage acting didn't apply in any way to film. All I was probably doing in that audition room was proving myself to be insane in front of the other actors. I wasn't actually intimidating anyone."

But it worked.

JAMES: "It worked because I was confident, I was cocky, so I was really in character by the time I walked into that room."

At some point you had to realize just how crazy the fans were about Spike. Do you remember when you became aware that the character was really working?

JAMES: "I remember recognizing that the character was working for myself. I've done a lot of characters, and sometimes you feel like, *This is kinda working. This is okay*, but there are other times when you think, *This one is really clicking. This one kicks ass*. And I remember Spike being one of those characters that from the very first scene I played I thought, *Holy crap, this is really working well*, and when I saw the first episode, I said, 'Yep, I knew it. This is kicking ass.' That's on a personal level or an artistic level. At that point, I would've been very surprised if the character hadn't been really popular. That sounds like more cockiness, but it's not. I've produced a lot of plays and I've directed plays, and you can be sitting there on opening night thinking, *This one's gonna hit. This is gonna get great reviews*. You're watching it, and you just know."

At some point you began to attend conventions and you must have recognized that Spike was as popular or even more popular than some of the core characters.

JAMES: "I remember going to the Posting Board Party (thrown by the people who ran the *Buffy* forum *The Bronze*). The first one I attended was at the American Legion Hall in Los Angeles, and it was insane. There was so much excitement in the room that I was afraid for my safety. I had been in a situation like that once before, when I was seventeen, and people were surrounding me and people were trying to rip at my clothes to get a piece for themselves."

What were you doing at seventeen that caused people to tear your clothes off?

JAMES: "It was a production of *Godspell* for the International Thespian Society convention, which happens every two years at Ball State in Muncie, Indiana. Every two years all the drama nerds from around the country congregate in Indiana. There are, like, two thousand high school drama nerds who go there, and they cast a play from around the country to perform only at the conference. That year it was *Godspell*, and they cast me as Jesus. In high school circles it's a big deal to be in that. You do one performance in front of two thousand people and that's it. Within the confines of Ball State University, I was like Justin Bieber at his height. It was a madhouse, and I had to have security—the whole cast, we had to have security at all times. People would break into our living quarters and steal stuff. People would bust into bathrooms and try to look at our junk. We had to eat separately, and after the show was performed, the audience just swarmed onto the stage before we could get off, and I remember being surrounded and people were trying to rip at my costume to get a piece of it. . . . It was the strangest thing."

Then you moved from that, in which there are a finite number of people who could possibly recognize you from that performance, to being on television every week, where it's shown all over the world. There's nowhere to go, at that point, where you might not be recognized anywhere, at any time. How did your life change when it really happened, when that celebrity really hit?

JAMES: "I hid from the world. I was not comfortable with that level of fame at all. After the *Godspell* experience, I remember thinking, *Well, I guess I'm glad that happened, because now I know I'm not really into that level of fame. I don't really want to chase that, so I'm going to do stage, where there's a smaller audience and the excitement level is a little more subdued. And now I know that I don't want to go to Los Angeles.* And I had many good years. It was great because you'd be out jogging or walking around and someone would stop you and say, 'Oh, Mr. Marsters, I saw your *Macbeth* last night, very nice,' and you'd say thank you, and you'd go on your way. And it felt really good. That was the level of fame that I enjoyed. I came to Los Angeles because I had a son and I had to actually make money, which they don't have a lot of in theater. I came down here for diaper money, not expecting at all to get famous. I thought I was going to do a couple of guest spots, get a little chunk of change in the bank account, and that'd be it. And then I met Joss Whedon and everything just exploded.

"So I hid, but the problem was I had white-blond hair, which is like a neon bulb, and it just draws the eye. When I was out on the street every eyeball just got visually pulled to the freak in the white hair. And if you look for more than a few seconds and you've ever seen the show, then you know 'Oh, that's the guy from *Buffy*.' It was usually between five and fifteen seconds that I had on a sidewalk anywhere in the world, then I had to get away from that sidewalk or a crowd would form and just get bigger and bigger, and it wouldn't stop. There was no way I could meet everyone and get everyone satisfied and just move on. It would continue to grow. It was a low-grade panic for me.

"I remember I was dating a girl and I constantly wanted to take her back to my apartment, and she was like, 'I don't want to go to your apartment, masher!' And I kept explaining to her that I couldn't just walk around the streets of Santa Monica. I couldn't just hang out and go to a restaurant or something. 'I'm not really comfortable out in public right now. I'm not really relaxed, you know, so if we could just go back to my place, I could have a good evening.' Ultimately I think we broke up over that—she thought I was just trying to get on to second base.

"The thing that happened was I did a TV movie with Roger Daltrey, who was the lead singer of The Who, and he taught me how to be famous."

What does that mean? How did he teach you how to be famous?

JAMES: "He described himself as a worm farmer. He said, 'I used to be a rock star, but now I farm worms for silk.' The world still thinks of him as a rock god. We were shooting a project called *Strange Frequencies*, where he played the devil and I played a guitarist. We'd be out on location filming and people would just be coming up to him constantly, saying, 'Oh my God, it's Roger Daltrey. Can I have a picture? Oh my God, can I have an autograph?' And he would be talking to me about worms, and he would graciously turn to the person, give them the picture, give them the autograph, and then move on. He had a very gracious way of letting them know that's over now, and he'd turn back to me and have his conversation. He had integrated this into the rhythm of his life. He wasn't running from it, he wasn't ashamed of it, he wasn't angry about it. He was having fun with it, but it wasn't feeding his ego either. And watching him do that, I thought, *That's how you do it.* He told me, 'It's not going to go away, so you can choose to take it seriously—which will make you an egotistical jerk—or you can choose to be afraid of it—which will make you unhappy—or you can just say, "This is part of my life," and it is kind of weird and fun, but it's not all of what you are.'"

Obviously the popularity and longevity of Spike going from a one-off to a recurring character to a regular on *Buffy* to a regular on *Angel* is a testament to your abilities as an actor, but it seemed that the funnier Spike became, the more popular he became.

JAMES: "I think you're absolutely right. If you're a character in Joss Whedon's world, if you want to last, you'd better be funny. People are funny in real life. People are humiliated, and they are afraid, and they are silly. Every human is, and I think Joss sees that. And I think that if you want to live in his world, you have to be able to reflect that. I remember he walked up to me at one point and said, 'James, you're funny! I didn't know how funny—you're, like, Emma Caulfield funny,' and I knew that meant that he thought that I was really, really funny. If he thought you were 'Emma Caulfield funny,' you had arrived."

Were there other factors you think contributed to Spike's longevity?

JAMES: "I think the principal one is that evil is not cool to Joss Whedon. I don't think evil is cool in real life—I think evil is pathetic, pitiful, and I think that Joss sees it that way too. Hollywood quite often does a disservice by making evil look cool. It works for a story to make the villain cool, and everyone likes a villain that you love to hate, but it sets up a strange message sometimes. So in Joss's world on *Buffy*, vampires were not supposed to be sexy. They were not supposed to be cool. They were supposed to be metaphors for the challenges that you meet when you're a teenager. So we were supposed to be ugly and very quickly killed off. That's why he had us 'vamp out' when we bit someone, because he didn't want it to be sensual at all; he wanted it to be horrific. He got talked into one sexy vampire by his writing partner David Greenwalt, and that was Angel. It was not his idea—that wasn't an original part of his vision for the show, but he got talked into it, and Angel took off like a rocket ship. Which is not surprising, because the audience wants that sexy vampire. There's a hunger for it whenever you do a vampire show, so he was satisfying that. And he told David, 'Okay, I gave you Angel, but that's the only one. We're not doing any more than that. We're gonna keep to my theme.' But for whatever reason the audience perceived Spike as a romantic character even though Joss very much did not. I was supposed to be a dirty, skanky, punk-rock character that Angel was gonna kill so that he'd look cooler. So for a long time Angel and I were the only two sexy vampires, and we were filling a need that Joss was denying the audience everywhere else on the show. I think that's a big part of the character's success.

"I think that both Joss and I are by nature subversive artists. I produced a lot of theater that was subversive. I really enjoy subversive art; it's my favorite stuff. Subversion, by the way, is not trying to make people feel upset or uncomfortable, but that often happens if it's working. Subversion is all about divesting the audience of lies they get taught in childhood. Some of these lies are things like violence works, old people are boring, you can buy yourself identity. *Buffy* was subverting the idea that females can't defend themselves. Another part of subversion is undercutting the powerful. Because the truth is that all human beings are equal, but in society we don't treat each other that way. So when a subversive sees a powerful institution or a powerful person there's a real instinct to even the playing field, to rip the powerful down somehow.

"That's where, artistically speaking, both Joss and I live. So in some way he got a great mouthpiece for his style because I instinctually understand what he's doing and I really like it. He hired a real original punk rocker to play a punk-rock vampire. You know, when he told me he wanted the Sid Vicious of the vampire set I told him, 'No, you don't. You don't want Sid; you want Johnny Rotten.'

"Sid was an idiot—he really was. He was not a smart man; he was not a talented musician—I'm not saying he was a bad person, but he was not a force of nature in any way. He didn't play on the one album that the Sex Pistols recorded. He pretty much ruined the tour because he was not a good musician. If Sid had played on the album, it would not have been a hit. Johnny Lydon, on the other hand—Johnny Rotten—is a frickin' genius. If you see any interviews with him, he is a maniacal, fiery subversive, and howlingly funny, and he was always the Sex Pistol that I was drawn to."

Speaking of musicians, you've been traveling the world for years as an actor, but also performing music that whole time, both with Ghost of the Robot and as a solo performer. So are you an actor moonlighting as a musician or a musician moonlighting as an actor?

JAMES: "Ha-ha! I don't have to choose! I'm having my cake, and I get to eat it at the same time."

You're also a writer. Do you have any writing projects in the works?

JAMES: "I love to sit down at a keyboard and try to arrange words in a way that they have an effect, and it is delicious when I can read something back that I'm working on and it seems like the engine is starting to hum. There's a joy that I have when I'm doing that. I am not an experienced writer. I've had a few little successes with it, but I love it.

"I was working on a Web series about an alien getting stranded on Earth—this idea that the alien really could be—he could be the mouthpiece for this thing that I feel, that as human beings we are so close to saving ourselves, that technologically speaking we are so close to *Star Trek*. We could do it; we could fix all the problems that we have. There are just a couple of pieces of research and development that if we got, we could heal the planet and march toward a great future, and we should not give up. We should not lose hope; we should not fall into despair in any way. It would be so tragic if we don't turn the corner because we're so close. And I would love for an alien to say that: 'Wait a minute, if you don't do it now, it'd be like quitting college on the last day before you get your diploma. You're so close.'

"I'm also working on helping to adapt the Shakespeare play *Macbeth* into a TV series that would be a western. I'm not usually a fan of doing Shakespeare in any way except exactly the way Shakespeare wanted to do it, but the idea these people came up with about exactly where to set it really excited me."

With all the time that has gone by, what behind-the-scenes memories really stand out to you from your time as Spike?

JAMES: "I remember the dichotomy of what was on-screen and what was happening on the day we shot the scene where Sarah and I finally get into it, and we are so passionate that we knock down a house around us. A lot of people remember that scene; it's one of the scenes that people like to talk about. The truth is that while we were filming that, we were worried if our stunt coordinator was alive or not. In the beginning of that scene, Spike jumps onto a chandelier and kicks Buffy in the face. In order to get that shot, they needed to make a chandelier that wouldn't sway very much while that gag happened. And to do that they had to make it extremely heavy, heavier than the human body. For the shot they wanted, it had to remain fairly still. And I remember talking to Jeff Pruitt, the stunt coordinator, saying, 'Hey, I'd like to do that gag. That's a pretty simple gag, I wouldn't mind doing that myself.' And I remember Jeff being very specific in saying, 'James, no—the chandelier is really heavy, and it's a little dicier than that.' I remember being kind of frustrated.

"So Jeff doubled me, put on the coat and the hair and everything. He did the gag, and the worst thing in the world happened: the chain broke. As he had his legs up at the apex of the kick, the chandelier released from the ceiling. It was concentric circles of metal that came down to a point—and the point landed on his face. They carried him to the hospital, and the entire time that we were shooting the scene, we didn't know if he was alive or dead. The moment the scene was over the entire company—cast and crew—invaded the hospital to check on Jeff. And Jeff is a stuntman, so when we get to the hospital, his whole head is bandaged, and he's like, 'Hey, guys! What's up! Man, that sucked.' He was back to work in record time, a month or something like that.

"I also remember trying to get off the set without letting people know how badly I'd hurt myself when I wanted to do the fire gag. I was only in one episode in season four, and I asked to do the gag where Spike's hand is lit on fire by the sunshine. It's a funny little scene. He falls asleep drunk because he's heartbroken, but he falls asleep outside and he's only woken up because the sun is lighting him on fire, and it's kind of funny. They had designed it so the stuntman's arm would be in the shot for the close-up of Spike's face when he wakes up and sees his hand is on fire. I asked Jeff if I could have that stunt, and he said, 'Well, James, you know that is one of the most dangerous gags in Hollywood because it's an unprotected fire gag. Usually when we do fire gags, it's on top of clothing so you can have a protected suit under your clothes, and you also have the clothes as protection, so it's really the clothes burning, not you, but in this instance it's just the skin, dude, so we dunk the hand in a protective gel and then we dunk the hand in the fuel and then we light you on fire. And the thing is, the protective gel is burning off really fast so the timing is crucial.' And I kept pressing for it. I really wanted that gag. I think they only relented because I was only in one episode that year, and they didn't have any plans to have me back for more. And so they let me light myself on fire.

"I'm not a professional stuntman. I'm an actor and I'm a fool, so I decided that the longer it took Spike to realize that he was on fire, waking up from being asleep, the funnier it would be. If you just had that moment where Spike was awake being like, 'Oh, wow, fire. That's beautiful. What a nice little image—OH, FIRE! . . .' That is hilarious. So I let the gag go on. It's supposed to be a four-second gag, and I let it go for eight. And that was all the difference in the world. I remember going off the set and it's starting to hurt, getting into my trailer and it's hurting a lot, getting into my street clothes and it's starting to blister, and then trying to walk to my car and trying to smile to people who were saying good-bye, because they were saying good-bye forever, really. 'James, love you, good-bye!' And I'm just thinking, *Don't tell the set medic that you've hurt yourself, just go straight to the hospital, because if they find out that you blew this gag so bad, they're never gonna trust you; if you ever get back on the show, they'll never let you do another gag at all.* And I did it. I made it. I drove to the hospital with, like, . . . eighteen quarter-size blisters on my forearm. It was really pretty gross."

Did you ever tell Joss that story?

JAMES: "No! Hell no!"

Everyone says working on a long-running TV series is a lot like a high school. You have your circles of friends, and there are always people you wish you could've hung out with more once you've graduated. So who do you wish you'd hung out with more?

JAMES: "Charisma Carpenter. I had assumed she was like her character on *Buffy*—I thought she was that cheerleader who brutalized me in high school. So I was not interested in getting to know her at all, and I avoided her like the plague, and what I didn't realize was that she was just a phenomenally good actor. Years later I was shooting . . . *Supernatural*, and we were playing husband and wife, and I finally got to know her and realized what a sweetheart she is. We spent the day talking about our kids—and I remember thinking, *My God. She's one of the nicest people in the entire cast, and I thought she was so mean and I never got to know her.* I think she'd be the one that I'd regret not having gotten to know better.

"At the same time I think it was only in season two where we were in the same cast, because by the time I was on *Buffy*, she was over doing *Angel*, and by the time I was on *Angel*, she wasn't there anymore. Actually, the reason why I got on to the show, both shows, was that I was her replacement. I was the new Cordelia on *Buffy*. I was the character that was supposed to tell Buffy that she was stupid and we were all gonna die. And I think that's kind of why I ended up on *Angel*."

I'm sure that when you've had encounters with fans at conventions and things, you've had some uncomfortable things happen, but what are the best ones? What sticks with you?

JAMES: "I have met the most interesting people. I met a person who helped design the Mars rover. That's still up there doing science on Mars as we speak. I met four other people who work at NASA. I've met people who've worked for the NSA, CIA, the State Department, many physicists—I'm a science fan, so I remember those jobs. And every time I go out and meet fans I meet at least one person with a job that I wish I could do.

"I love it when someone tells me how *Buffy* was the thing that brought their family together in some way. People will say, 'That's the thing that I had with my mom—we watched *Buffy*.' I love when you see a twelve- or thirteen-year-old girl who is discovering *Buffy* for the very first time and you can see in her eyes that she is getting empowered by that. It's really wonderful. That is an age where girls start to get put into the vise of our culture, and [there is] the expectation of being a Barbie doll, the expectation of not being sexual, or the shame that comes with sexuality. There's a lot of stuff that can be crushing to young females, and a lot of them go a little crazy when they wake up and childhood ends and they're twelve or thirteen years old. It's not a good time for girls. And to have a show that is pushing back against that really hard is a glorious thing."

You've worked in all sorts of film and TV projects in the years since *Buffy* and *Angel*, including *Hawaii Five-0*, *Without a Trace*, *Torchwood*, and *Smallville*. What's been your favorite post-Spike role?

JAMES: "A high point was playing Buzz Aldrin in a movie called *Moonshot* that you can get on iTunes. That was a really hard shoot. The director explained that he wanted to do a movie that showed what a difficult mission that was. These people were fighter pilots, and they always radio back to NASA so calmly that it appears that it's just a cakewalk to get to the moon, but it really wasn't. It was really uncomfortable and really dangerous and they only gave them a 50 percent chance of survival, and they went. Like the LEM—the lunar excursion module—the walls of that vehicle were only as thick as three pieces of aluminum foil. If they had stepped the wrong way, it would have blown the vehicle apart. It would have depressurized and destroyed them. When Buzz and Neil landed on the moon, their computers were freaking out, and Neil Armstrong had to take over control of the vehicle and land it manually, which was not part of the mission. When they landed, they only had a handful of seconds of fuel remaining. And when they went to press the blast-off button—the engine-ascent button to leave the moon—it wasn't working. They had to figure out how to fix that button, and they ended up doing it with a felt-tip pen. It was really fly-by-the-seat-of-your-pants Lewis-and-Clark stuff. The director said that whenever they've shown the capsule in these movies about *Apollo*, it's always a spacious capsule. It looks like *Star Trek* because they have to fit a big camera in there. For the first time, we were doing it with digital cameras—they can be as little as a ChapStick, some of these cameras—so they built this set to the exact specifications of NASA. It was a very cramped, difficult shoot, but when NASA saw it, they said it finally looked like the mission, which was cool.

"*Torchwood* was also a high point because *Torchwood* is a subversive show. It was done by Russell T. Davies, who is also a *Buffy* fan. He reawakened the whole *Doctor Who* franchise. Without him we wouldn't have the modern *Doctor Who*. But he said that *Torchwood* was his *Buffy*. It took me a long time to realize what he meant was that *Torchwood* was a subversive show. *Buffy* was subverting the idea that women can't defend themselves, and *Torchwood* was subverting the idea that gay people can't be heroes or that LGBT people can't be heroes."

JULIET LANDAU (DRUSILLA)

You've established yourself as a documentarian in recent years, beginning with *Take Flight*, a documentary focused on Gary Oldman, and now with *A Place Among the Dead* and *A Place Among the Undead*. What prompted the first foray into the medium?

JULIET: "Yes, my directorial debut was *Take Flight*, a documentary about Gary Oldman's creative process. That was the first time I worked with Gary, and we had a lot of fun! It started as a behind-the-scenes 'making of' and developed from there. Next my husband, Deverill, and I co-directed *Dream Out Loud*, about makeup artist Kazuhiro Tsuji, who was branching into the world of fine art. The film captured one of his creations from inception to culmination. It showcased interviews with Guillermo del Toro, Joseph Gordon-Levitt, and Rian Johnson.

"Currently, Dev and I are co-directing *A Place Among the Undead* and *A Place Among the Dead*. We are doing something very special with these projects . . . making film history. *A Place Among the Undead* is the definitive docuseries on vampires, featuring previously untapped intimate conversations and insights from the top of the A-list, between one person who has earned her place among the undead—me—journeying into the minds of our pop-culture icons and innovators, who have never been gathered together to discuss their place among the undead. So far we have interviewed Joss Whedon, Tim Burton, Gary Oldman, Willem Dafoe, Anne Rice, Ron Perlman, and Charlaine Harris, among many others—including you, Christopher! We probe our deep-seated need for vampires and how they help us look at different aspects of ourselves: sex, loss, death, violence, addiction, obsession, the dark side of our natures, [and] being outsiders, to name a few. Each episode culminates in a five- to fifteen-minute film, which explores one of these metaphors. It is exciting to be writing and directing narrative content as well. While making the series, we discovered an underbelly, true-crime stories, in which people have taken the fantasy of vampirism too far. We profile one such case in the feature-length [project] *A Place Among the Dead*."

What's the status of when folks will be able to see the finished product of both of those projects, and what have been your favorite moments from this odyssey?

JULIET: "They have continued to grow beyond our wildest expectations. *Undead* started as a feature, but so many people have come aboard that the project developed into a series. Some of the new interviewees include Lance Henriksen (*Near Dark, Aliens, Millennium*), Nathan Fillion (*Dracula 2000, Buffy, Castle*), Kristin Bauer van Straten (Pam from *True Blood*), David Slade (director of *The Twilight Saga: Eclipse, 30 Days of Night*), Kevin Grevioux (creator of the *Underworld* franchise), Marv Wolfman (creator of *Tomb of Dracula* and *Blade*), Lara Parker (original *Dark Shadows* TV series), Kathryn Leigh Scott (original *Dark Shadows* TV series), Gary Shore (director of the Universal blockbuster *Dracula Untold*), and Christian Kane (*Angel*). We are creating a companion book called *Book of the Undead*. Deverill has been shooting the stills for it along with Gary Oldman, who has been shooting tintype portraits of our *Undead* interviewees on his camera from 1853. We are still fund-raising and shooting, so it's looking like [the end of 2017] for the release of both projects."

Have you always been fascinated by vampires and the supernatural, or was this something that sprang from playing such an iconic vampire yourself?

JULIET: "It started when I was on the *Buffy* set and continued from there. Whenever I have hung out with creators, writers, directors, artists, and actors who have played in the vampire universe, we have had the best conversations. There is a real camaraderie amongst us."

You come from what many would consider geek royalty, and with your work in video game and animation voice-over added to your time as Drusilla on both *Buffy* and *Angel*, you're an indelible part of our pop culture. But what are *you* a geek about?

JULIET: "I'm not really a geek in the classic sense of the word, but I'm kind of a geek about work. I am a perfectionist, although I have eased off of trying to make things perfect and just try to do them to the best of my ability. I obsess on every detail . . . whether it is performance, editing, sound design, score, color correction. I push myself and our team to go beyond the work we have done before. . . . My sound editor nicknamed me 'Kubrick,' but as far as I am concerned, there are worse things than being likened to one of the best filmmakers!"

The first time I met you was on the set of *Buffy*. I interviewed you between scenes for the first Watcher's Guide, and while we talked, you kept up some of Drusilla's mannerisms, including hand gestures and some of her vocal cadence. Were you sticking with method and staying in character, or did you just like to freak people out?

JULIET: "Oh, that's funny! I don't think it was either! Sometimes James and I would keep the Spike and Dru dialects because it made it easier not to have to think about it at all. But as far as mannerisms and gestures, maybe it was leftover residue from the work. I hope I didn't freak you out too much!"

You've had all sorts of roles in your career, both on camera and voicing animation. Aside from Drusilla, what has been your favorite? And which role would you hope *Buffy* fans would track down and watch, if they haven't seen it?

JULIET: "I have been so fortunate getting to play a diverse range of characters. I loved playing Loretta King in *Ed Wood*. It was my first big movie and working with Tim Burton was brilliant. The role I am working on whenever I am asked tends to become my favorite at that time! For me the exploration phase is what I love best. I did an episode of *La Femme Nikita*, directed by Joel Surnow, who created *24*, in which I played two characters. It was an actor's dream! I loved voicing Tala in *Justice League Unlimited* and the Little Sisters in *Bioshock*. I just recorded an animated feature for DC, which I am excited about but can't talk about yet! Two of my favorite roles ever were onstage . . . Roberta in *Danny and the Deep Blue Sea* and Blanche in *A Streetcar Named Desire*. See . . . I told you it was hard to pick!"

You have a theater background. How has theater been a part of your life both before and after Drusilla, and do you have plans to return to the stage?

JULIET: "I *love* doing theater. It has been a huge part of my career. Dev and I produced *Danny and the Deep Blue Sea* in Los Angeles a few years ago. We were supposed to run for six weeks but kept getting extended and ran for six months. We got twelve out of twelve rave reviews, including the *Los Angeles Times* Critics' Pick and multiple awards. I don't have plans at the moment for a stage production, because of the time commitment and scope of our two current projects, but I will absolutely be returning to the stage."

Looking back now, what stands out to you about the process of being cast as Drusilla—about the audition or your first look at the script, or both?

JULIET: "I never auditioned for the role. Joss had seen me in *Ed Wood* and another movie. I had read a few pages before going in for a meeting, which was the scene with the Anointed One. I went in and had the most amazing creative meeting with Joss, David Greenwalt, Gail Berman, and Marcia Shulman, who was the head of casting at Fox. Joss said the character could be British or American. I remember saying, 'She has to be English!' and then I did a little of Dru. I wafted up to the ceiling and talked to it in what became Dru's singsong cadence. He said if they could find an actor who could play Spike [as] British, it would be so. He explained that he'd had Drusilla and Spike running around in his head for ten years! The meeting was a free-form conversation and very inspiring. My cell phone rang before I had even reached my car in the parking lot. It was my agent saying they wanted to hire me. I couldn't wait to get on set to work with Joss and the gang!"

Did you have any idea after that first episode that Drusilla would be back or that she'd come to play a pivotal role in the series?

JULIET: "Yes. They weren't sure the number of episodes, but they told me in that initial meeting that Drusilla would be throughout season two. I think it developed past that as we went along."

I'm sure you get recognized on the street. How did your life change once Drusilla became part of pop culture?

JULIET: "It is extraordinary when people respond deeply to a character which you have played. They often echo back to you the very elements you were imbuing the role with, and that is extremely rewarding and satisfying. *Buffy*, *Angel*, and the Whedonverse have such a phenomenal fan base. I think the main change is that I've gotten to meet so many varied and interesting people because of being a part of it."

Conventions and public appearances—and just being in public—must come with some pretty strange fan interactions. If you're willing to share . . . what are the best and worst fan moments you can remember?

JULIET: "Most *Buffy* and *Angel* fans are supremely smart and discerning. The shows were so intelligently conceived and written that the people who respond are very much in kind.

I did have one fan run down the street screaming, 'Aaaaah, Drusilla!' as she went. I kept yelling, 'I'm an actress! I'm not a vampire!' But it was to no avail. Her bellows could be heard down the block. . . . And it was daylight, too! Sometimes people have tattoos done of your visage or your signature. I was at London Comic Con and a gal named Victoria Louise asked me to sign a picture: 'John, will you marry me?' I asked her if she was sure she wanted me to be in the middle of this intimate moment, and she said yes. As I was signing, she took out a ring box *and* so did he! He had been planning to propose at the very same moment! *Buffy* brought them together, and it was tremendously moving to be part of their special union. I am often touched by how many people say *Buffy*, *Angel*, and/or Drusilla got them through a really hard time, like an illness or bullying—all sorts of life challenges."

It's been a long time since *Buffy*. What are your favorite behind-the-scenes memories of your time on the show?

JULIET: "There are so many! Joss is a genius. It was a sensational group of people. On season two of *Buffy*, we got the scripts about a week ahead of time and we would sit down to table reads with all the cast. James, like me, has a theater background, so we'd get together and rehearse before shooting. We always came in rife with ideas, including blocking (where one moves in a scene) and it made the shoot days fluid and full of discovery, which can be unusual in television. Joss changed the genre with his vision and creativity, and he nourished and inspired us to bring our A-game to the set every day."

Everyone says that working on a long-running TV series is a lot like high school, with circles of friends and then those people you wish you'd hung out with more. Who do you wish you'd hung out with more?

JULIET: "I got to hang out a lot with Joss, James, David, Julie, Sarah, Alyson, Nick, and Charisma, which was fabulous! I never thought of it like high school. . . . For me it was more like the run of a play, where you get to live with a character for a long time and learn new things. The difference in theater is that the text is the same, whereas in a series every episode is new, but in both, the understanding and the layers of the character deepen and grow."

What are you working on now, and what does the future hold for Juliet Landau?

JULIET: "As discussed, I am co-directing *A Place Among the Undead* and *A Place Among the Dead*. I am starring in the narrative sections of *Undead* alongside many people's favorite performers. Dev and I are working on the *Book of the Undead*. I'm currently starring in a film on Netflix called *Where the Road Runs Out*, which I shot in Africa. I have a number of really cool projects brewing and a couple in the can, but I am not allowed to announce those yet!"

CYNTHIA BERGSTROM (COSTUME DESIGN)

Your first costuming job—at least that I can find a record of—was working in wardrobe for a Virginia Madsen movie called *Zombie High*. I need to see this film. What do you remember about that experience, and how did you get your first job on set?

CYNTHIA: "Yes, *Zombie High* was my first experience in film. I was friends with one of the producers. At the time I was working as a sales rep for a fashion line. My friend asked to use some of my samples for the film and brought me on board as the costume designer. It was a super-low-budget project and so much fun. I felt right at home and knew I had found my calling. I had no experience, yet everyone from each department filled me [in] on what a costume designer does beyond simply creating the look of the show. The accountant showed me how to devise a budget, the script supervisor showed me how to break down a script, the assistant directors filled me in on how to work with extras . . . and so on. I was also Virginia's stunt person. I recall being thrown across the room into a bookcase. I was then to get up and hit an older gentleman (a zombie) over the head with a balsa wood bat. Unfortunately, I was given the real bat and not the prop bat. . . . I'll never forget my horror when I realized the mistake when I heard the crack of the bat hitting his skull along with the shrill of his scream. The man was sent to the hospital. I believe he suffered a small concussion, yet was fine. Thank heavens I didn't have a very powerful swing!"

In addition to an incredible run as costume designer on one hundred and ten episodes of *Buffy*, you also had long runs with series like *Medium*, *Private Practice*, and *CSI: Miami*. When we first met, and reading other interviews with you, it seemed obvious that your work helped define the characters on *Buffy*. I'm sure the degree to which that's possible, the freedom a costume designer has, must vary from job to job. How would you compare the experience on *Buffy* to others you've had?

CYNTHIA: "After I left *Buffy*, I soon came to realize that costuming *Buffy* was a unique experience. I was given a great deal of freedom, trust, and respect. Every show is different. It's a different group of people as well as a different concept. I found that each show has its own rhythm and way of uniting departments. Once that rhythm is found, then everything flows and all departments usually work together in a cohesive manner. After the first episode, I would again begin to see the same level of freedom, trust, and respect. I loved the other shows that I designed. The creative environment was different and that was okay. But *Buffy* was hugely creative—it was fantasy and make-believe and traversed different realms. I loved imagining the fantastical. I loved building the costumes from imagination."

Who was your favorite character to dress, and why?

CYNTHIA: "I am asked this question still to this day. It's a fan favorite. My answer is always the same. I loved dressing them all. Each character was so defined and individual. Each was an extension of my imagination and creativity. I loved it all and loved them all."

All these years later, do you have a favorite outfit from the series and a favorite moment when you knew your work on an episode really hit a home run?

CYNTHIA: "Episode six of season two. I think it was called 'The Wish.' I only know that because I recently moved. As I was unpacking boxes from storage, I found my old sketches from the show. I remember showing Sarah the sketch of the dress I designed for her. Her face was so precious and appreciative of the gorgeous gown that was being created for her. She was stunning in it. I recall that being a pinnacle moment in my evolution as a designer."

So much time has passed. What are your favorite behind-the-scenes memories of your time on *Buffy*?

CYNTHIA: "I loved it when the actors would come into the costume department and hang out just to chat. We had couches throughout the department where people could just come in and relax. I usually had my two dogs with me. The cast and our producer, Gareth Davies, would show up daily to play with the dogs. It was always so much fun and so joyful with lots of laughs, giggles, howling, and barking."

Everyone says that working on a long-running TV series is a lot like high school, with circles of friends and then those people you wish you'd hung out with more. Who do you wish you'd hung out with more?

CYNTHIA: "That's a great question. In high school, I was a spirit leader, which meant at games and throughout the year, along with my co-spirit leader, we would help to raise the morale and lift the spirits of others. I'm still doing this in life and most certainly did this on the set of *Buffy*. I was able to spend time with almost everyone in every department. I love getting to know people, seeing who they are and what makes them tick, and hopefully bring a little light into their lives."

Overall, how would you characterize the influence of your time on *Buffy* on your life?

CYNTHIA: "*Buffy* was a great time in my life. It was a special group. We all had so much fun together. . . . We shared in each other's lives. We really cared about one another. Other shows were not like that. . . . There was caring; it was just different. On *Buffy*, we were creating something really special and unique. It wasn't always a bed of roses—I mean, it was hard work, and, of course, with hard work and long hours, personalities get pushed to the brink. But we were family. I loved going to work every day . . . even the days I didn't love going to work."

You've taken a new path in your life and left costume design behind. What are you up to, and what does the future hold for Cynthia Bergstrom?

CYNTHIA: "Yes! I am complete with costume design. I left the business in 2014 after twenty-seven years. I went back to school to get my master's in spiritual psychology. I now work with highly motivated individuals who are seeking deeper meaning, purpose, joy, and fulfillment in their lives. I also recently discovered I have this amazing, powerful, and soulful singing voice. So I am singing professionally. I am writing two children's stories on spiritual transformation and have created workshops for adults on the same subject. Life is really good. My future is bright and, of course, as always, extremely creative."

SEASON 3

Lovers Walk
Episode 3.8

Arguments for the "best season" of *Buffy the Vampire Slayer* are unwinnable. Every fan is entitled to their own opinion. But if you were to make a list of the best twenty or so episodes of the series—as we did—it would be hard to argue with the position that season three contains more of those episodes than any other. Who can argue that "Lovers Walk" isn't a vital turning point, particularly for Spike? When—at the end—he mocks his own anguish along with the pain of the Scoobies, his comment isn't just one of the character's best lines, it's also a commentary on their drama: "I may be love's bitch, but at least I'm man enough to admit it."

WRITTEN BY: Dan Vebber
DIRECTED BY: David Semel
GUEST STARS: Kristine Sutherland as Joyce Summers, Harry Groener as Mayor Richard Wilkins III, James Marsters as Spike
CO-STARS: Jack Plotnick as Deputy Mayor Allan Finch, Mark Burnham as Lenny, Suzanne Krull as Clerk

THE PLOT THICKENS:
Xander comforts Willow, who is devastated by her self-perceived poor performance on the SATs. Buffy's unanticipated high scores are a shock to all, causing her to reevaluate her thoughts on her future. Cordelia points out that non-Hellmouth options are a good thing, asking, "What kind of moron would want to come back here?" Spike's drunken arrival answers that.

Spike mopes for Drusilla in the abandoned factory. Cordelia, Xander, Willow, and Oz plan a double date for bowling. Cordy actually has photos of Xander in her locker, and Oz gifts Willow with a Pez candy-dispenser witch—true love! Buffy shares Joyce's enthusiastic response to her high test scores with Giles, on his way to a retreat. He unexpectedly responds in the positive when Buffy mentions the idea of school outside of Sunnydale. Willow decides to solve her romantic dilemma of the secret trysts with Xander through an anti-love spell. Spike is in the magick shop looking for a curse to torment Angel; when Willow enters, he gets a better idea.

The Mayor authorizes Deputy Mayor Allan Finch to seek Mr. Trick's assistance in ridding Sunnydale of Spike. Angel endorses Buffy's tentative plan to leave Sunnydale, much to her chagrin. Willow tries to perform her de-lusting spell on an unknowing Xander, but he refuses to cooperate. Spike ends their debate by kidnapping both of them, knocking Xander unconscious, and informing Willow she is to perform a spell to draw Drusilla back to him—or they're both dead, Xander first. She persuades him she can't possibly cast a successful spell without more ingredients and a spell book. Oz and Cordelia alert Buffy about Xander and Willow's disappearance; she sets them on the road to retrieve Giles and is phoning Joyce when she hears Spike greet Joyce on the other end of the line.

Joyce is lending Spike a sympathetic ear when Angel spots them over their cocoa. Spike is so delighted by Angel's impotent attempts to convince Joyce to invite him in, he doesn't notice Buffy until she knocks him to the ground. While Joyce watches in confusion, Buffy invites Angel in and prepares to dust Spike, halting only when he reveals he is holding hostages. Oz and Cordelia are diverted from their frantic Giles retrieval by Oz's detecting Willow's scent. Spike, Buffy, and Angel search the magick shop for spell components. Spike decides misery loves company and spells out Buffy and Angel's romantic contradictions, leaving them "comeback deficient." Willow comforts a revived Xander; they rationalize the comfort's turn to romance through invoking their dire situation. A situation that is dire in new ways, as Oz and Cordelia arrive to rescue them, only to discover them kissing. Cordelia's hasty exit from the warehouse is cut short as she falls through a rotten stair, impaling herself on a sharp spike. While an anxious Willow watches, Xander descends to check her condition. Oz goes for help.

Buffy, Angel, and Spike's return to the warehouse is interrupted by the appearance of ten vampires sent by Mr. Trick, led by Lenny, an old acquaintance of Spike's. It takes a while, but the ten-to-three odds aren't in the vampires' favor, especially when Buffy and Angel discover an assortment of bottles of holy water. Spike finds the rush of the battle improves his spirits to such a degree he no longer feels the need for Willow or her spell. Revived, he heads off to Brazil to "tie [Drusilla] up and torture her" until she cares for him again. Buffy consoles Willow, grieving over betraying Oz. Xander attempts to make peace with the hospitalized Cordelia, who summons her strength just long enough to dismiss him absolutely. Buffy tells Angel she can't continue their relationship, that she has to be honest with herself. The episode closes with "a series of images: the kids in misery," as Willow, Oz, Xander, Cordelia, and Buffy all face the future with sadness and uncertainty.

QUOTE OF THE WEEK:
Giles worries Joyce has had an *Exorcist* moment over Buffy's high SAT scores:
  BUFFY: "She saw these scores and her head spun around and exploded."
  GILES: "I've been on the Hellmouth too long. That was metaphorical, yes?"

THE AGONY AND THE ECSTASY:
Everyone in this episode is "love's bitch" in one way or another. Willow and Xander struggle with the opposing desires to act on their attractions and be faithful to their chosen partners. Buffy and Angel struggle with admitting their continued love, as they've been cloaking it in the guise of her playing nursemaid to a friend in need. Cordelia makes the momentous leap of publicly displaying Xander's photo in her locker, only to find herself cuckolded, as does Oz. Spike pines for Drusilla the fickle (Angel/Chaos Demon/Fungus Demon). Joyce continues to struggle with Buffy being a Slayer, her enthusiasm for the SATs a reflection of her continued desire for Buffy to have a normal life.

> Spike's choice of Sinatra lyrics was changed in the final aired version, but the closed captioning still reflects the quote used in the original script: "Mistakes . . . I've made a few . . . I ate it up . . . and spit it out . . . and did it my way. . . ." instead of: "More . . . much more than this . . . I did it my way. . . ."

POP-CULTURE IQ:
Bemoaning her "low" SAT scores, Willow compares herself to the stereotypically uneducated character from *The Simpsons*:
   "I'm Cletus the Slack-Jawed Yokel."
Buffy implores Giles to back up during his discussion of her leaving Sunnydale to go to college. She's using video store vernacular:
   "Be kind. Rewind."
Buffy may mean either the 1985 film or the 1994 television show as she inspects Willow's abandoned spell ingredients after Spike abducted her:
   "I'm thinking *Weird Science*."
Angel's long life and international experiences allow him to read philosopher Jean-Paul Sarte's *Nausea* in the original French (*La Nausée*).

CONTINUITY:
Spike's return is a fractured mirror of his original arrival in "School Hard," and a reverse of his departure in "Becoming, Part Two." Buffy's comment "Faith could be Miss Sunnydale in the Slayer pageant" evokes "Homecoming." The Mayor knew of Spike's activities in Sunnydale during the second season but didn't take exception to them before. Xander is nervous about Willow's "de-lusting" spell after Amy's love spell misfired in "Bewitched, Bothered, and Bewildered." Drusilla leaves Spike for a Chaos Demon this time; in "The Harsh Light of Day" Harmony reports that she left him for a Fungus Demon instead. Spike nuzzles Willow's neck, a moment they'll relive when he unsuccessfully attacks her in "The Initiative." Joyce has no reason to fear Spike, introduced to her as a singer in a band in "Becoming, Part Two." Joyce hears in passing that Willow is a witch, but doesn't take it seriously until "Gingerbread." Oz's were-abilities manifesting when he's human are a pivotal plot point in "New Moon Rising." The events of "The Wish," "Doppelgangland" and Anya/Anyanka's presence in Sunnydale are all consequences of

Xander and Willow's factory embrace. Spike's speech about how impossible Buffy and Angel's relationship is will be echoed by the Mayor ("Choices") and Joyce ("The Prom"), eventually resulting in Angel's departure.

FROM THE ORIGINAL TELEPLAY:

Script directions for the teaser:

[A shot-by-shot recreation of Spike's arrival in "School Hard." There's that "Welcome to Sunnydale" sign. And here comes Spike's car, crashing into it as it screeches to a stop. Growling rock cue as the door opens. Except instead of one boot, an entire Spike falls bodily out of the car. A clatter of empties, beer bottles and cans, accompanies him. Our boy's bombed.]

SPIKE: "Home sweet . . . home."

[A moment of looking blearily around, then his head drops back and hits pavement.]

The Wish
Episode 3.9

Continuing our argument that season three is the best of the series, "Lovers Walk" was followed immediately by "The Wish." A week after the broken hearts and plot twists of "Lovers Walk," with everyone hurting and in disarray, the series introduced two elements that would—in time—change everything. First we meet Anya, a.k.a. the vengeance demon Anyanka, who offers Cordelia a single vengeful wish. Spurned and betrayed, Cordelia blames Buffy and wishes she'd never existed . . . with results even Anya couldn't have foreseen. Not only does the arrival of Anya give us the introduction of one of the series's best loved and most indelible characters, but it introduces the character of Vampire Willow, who will reappear later this season in "Doppelgangland" and inspire the real Willow to begin questioning her sexuality—setting up major changes down the line.

WRITTEN BY: Marti Noxon
DIRECTED BY: David Greenwalt
GUEST STARS: Mark Metcalf as the Master, Emma Caulfield as Anyanka/Anya, Larry Bagby III as Larry Blaisdell, Mercedes McNab as Harmony Kendall
CO-STAR: Danny Strong as Jonathan Levenson

THE PLOT THICKENS:
Xander and Willow help Buffy slay as a distraction from their broken hearts. Cordelia, mending physically, burns Xander's photos. On Cordelia's first day back at school, fashion-aware new girl Anya doesn't harass her for having dated Xander like the other Cordettes do. Evening at the Bronze finds Buffy, Willow, and Xander moping over chocolate while Cordelia shows Xander she's moved on. Cordelia heads home when her rebar wound cuts her demonstration short. Buffy tries to intervene with her on Xander's behalf. A random vamp attack ends their debate, and Buffy's successful vamp staking dumps Cordelia in the trash. The next day a sympathetic Anya lends a furiously venting Cordelia her necklace, and Cordelia speaks the fateful words "I wish Buffy Summers had never

come to Sunnydale." Anya reveals her demonic visage, and Sunnydale transforms.

Sunnydale High with no Buffy Summers has a series of deceased principals, monthly memorial services, and students uniformly choosing to dress in subdued, non-vampire-attracting colors. Cordelia makes several adjustments in her new reality: curfew, no car, and a vamp-infested Bronze. Harmony tells Cordelia that Xander and Willow are dead; actually, they're undead vampires. Cordelia, desperate for someone called the Slayer, is rescued from Vamp Willow and Vamp Xander by Giles, Oz, and Larry. Vamp Willow and Vamp Xander visit the Master at the Bronze, who reprimands them for not killing Cordelia outright when she mentioned the Slayer. They cruise to the library, cage Giles, and drain Cordy.

The white hats report other losses to Giles, who manages to free himself and remove Cordelia's body. Giles retains Anyanka's amulet. The Master rewards Xander and Willow, granting Willow permission to "play with the puppy." Translation: torturing a captive Angel for sexual entertainment. Giles makes progress researching Anya and her pendant. He stops to battle vampires who are rounding up citizens, and is losing when Slayer Buffy Summers arrives from Cleveland.

This scarred Buffy has little patience with Giles's research, preferring to find something to stake to solve their problems. When Giles reveals that the Master inhabits the Bronze, she is on the hunt. Angel manages to overcome Buffy's mistrust of him and lead her to the Master and Co. at the factory, where the Master has perfected a technique to harvest blood from Sunnydale's remaining human population. Giles invokes Anya and takes steps to destroy her power center as Buffy and Angel lead an attack on the Master and his minions. Just as the Master kills Buffy, Giles succeeds in reversing Cordelia's wish by destroying the amulet, leaving Anya powerless and bewildered.

QUOTE OF THE WEEK:
Larry in Bizarro Sunnydale delivers the eulogy for dead Bizarro Cordelia, recently killed by Vamp Willow and Vamp Xander:
"Okay, the entire world sucks because some dead ditz made a wish? I just want to be clear."

THE AGONY AND THE ECSTASY:
Demon Anyanka grants wishes for women scorned. Death as a metaphor is at work for almost every character with a broken heart in this episode. Vamp Willow and Vamp Xander drain Cordelia. Vamp Xander dusts Angel. Buffy stakes Vamp Xander. Oz slays Vamp Willow. Giles grieves for the Slayer he never Watched, who dies at the hands of the Master (again).

> "Cordette #1"—Nicole Bilderback—played opposite Seth Green in the 1998 film Can't Hardly Wait.

POP-CULTURE IQ:

Xander, watching Cordelia not missing him, quotes Smokey Robinson and the Miracles:

"Look at her. Tears of a clown, baby."

Anya's old enough to be quoting both William Shakespeare's play *The Tempest* and Aldous Huxley's novel *Brave New World* in this reference to Cordelia's wish that Buffy had never come to Sunnydale:

"I had no idea her wish would be so exciting. Brave new world."

CONTINUITY:

Wicca girl Amy Madison doesn't appear in this episode, but tells Willow off-screen she saw the recovering, betrayed Cordy at the mall. Cordelia and Amy bond over distaste for everything Harmony. In regular continuity, Oz rebuffs Willow's overtures and Buffy advises Xander and Willow about doomed romance. Anya tries to reverse events and regain her powers in "Doppelgangland."

Even in the alternate reality Angel has been summoned to Sunnydale to assist Buffy the Slayer. The Master emerges victorious over Buffy, reversing the events of "Prophecy Girl."

FROM THE ORIGINAL TELEPLAY:

Giles's exposition was changed:

"Anyanka raised a demon to ruin her unfaithful lover. The demon did her bidding—but then cursed her and turned her into a sort of patron saint for scorned women. Apparently the cry of a wronged woman is like a siren's call to Anyanka."

Amends
Episode 3.10

Completing the season three trifecta of awesome, "The Wish" is followed by "Amends," in some ways the most romantic episode in a series full of them. With Angel coming to terms with the horrors he committed as Angelus, and being driven mad by The First Evil, Buffy's selfless expression of love toward him and their daytime walk through the seemingly miraculous snowstorm at the end is doubtless one of the sweetest and hardest-earned moments in the series. And that's three standout episodes *in a row* in a standout season.

WRITTEN AND DIRECTED BY: Joss Whedon
GUEST STARS: Kristine Sutherland as Joyce Summers, Saverio Guerra as Willy the Snitch, Shane Barach as Daniel, Edward Edwards as Travis, Cornelia Hayes O'Herlihy as Margaret, Robia LaMorte as Jenny Calendar, Eliza Dushku as Faith

THE PLOT THICKENS:
It's a typical balmy Southern California Christmas season. No one seems to have the proper spirit except for Cordelia, headed for the slopes of Aspen and "actual snow." Willow's Jewish and still Oz-less. Xander plans to sleep outside, away from family battles. Joyce guilt-trips Buffy into inviting Faith to join their festivities. Giles is somber, despite the "Mr. Giles" stocking hanging from the library door. And the apparitions of three of his victims, including Jenny Calendar, are haunting Angel.

Buffy and Joyce shop for a tree, avoiding the large circle of unpleasantly dead ones in the tree lot. Angel tries to get information from a wary Giles about his nightmarish visitors but flees when Jenny's apparition appears in Giles's apartment. He dreams of another victim, and this time shares his dream with Buffy, who also appears in it. Angel is still tormented by Jenny and the others even when he awakens. Buffy seeks Giles's help, sharing the research load with Xander and Willow. The apparitions remind Angel he lacked integrity in life, and whisper to him of the evil he is capable of, with or without his demon. Buffy and Angel share a nightmare, which ends with Angel vamping out and biting her. Jenny appears and taunts Angel by telling him the dream reflects his true desires.

Buffy and Giles's research pays off with info on the three Harbingers, eyeless priests who draw on the power of an unimaginably ancient evil, The First. Even the powers of the Slayer won't be able to affect The First, so Buffy's tactic is to try to find its priests. Willy imparts that the priests are rumored to be somewhere underground—not much of a lead in tunnel-infested Sunnydale. Buffy and Joyce decorate their tree in front of an unnecessary but cheery fire. Faith accepts the Summerses' invitation, and Buffy heads upstairs to retrieve presents. Angel waits in her room and delivers an incoherent warning to stay away from him. Buffy leaves Faith to guard Joyce. The spirit of Jenny continues to torment Angel, encouraging him to kill Buffy.

The passage "the harbingers of death, nothing shall grow above or below" tips Buffy off to the Harbingers' location. Buffy takes out all three priests almost effortlessly but cannot physically assault The First, who, in the guise of Jenny, promises her that Angel will be dead by sunrise, when he plans to end his torment and hers. Just before dawn Buffy tracks Angel to an exposed bluff. Unable to persuade Angel to continue to be undead, Buffy moves from pleading to anger. As they prepare for sunrise, an unprecedented snow falls on them from the sun-obscuring cloud cover. Buffy and a rescued, stronger Angel walk silently through the snowy streets. "Not saying a word. Not needing to" [from the stage directions].

QUOTE OF THE WEEK:
Buffy, trying to talk Angel into coming in out of the sun before it rises:
"Strong is fighting. It's hard and it's painful and it's every day. It's what we have to do, and we can do it together, but if you're too much of a coward for that, then burn."

> The weatherman who appears on a TV screen in the episode, discussing the freak snowstorm, is actually KTLA weatherman Mark Kriski, who reports for the Los Angeles WB affiliate. His then colleague, KTLA anchorman Carlos Amezcua, appeared in "Hush."

THE AGONY AND THE ECSTASY:
Oz and Willow reunite, but Oz gently puts Willow's adorable attempted seduction of him on hold. When a guilty but needy Angel approaches him for help, Giles strives to forget "that whole Angel-killed-his-girlfriend-and-tortured-him thing." Buffy and Angel have a chance to air all the unspoken feelings that have been simmering between them since his return from Hell.

POP-CULTURE IQ:
Buffy envisions Christmas dinner with *The Grinch Who Stole Christmas*, written in 1957 by Dr. Seuss:
"Tree. Nog. Roast Beast."

During Willow's planned seduction of Oz, he appreciates fellow musician Barry White, the "King of Love," who began performing in the '60s:
"And you got the Barry working for you."

> Ironically, "Amends," billed by the network as "A Buffy Christmas," began filming 10/31/98—Halloween—although it did air 12/15/98, during the holiday season.

CONTINUITY:
Angel killed Jenny Calendar in "Passion." She also appeared in "Becoming, Part Two" as part of Drusilla's spell to ensnare Giles. However, the script makes clear that this is not the vengeful ghost of Jenny, but simply a form The First Evil has taken in order to provoke guilt in Angel. The scenes from 1753 Ireland and 1838 Romania establish more of the timeline of Angel's past. Xander provides research snacks, a theme echoed in "The Zeppo." Joyce is not anxious to invite Giles to Christmas dinner following the events of "Band Candy."

FROM THE ORIGINAL TELEPLAY:
Buffy's response to Joyce is more prophetic in the original version:
JOYCE: "You know, honey, I was thinking—maybe we should invite Faith to spend Christmas Eve with us."
BUFFY: "I'll ask her. Worst she can do is—well, the worst she can do is serious bodily harm, but she'll probably just say no."

> The Mutant Enemy logo monster gets in the seasonal spirit with a Santa cap and jingle bells in the background. He was also altered in "Becoming, Part Two," when he requested a hug, and "Graduation Day," when he wore a graduation cap.

The Zeppo
Episode 3.13

No list of the series's best episodes is complete without the unique wackiness of "The Zeppo." The title is a reference to Zeppo Marx, widely considered the least interesting member of classic film comedy team the Marx Brothers. In this case, it refers to Xander and focuses on his feelings of isolation and impotence among a group of people far more suited to saving the world than he is. In the background of this episode, the rest of the gang is stopping yet another apocalypse, but Xander not only has an adventure of his own—slightly easing his discontent with his position in the group—he also has sex with Faith, a twist fans certainly didn't see coming.

WRITTEN BY: Dan Vebber
DIRECTED BY: James Whitmore Jr.
GUEST STARS: Saverio Guerra as Willy the Snitch, Channon Roe as Jack, Michael Cudlitz as Bob, Eliza Dushku as Faith
CO-STARS: Darin Heames as Parker, Scott Torrence as Dickie, Whitney Dylan as Lysette

THE PLOT THICKENS:
Buffy and Faith slay several of the Sisterhood of Jhe, with the assistance of Willow and Giles. Concerned for his safety, they all suggest the badly beaten Xander should stay out of future battles. He doesn't fare any better the next day at school, when he misses catching a football that hits Jack O'Toole ("a subliterate that's repeated twelfth grade three times," according to Cordelia) and gives Cordelia ample opportunity for Xander bashing. Xander develops what Oz describes as "an exciting new obsession"—how to define and achieve coolness. He starts by driving his uncle Roary's 1957 Chevy Bel Aire, which attracts the attention of both car fan Lysette Torchio and his new best friend Jack. The rest of the gang tries to find ways to stop the Sisterhood of Jhe from opening the Hellmouth and bringing about the end of the world, asking Xander to remain out of the way except for the occasional doughnut run.

Xander finds himself "having a very strange night." Under duress, he travels with Jack to three cemeteries to revive Jack's gang members. He discovers that Jack is also recently dead and revived, although prior to that he was a living, breathing high school bully. They decide to follow Dickie's plan to "bake a cake." Xander's attempts to get Angel, Giles, or Willow to rescue him from his predicament are rebuffed. He flees for his life when Jack threatens to make him the fifth dead member of the gang.

Xander assists Faith by slamming into a member of the Sisterhood of Jhe with the car. Back in her hotel room she assists him in losing his virginity. She then tosses him out, pants in hand, and as he climbs back in the car, he realizes "baking a cake" is a euphemism for building a bomb. A new man, he drives past the gang and persuades one of the gang members to divulge the location of the bomb before he loses his head. Everyone ends up back at Sunnydale High, with Xander and his zombie buddies chasing one another through the halls as the rest of the Scooby Gang battle the demons emerging from the Hellmouth. Xander faces his final opponent, Jack, over the bomb as it ticks down its final seconds. Xander convinces Jack to pull the plug on it, then departs, with nothing more to prove. A surly Jack chooses the other exit, running into Wolf Oz. The next day the library warriors gather to examine their wounds, and Xander gives Cordelia the Teflon treatment, secure in his role in the universe.

QUOTE OF THE WEEK:
Willow suggests a use for burning demons after Buffy and gang toast the Sisterhood of Jhe:
"I brought marshmallows! Occasionally I am callous and strange."

THE AGONY AND THE ECSTASY:
Xander and Cordelia's relationship is still strained and bitter following "Lovers Walk" and "The Wish." Xander's attempts to lose his virginity have been around since "Teacher's Pet." Buffy and Angel pledge to love each other, even beyond death, with shades of both "Becoming, Part Two" and "Amends."

POP-CULTURE IQ:
Xander, feeling useless, makes a Jimmy Olsen reference, which is lost on Giles:
"But, gee, Mr. White, if Clark and Lois get all the big stories I'll never be a good reporter."
Cordelia gets *Superman* references and isn't afraid to use them if it will give Xander pain:
"It must be hard when all your friends here have, like, superpowers. Slayer, werewolves, witches, vampires, and you're like this little nothing. You must feel like . . . Jimmy Olsen."
The Queen of Mean compares Xander to the fifth Marx brother, who may or may not also have been sent to get the doughnuts:

"You're the useless part of the group. You're the Zeppo."

When he rises from the grave, Dead Bob needs his Chuck Norris fix:

"*Walker, Texas Ranger*. You been tapin' 'em?"

Xander chooses the All-American singing group as a euphemism . . . or is it a metaphor? . . . to describe his currently virgin state:

"It's just, um, I've never been up with people . . . before. . . ."

And the musical references keep coming as Xander quotes the Beastie Boys at the bomb:

"Hello, Nasty."

CONTINUITY:

Giles continues to assist his Slayer, despite being "unofficial." The gang re-explores the concept of "cool," also discussed in "Gingerbread." The book cage has once again been deemed secure enough for Wolf Oz ("Beauty and the Beasts") and proven otherwise. Giles and Buffy mention her dying at the hands of the Master the last time the Hellmouth opened, complete with demon now returning. Faith has returned from her "walkabout" activities in "Helpless" to actively slay with Buffy. The theft from the hardware store echoes both "Band Candy" and "Bad Girls." Rival gang the Jackals is mentioned, perhaps cousins to the hyena kids in "The Pack." Giles works to keep Willow safe, Angel acts to keep Buffy safe, Willow tries to keep Oz safe, and everyone acts to keep the world safe.

FROM THE ORIGINAL TELEPLAY:

Jack changes his mind about Xander's coolness factor in this comment cut due to length:

"That's it. No way am I bringing him back after I kill him."

The Prom
Episode 3.20

WRITTEN BY: Marti Noxon
DIRECTED BY: David Solomon
GUEST STARS: Kristine Sutherland as Joyce Summers, Alexis Denisof as Wesley Wyndam-Pryce, Brad Kane as Tucker, Emma Caulfield as Anya
CO-STARS: Danny Strong as Jonathan Levenson, Mike Kimmel as Harv

THE PLOT THICKENS:
Buffy discusses prom and housekeeping plans with a reluctant Angel. Anya asks Xander to the prom. Joyce visits Angel and tells him if he loves Buffy, he should end their relationship. Prom plans are discussed in the library as Giles tries to focus everyone on the Ascension. Angel and Buffy are on patrol in the sewers when she brings up the prom again. He not only turns her down for the prom, he tells her they have no future. If they survive the Ascension, he will leave Sunnydale. Willow consoles Buffy as Buffy faces her heartbreak and going stag to the prom.

Xander enters the dress shop to tease Cordelia until he discovers that she has been reduced to a working girl trying to earn her prom dress. As they bicker, a Hell Hound bursts through the window and savages a youth in a tux before disappearing as abruptly as it appeared. The gang views the shop's videotape of the incident and realizes the Hell Hound was drawn to the victim by his formal attire. They also spot Tucker, apparent master of the Hound. Buffy squashes any thoughts of the gang missing the prom to assist her in Hell Hound roundup. Buffy and Angel have an uncomfortable run-in at the meatpacking plant, where Buffy gets Tucker's address. Buffy sends the others off to the prom; Giles remains behind to offer sympathy.

At the dance Willow and Oz, Xander and Anya, Cordelia, and Wesley (Faith's Watcher) mingle and keep an eye out for disaster. Buffy subdues Tucker only to find he has already released three of his Hell Hounds. Buffy manages to take them out one at a time before they can enter the dance floor. She changes into her "kick" pink prom dress. The Class Awards are given, including a new and unexpected one: "Buffy Summers, Class Protector." Giles and Buffy quietly contemplate the significance of her work being appreciated by her peers while the others dance. Angel arrives in his tuxedo to help Buffy capture at least one "perfect high school moment."

QUOTE OF THE WEEK:
Giles prefers slaying to shopping, though Willow and Buffy would rather discuss what to wear to the prom:
   "I will be wearing pink taffeta, as the chenille does nothing for my complexion, and can we PLEASE talk about the Ascension?"

THE AGONY AND THE ECSTASY:
Buffy sleeps in Angel's bedroom. Anya is drawn to Xander despite blaming him for her mortality ("The Wish"). Angel dreams of wedding Buffy, then seeing her destroyed as their life together tries to withstand the harsh light of day. He makes the hard choice to leave her rather than see their relationship ruin her chance for a normal romantic life. Wesley is jealous when he sees Xander and Cordelia together on the tape. Xander rises to the occasion by not revealing Cordelia's "shame," and by dipping into his road fund to purchase her dress. Wesley asks Cordelia to dance at the prom, one more step in their mutual attraction. Willow and Oz's romance continues to blossom.

> Variations of Hell Hounds abound in world mythology. The most famous is Cerberus from Greek mythology. Ray Harryhausen depicted a fierce two-headed Cerberus in 1981's Clash of the Titans.

POP-CULTURE IQ:
Cordelia compares Wesley to James Bond, prompting him to volunteer for chaperone duty at the prom:
   "I bet you'd look way 'double oh seven' in a tux."
Buffy quotes Robert Frost's "Stopping by Woods on a Snowy Evening," meaning that she has lots to do before she can fully appreciate the fashion choices associated with prom worthiness:
   "Giles, we got it. Miles to go before we sleep."
Xander believes in pet treats for Hell Hounds and wants to employ a clever strategy to find same:
   "Or check and see who's been stocking up on Hell Hound Snausages."
Buffy conjures visions of bloody dripping golden arches when she finds Angel with some takeout down at the butcher's dock:
   "I mean—where did I think you got your blood? McPlasma's?"
Buffy refers to Stephen King's 1974 debut novel, comparing the imminent attack on promgoers to the carnage that psychokinetic Carrie caused after being humiliated at the prom:
   "I've got to stop a crazy from pulling a Carrie at the prom."
Buffy references the Prince song that was quoted widely in 1999, when confronting Tucker:
   "I'm going to lock you up in here, and then I'm going to party like it's . . ."

CONTINUITY:
Xander reminds everyone of Willow's brave acquisition of key parts of the Books of Ascension ("Choices"). Joyce's conversation with Angel is a kinder version of the Mayor's ("Choices"). Angel refers to his post-sex reversion to Angelus in "Surprise" and "Innocence." Willow's low opinion of guys who break up with their girlfriends and leave town will be heard again ("Pangs"). Jonathan has special reason to think of Buffy as the Class Protector ("Earshot"). Other students refer to incidents with zombies ("Dead Man's Party") and hyena people ("The Pack"). Buffy takes her umbrella to UC Sunnydale with her, where it is mistreated by Sunday ("The Freshman").

> *During the days when the actual prom scene was shot, the weather varied from drizzle to pouring rain, making makeup, hair, and costumes that much more difficult.*

FROM THE ORIGINAL TELEPLAY:
Stage directions indicate the process Tucker uses to train his Hell Hounds:
   [His eyes held open with metal clamps (à la *A Clockwork Orange*).]

Giles endeavors to comprehend adolescence in this exchange cut due to length:
   GILES: "Fine. You're all suffering from a touch of spring madness, if you ask me."
   OZ: "Mine is more space madness. But I'll feel better once I get used to the weightlessness."
   WILLOW (TO OZ): "Promise me you'll never be linear."
   OZ (A PLEDGE): "On my trout."

Graduation Day, Part One
Episode 3.21

WRITTEN AND DIRECTED BY: Joss Whedon
GUEST STARS: Kristine Sutherland as Joyce Summers, Harry Groener as Mayor Richard Wilkins III, Alexis Denisof as Wesley Wyndam-Pryce, Mercedes McNab as Harmony, Ethan Erickson as Percy West, Emma Caulfield as Anya, Eliza Dushku as Faith, Armin Shimerman as Principal Snyder
CO-STARS: James Lurie as Mr. Miller, Hal Robinson as Lester Worth

THE PLOT THICKENS:
Xander is facing graduation day and the Mayor's Ascension with a sense of certain doom. Buffy tells Willow she doesn't find the graduation ceremony significant and may not attend. She changes her mind upon hearing that the Mayor will be the commencement speaker. Faith pays a fatal call on the seemingly innocuous geology professor, Lester Worth, and steals his papers, which have details of the last Ascension. Buffy recognizes her MO from the news report and decides to investigate. Xander learns Anya witnessed an Ascension in the past. Anya recalls the devastation that resulted when a human became a demon in pure, not hybrid, form. She is striving to contribute specifics when the Mayor braves "the inner sanctum" of the library. The Mayor's threat to Buffy goads Giles into stabbing him, to no avail.

Buffy packs up Joyce and sends her safely out of town. Giles sends Angel to help Buffy look for clues at Professor Worth's. As Buffy and Angel argue on the street, Faith shoots Angel in the chest with an arrow. Giles and Buffy do first aid on Angel's wound as Wesley reads Professor Worth's papers. They learn an eruption killed an earlier demon. Angel collapses from the poisoned arrow, distracting Buffy per Faith's plan. Anya makes plans to leave town pre-Ascension and invites Xander to join her. The Watchers Council will not share information on healing Angel. Buffy reaches her breaking point and disassociates herself from the organization. Oz succeeds in tracking down a cure for Angel: "to drain the blood of a Slayer." Buffy heads out to sacrifice Faith to the cause.

Faith is chillin' when Buffy enters her apartment and informs her of both Angel's cure and her intent to see he gets it. They fight, no holds barred, with everything they value at stake. The fight extends violently through the window to the rooftop, where a determined Buffy handcuffs herself to her dark counterpart. Faith has enough energy to break the cuffs but is tiring as Buffy draws a familiar knife. Buffy stabs Faith. Faith knocks Buffy back from the edge of the roof, then falls out of reach onto the bed of a passing truck, denying Buffy her hard-won victory.

QUOTE OF THE WEEK:
What's a little hooky compared to the end of the world?
> **XANDER:** "The Mayor's going to kill us all during graduation."
> **CORDELIA:** "Oh. [beat] Are you gonna go to fifth period?"
> **XANDER:** "I'm thinking I might skip it."

THE AGONY AND THE ECSTASY:
The Mayor and Faith continue to bond in their own mega-dysfunctional family manner; she responds to his praise and assurances he will still need her even after his Ascension. Anya strives to better understand herself and her attraction to Xander, despite her centuries of anti-male actions. Joyce hates leaving Buffy in Sunnydale to face danger without her, but recognizes she is a liability. Willow and Oz make love for the first time, seeking comfort in the face of danger. After their breakup Buffy can't stand being with Angel or separated from him. Either way she is not willing to let Faith or anyone else take the choice away from her. Xander's mature concern for Buffy's emotional well-being if she kills Faith is a mark of his growth.

> Faith shoots Angel from atop the Sunnydale cinema, proving once again "The Sun" is bad for vampires.

POP-CULTURE IQ:
Willow's dream commencement speakers are Las Vegas headliners, but no such luck. They're getting the Mayor:
> "Siegfried? Roy? One of their tigers?"

Xander references *Jaws* when he sees a picture of what the Mayor plans to transform into:
> "We're gonna need a bigger boat."

CONTINUITY:
Willow and Harmony pledge to keep in touch; the undead Harmony returns in "The Harsh Light of Day." Percy thanks Willow for refraining from assaulting him again ("Doppelgangland"). Amy is still a rat, but with a "swinging habitrail" ("Gingerbread"). Buffy tells Angel he's her "last office romance" but changes her mind for Riley in season four. Faith shoots Angel from a rooftop with her longbow, the same MO she used for

the courier ("Choices"). Anya questions Xander's contributions to the group efforts, echoing Cordelia's taunts in "The Zeppo." Buffy collected Faith's knife in the cafeteria after Faith killed an escapee from the Box of Gavrok ("Choices"). Anya and the death of Professor Worth provide essential clues to the demon's destruction, and Anya clarifies pure versus "hybrid" (tainted) demons.

FROM THE ORIGINAL TELEPLAY:
In the opening dialogue Cordelia has lobbied for red graduation robes, and Xander prefers blue. Buffy later describes her gown as dark blue. The robes ended up being Sunnydale's maroon color.

Graduation Day, Part Two
Episode 3.22

WRITTEN AND DIRECTED BY: Joss Whedon
GUEST STARS: Harry Groener as Mayor Richard Wilkins III, Alexis Denisof as Wesley Wyndam-Pryce, Danny Strong as Jonathan Levenson, Larry Bagby III as Larry Blaisdell, Mercedes McNab as Harmony, Ethan Erickson as Percy West, Eliza Dushku as Faith, Armin Shimerman as Principal Snyder
CO-STARS: Paulo Andres as Dr. Powell, Tom Bellin as Dr. Gold

THE PLOT THICKENS:
The Mayor's confidence is shaken by Faith's empty post-battle apartment. Cordelia gets the skinny on Buffy's quitting the Council from research fiends Giles and Xander. Buffy relieves Oz and Willow from Angel watch. She forces Angel to drink her blood so that he can recover from the "Killer of the Dead" poison. Angel rushes the unconscious Buffy to the hospital, where she is treated just a few rooms down from the comatose Faith. The Mayor tries to suffocate Buffy, but Angel and the hospital staff rescue her. Angel assures the arriving Scooby Gang that Buffy will recover and will not turn into a vampire, but they're angry with him for nearly killing Buffy. Buffy and Faith share a dream, and a subdued Faith tells Buffy to use the Mayor's human weakness to destroy him. Buffy visits the recumbent Faith, then leads her team into preparations for war.

The gang meets in the library to formulate their attack plans. Suggestions include attacking the Mayor with hummus and a fake Ebola virus. Wesley joins them in a non-Watcher capacity, and they make do-it-yourself volcano arrangements. A scheduled eclipse means both Angel and the Mayor's hench vamps can join in the battle. Xander and Willow spearhead the effort to recruit other students.

The graduation ceremony begins. Snyder gives a completely uninspiring intro to the Mayor, who lectures his captive, about-to-be-devoured audience on Sunnydale history. The eclipse occurs, and he transforms into an "unholy big-ass snake thing." Snyder's dismay at this chaos is brief, as the Mayor swallows him. The students drop their robes to reveal an assortment of weapons, the Mayor's vampires attack from the flank, and the battle is joined. Casualties are inflicted on both sides as Larry is slammed by the Mayor's tail and Harmony is bitten by a vampire. Buffy engages the Mayor in some David and Goliath action, taunting him with Faith's knife, then fleeing for her life and everyone else's. She charges through the school halls and into the library with the Mayor snake-demon in hot—and destructive—pursuit. She bursts out of the library's rear window, and as the Mayor enters, the library is blown to bits by explosives placed there by the gang earlier that day. Giles presents Buffy with her charred diploma. Buffy, Willow, Xander, Oz, and Cordelia contemplate the fact that they have a post–high school future. The final shot is of a yearbook lying on the ground, captioned "Sunnydale High '99—The Future Is Ours."

QUOTE OF THE WEEK:
Cordelia employs her usual tact when discussing Wesley's planned departure for England:
> GILES: "Buffy no longer needs a Watcher."
> CORDELIA: "Well, does [Wesley] have to leave the country? I mean, you got fired and you still hang around like a big loser, why can't he?"

THE AGONY AND THE ECSTASY:
Willow and Oz are glowing with romantic contentment even with the arrival of the Ascension. Giles and Willow both show compassion for Angel despite the harm done to them by Angelus ("Passion" and "Becoming, Parts One and Two"). Buffy is willing to risk her life to save Angel, even knowing they have no future together. Cordelia and Wesley get a chance to act on their attraction but the resulting kiss is really, really bad. Angel tells Buffy he won't prolong their good-byes—in some ways they've been saying good-bye since "Choices." After the destruction of Sunnydale High and the Mayor, Buffy and Angel confirm each other's physical well-being with a look, and then he departs without another word.

> *It's graduation time for everyone as the Mutant Enemy logo monster dons his mortarboard as well.*

POP-CULTURE IQ:
Faith's dream speech refers to both Robert Frost and Mother Goose:
"Oh, yeah. Miles to go. Little Miss Muffet counting down from seven three oh."

CONTINUITY:
Angel's vampiric nature rising in response to pain parallels Oz's wolf nature responding to emotional pain in "New Moon Rising." Buffy kisses the comatose Faith on the forehead in unconscious imitation of Faith's gesture in "Enemies." The battle plan discussions include a reference to Xander's pseudo-military knowledge ("Halloween") and Buffy's use of a rocket launcher against the Judge ("Innocence"). Wesley and Cordelia box the library books, which were recently returned after being removed in "Gingerbread." Buffy retrieves the knife she used on Faith ("Graduation Day, Part One"), which was originally a gift from the Mayor ("Choices"), and uses it as the bait to lure the Mayor. Oz and Willow have sex again right before the graduation ceremony. Buffy's post-explosion verbal skills—"fire bad, tree pretty"—will resurface in "Beer Bad."

HARRY GROENER (MAYOR WILKINS)

Though you've been acting in film and television through most of your career, you've had enormous success as a theater actor, including three Tony Award nominations (for *Cats*, *Oklahoma*, and *Crazy for You*). Is the stage where your heart is?

HARRY: "Well, I started out in the theater, and so you could say it's really my first love, although I do enjoy working in front of a camera. But they're two different disciplines. What working in front of a camera can do for the theater actor is that it can teach you how to economize and be simpler, because you don't need to do a lot of indicating for the audience about what's going on onstage and how you're feeling. You have to be a little bigger onstage to make sure that everyone understands what you're doing. You don't have to do that in front of a camera. What you bring from the theater to television and film is a kind of discipline, because in the theater you have to be so much more aware of how to communicate the story. You have to worry about being heard, being seen—there's no script person, no costume person; there's no audio engineer that can come and fix something. You have to take care of it. In television and film, everything is done for you. You don't have to worry about being seen or heard. They all light it, they all make sure that your microphone's in the right place, they make sure that you're heard, and so you can just focus on trying to create a scene that is as real as you can make it for the audience to be able to believe it."

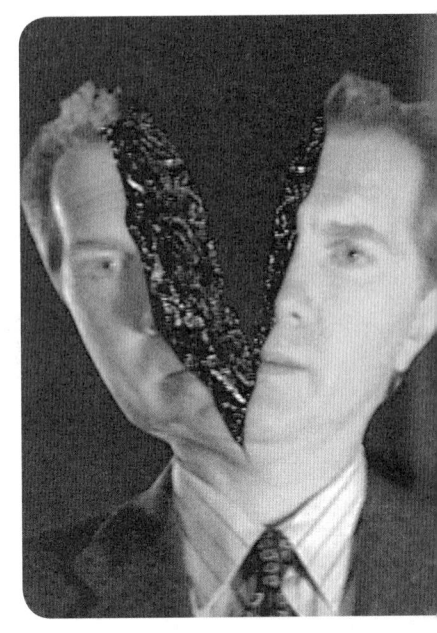

It's clear you take lessons as an actor from both disciplines, but do you find one more pleasurable than the other?

HARRY: "The theater's more immediate. It's right there every night. You hear whether you're communicating, whether you're being successful or not, by the response of the audience. You don't get that in television and film until it airs, and that could be—in film, it could be a year later, year and a half later; if it's a low budget, it could be ten years. But on television, if you have a series and you have friends watching it, then they'll call you and say, 'I saw you, and it was a good episode,' or whatever it is. It's much more immediate, of course, with the theater, and you have more control over everything. In front of a camera it's really a director's and editor's medium. They control it; they control the story. They can change the story; they can move things around to make it clearer, to make it better, make it more suspenseful, make it a more believable story. They can do all that, and it's actually quite exciting."

And what about when you step out the stage door after you've performed and you encounter the people who've just applauded you in the audience versus when you've met people who are fans of your work from television or they've seen you in a film? Is that experience different for you?

HARRY: "That's a very interesting question, because [the experience] really isn't. The people, the friends, that meet you backstage—hopefully they're complimentary about what you're doing, and they're supportive and all that. When you meet a fan of *Buffy*, let's say, and you meet them in the supermarket, you meet them on the street, it's equally wonderful. But with *Buffy*, in particular, I really enjoy it because it was such a fabulous time for me. That doesn't always happen, but every once in a while, you get a job where the role is really interesting. I've been fortunate enough to get a number of those, and *Buffy* is certainly at the top of the list. Being given that role was just so much fun. I was a fan of *Buffy*, and I love the vampire myth. It was only supposed to be an eight-episode arc, but because of the fans, because of how they responded, I got all those additional episodes, which was just fabulous.

"I loved being with the company. Sarah was unbelievably wonderful and such a pro and so disciplined; and the cast was terrific and nice and fun to be around. When I first started working in television or film, it was so foreign to me and very different, and initially I said, 'I don't think I can do this. I don't understand it. I'll try to learn, but I'm not really getting it. It doesn't make me happy; I don't feel part of a company.' And you can't, because you're just coming in to do one episode; you're only there for a few days at the most. If you're in the cast, you can start to get that kind of company feeling you can have in the theater. Well, the more you do—and, you know, over the years and going from one studio to the next—then a lot of the people overlap. All of a sudden you have sound people, costume people, [and] script people that overlap from different shows, and it becomes one big huge community and very familial. And I just love that."

You mentioned that you were only supposed to originally be on *Buffy* for eight episodes, but that it grew because of the reaction of the audience. It didn't seem that way. It seemed organic. Did you not have any inkling that they were going to keep you around?

HARRY: "No, they told me. They actually showed me right at the very beginning what the creature would look like. They had a model of it. I knew that there was going to be some transformation at the end, but I did not know how we got there."

So the additional episodes were added because the Mayor became popular, so they wanted to incorporate you more into that season?

HARRY: "That's right. They just added more to fill in the time before the actual graduation, before the actual transformation. And then, of course, the very, very last time we see him [in "Touched," season seven, episode twenty] . . . the only reason that that happened is because of my wife. We were in New York—at that time we lived in both places—and we had just come back to Los Angeles, and we were having breakfast out at some coffee shop and we found out that this was the last season of *Buffy*. My wife said, 'Why don't you call them up and tell them you're back and maybe they'll put you in.' I said, 'Oh God, don't be ridiculous. They're never gonna do that.' And she literally said, 'Don't be an asshole; call them up.' So I called my agent and he called them, and that's exactly what happened. But that would not have happened had it not been for my darling wonderful wife saying, 'Don't be an asshole; give them a call.'"

It's such a testament to what you do that people really loved that character. He's so evil, and yet I think everybody watching the show would have loved to have had coffee with him. They don't love him because he's evil; they love him because he's so much fun.

HARRY: "Yeah, he seems to have a pretty good sense of humor. He seems to see life a certain way that's really kind of pleasant. One of the things that the fans would always say, one of the reasons they like him, is that he's much scarier than the demons that have horns and teeth and scales and all that, but he's like the guy next door. He's like your uncle; he's like just a regular-seeming, just a regular guy, but he has all of this inside of him."

You sing, you dance, you have this history of musical theater. Were you disappointed that Mayor Wilkins was killed off before Joss decided to do the musical episode?

HARRY: "Oh my gosh, that would have been funny to see him do, in some kind of fantasy, some person's nightmare, right? But I'm not disappointed at all because Joss gave me all kinds of fabulous things to do, so many fun things to do. And that was at a time when I could still dance. I probably could still sing a little bit, but I can't dance anymore because of knees and ankles and particularly my back. I have a lower back injury that I sustained when I was in—if you can believe this—my mid-twenties."

You've appeared in great films like *About Schmidt*, *Road to Perdition*, and *Amistad* and have had recurring guest spots in so many TV series, including—I've noticed—three separate *Star Trek* series as three separate characters. But for fans who only know you from *Buffy*, what TV or film role would you love for people to track down and watch to see you in action in something else, and why?

HARRY: "Yes, I've done these films and they've been really fun to do, but they're not large roles. You'd have to see a number of things—you have to see just a number of different episodes of things so that you can see the range, the different kinds of characters that I've played. That's really the best way to see what kind of actor I am. From the beginning of my career, I've always wanted to be in many different roles and try to be unrecognizable. That's always the goal. You don't always achieve it, but you try, and it stretches you and it works the craft. Last year I got to do a Gore Verbinski film called *A Cure for Wellness*. I'm looking forward to that one because I got to do a little bit more in that film than I did in *Amistad* or something. I think it's kind of a thriller, but it looks so beautiful. I had such a good time. I went back and forth to Germany, and I just loved being there because I was born there. German is my first language, German and Russian. I don't speak either of them well, but those are the first two languages because I immigrated with my mother and my father when I was one and a half. And so going back to Germany, a lot of the language came back."

So much time has passed. Do you have any favorite behind-the-scenes memories of the time that you spent working on *Buffy*?

HARRY: "There was a funny moment during the graduation when the Mayor's transformation is supposed to happen. They built a suit that was supposed to break apart à la the Hulk. To try to accomplish that, they rigged it in a way that, to either side of me, away from the cameras, so you couldn't see it, there were two people. Each person had, I'd say, between ten and twelve fishing lines that they had to pull at a certain moment to make this effect happen. And they worked on this and worked on this and worked on this, the poor people, for the longest time. Well, we get to it, and it's supposed to happen, and I feel these tugs and things going right and left and right and left, and none of it happened. It did not work. So they yelled, 'Cut,' and they tried it again. 'Cut, cut,' and it just did not work at all. Over and over and over, these poor people. It was hours and hours setting that stuff up and figuring it out and trying to get it, and none of it worked.

"Eventually they [decided] to just shoot it in front of a green screen, and even then, it didn't really work the way it was supposed to work. It really was funny at the time. Everybody was watching—the whole graduating class sitting there with their weapons under their gowns, waiting to have this big huge final battle—and we'd get to that bit and it just wouldn't happen. And it'd be so funny; there'd be people cracking up: 'God, all right. Here we go. Let's try it again.' Oh God, it was heaven.

"And, of course, it was a night shoot, and it was a working high school that we shot it at, and we all had to get out before classes started. So when they finally yelled, 'Wrap,' and we had to all go, it was a mad dash to clear the set. What was funny about that was that the sun hadn't come up yet. It was slowly coming up, and so it seemed like everyone was trying to get underground before the sun came up, like vampires. We were all trying to get out before the sun came up! Oh God, that was funny, running around, trying to get away before the school starts."

You've already talked about *A Cure for Wellness*. What else are you working on now, and what does the future hold for Harry Groener?

HARRY: "I just finished a play by Jon Robin Baitz called *Vicuña* at the Kirk Douglas Theatre. This is a play that Robbie started working on in March 2016, and it was a play that reflected his feeling about what's going on now politically. I played a character that is based on Trump. It wasn't Trump; it was based on him. And all the circumstances were virtually identical: He was running against a woman; he has a daughter like Ivanka. He's getting ready for the final debate in three weeks' time, and he wants a fabulous suit. Vicuña—I didn't know this until we started, but Vicuña's a wonderful, very expensive fabric, and he wants this suit for the final debate. It was very interesting doing this play before the election and then after the election, because there really is no future for this play if Hillary had won. But now there is a future, and it becomes prescient. Robbie was very smart. So many of the circumstances that actually did happen that we heard about on CNN and MSNBC—he had already written in the play. He already saw it happening, I guess. At times it was almost as if Trump had read the script, because all of a sudden you'd go home and you'd see the news and he had done what was talked about in the play, that had already been there for months. It was really bizarre, but it was good to do the play. It became a very different play and seemingly more important and weighty after the election. We all had a really good time, but we were all very happy to finish because usually you do a play and you leave the theater and the world of the play stays in the theater. Well, in this situation, the world of the play was also the world outside, so you couldn't leave it. We were happy to finish telling the story.

"That's the last thing I did. Now my wife [Dawn] and I have a theater company, called the Antaeus Company, here in Los Angeles. We're founding members of the company. Right now we're building a theater in Glendale. There'll be two theaters, actually: a ninety-something-seat house and a forty-seat house. And we're going to open the theater with *Cat on a Hot Tin Roof*, and Dawn and I are playing Big Daddy and Big Mama."

JANE ESPENSON (WRITER, CO-EXECUTIVE PRODUCER)

You're one of the queens of TV—and certainly of geek TV. The list of TV series you've worked on as writer and producer is like a pop-culture tour of the past twenty years. *Star Trek: Deep Space Nine, Ellen, Buffy, Angel, Firefly, The O.C., Gilmore Girls, Tru Calling, Eureka, Battlestar Galactica, Dollhouse, Caprica, Game of Thrones, Torchwood, Husbands, Warehouse 13,* **and, of course,** *Once Upon a Time.* **I think it's clear you're "one of us," so what's your geek history, as it were? Where does your love of fantasy, sci-fi, and the supernatural come from, and how has that past served you in your career?**

JANE: "Wow—that list is long, isn't it? I must be very old! I do love fantasy and sci-fi, although I wouldn't say I have anything like an expert's knowledge of it. There are vast holes in my knowledge of sci-fi movies, for example. I just like what I like—some sci-fi, some regency romance, some true crime, some historical fiction. I guess I use science fiction, often, as more of a setting than anything—a backdrop for character interactions and emotions that are heightened by the extreme situations that the genre allows. But, of course, in the best cases, sci-fi also has something really special about it: stories that are driven by ideas, and I love that. That's what initially, as a kid, drew me to it. The stories of Ray Bradbury propelled me as a kid, and then in my teen years I found classic *Star Trek*. (Oddly, I'd been reading the *Star Trek* novels for years, but only dove into the original episodes later.) Then came movies like *Blade Runner* and *Alien* and *Aliens* and *Terminator*, that are obvious in their power. But I have to say that I loved TV comedy just as much as TV sci-fi, and I set out to be a comedy writer, not a genre drama writer. As it happened, though, *Star Trek: TNG* happened to be the open door to a career. This turned out to be a very good thing—I loved coming up with pitches for *Star Trek* series, because they hinged on finding that central hook of an idea, an insight about human nature, say, and I love thinking about that stuff. But other than at that very beginning, I've made myself useful on staffs not because of any kind of facility for sci-fi, but much more because of a love of humor. The point I try to make, over and over, in my writing, is that everyone is human (even when they're not human), and that a big part of that is being funny—accidentally and on purpose."

You'd been on staff for a handful of series before you came onto *Buffy*, but it certainly seems to have been the launching pad for you. Do you remember what it was like getting hired for the first time? How did that come about?

JANE: "I'd been on staff at five series: *Dinosaurs*, *Monty*, *Me and the Boys*, *Something So Right*, and *Ellen*, and I'd written a freelance *Star Trek: Deep Space Nine* and *Nowhere Man*. And yet you're absolutely right, *Buffy* was the launching pad. It was the first drama where I was on staff, and the first show that wasn't canceled during the year [when] I was hired. And it was the first place where I really felt I was contributing up to my abilities. I definitely remember being hired. I was brought in first for a preliminary meeting with two guys who were running Joss's company at the time, and all I remember about that meeting is that I was running late and in a bit of a panic about being late. I have a vague impression of bursting breathless into an office. But it went well enough that I was brought back to meet with Joss. I was asked to prepare some story ideas and I remember going over them with my friends until they were smooth. I remember that meeting more clearly. David Greenwalt was in the room, along with Joss, and I pitched my little ideas. One was the idea that turned into 'Band Candy,' my first script; although it was about a coffee shop, not candy, at the time. But the one that I think really helped me get the job was about a high school coach doing some kind of magic to make the football team start turning into cattle. At the time of my meeting, they had written the swim-team episode, but it hadn't yet aired, so I think I got big points for demonstrating that I was thinking along the same lines as the staff of the show. I got the call from my agent soon thereafter that I'd been hired. I was deliriously happy, of course. I sensed that this show was the right fit for me."

Some of the show's writers engaged regularly with fans and others didn't. It's no exaggeration to say that the *Buffy* fandom—particularly the core fans on posting boards like *The Bronze*—basically invented modern fandom. How much do you still interact with fans of the many shows you've worked on, and what are your thoughts on the relationship between modern TV and its fans?

JANE: "That's very true. There was actually a party every year at which the writers and producers would mingle with the fans from the *Bronze* posting board. That party is such an artifact of that post-Net, pre-Twitter time, it seems amazing that it happened. I love that it's so easy now to get a sense of what viewers are responding to, but I'm increasingly aware that it can easily get overwhelming. The more you know, the less you know, you know? You air an episode, and then you're flooded with every possible reaction to it, to the point where you lose even your own instincts to judge it. The individual writer needs to be able to keep their head clear and write with passion enough to make their story sing, instead of trying to write to please everyone. Above all, the one thing fan interaction has made clear to me is that there are so many people out there with the voice and the drive to create their own content. Increasing access to the means to create TV will result, I hope, in more shows with groundbreaking heroes."

You were a writer and co-executive producer on *Gilmore Girls*, which was recently resurrected by Netflix for a direct continuation. Do you think such a thing would ever be possible for *Buffy*, and what other shows you've worked on would you love to see return in the same way, with the original cast and no reboot?

JANE: "I was amazed when that happened. It strikes me as a one-in-a-million chance that the original creator and original cast would be available and interested in a reboot at the same time. *Buffy* ended when the people involved felt it was time—there wasn't a sense of having it ripped away unfinished—and the continuation of the show in comic-book form has probably fulfilled any sense of stories left untold. So I don't see that as a possible path for *Buffy*. *Firefly*, perhaps. It's a large cast, though, that has gone on to many other things—the logistics seem overwhelming. But if it did come back with Joss, I'd be the first one in line to be involved again. Other shows? *Battlestar* and *Torchwood*, yes, I'd do those again in a heartbeat."

As you noted, your first script for the series was "Band Candy," which remains one of my favorites for its sense of humor and for making Giles and Joyce adorably sexy. What's your favorite among the episodes you wrote for the series, and why?

JANE: "For a long time, 'Band Candy' was my favorite, because it had this glow around it of a story that started in my mind before I even got the job, and because it had such a comedic tone. But, looking back now, I'd choose 'Superstar' or 'Storyteller' or maybe 'Harsh Light of Day' or 'Pangs.' They all have a lot of humor in them, which I love. And I love a story where a supporting character, like Jonathan or Andrew, is given center stage. It's a reminder that in life there are no supporting characters; we're all the protagonist of our own story, which may be one of the most important lessons in all of life: everyone else is just as real as you. And I like Spike's role in 'Harsh Light' and 'Pangs'—a villain who earns our sympathy is a wonderful thing. I feel I should add that *Buffy* was a very creator-driven show. I wrote the dialogue for these episodes, but the stories came from the room as a whole, which usually means they came from Joss."

I've heard so many people talk about *Buffy* changing their lives—in many cases *saving* their lives. How do you feel when you hear that sort of thing, and have you had similar reactions to other series you've worked on?

JANE: "I used to hear this from girls, and now, more and more, from boys, who identify with Buffy and draw on her courage to help transcend their own situations and get through high school alive. We got a lot of letters at *Ellen*—and I'm sure Ellen personally got many more—with similar sentiments. I think *Ellen* might have had a bigger impact for a brief amount of time, but *Buffy* has persisted in the culture for longer. Television has the power to have a tremendous impact on people's lives, and I hope I've been a part of shows whose overall impact has been positive."

What are your favorite behind-the-scenes memories of your time on the show?

JANE: "Hmm, all of my memories are behind-the-scenes memories, I suppose. I usually don't love being on set, because it can be tedious and uncomfortable, but on *Buffy* you'd often get the sense that you were watching something iconic get made, and that was wonderful. I watched almost every frame of 'Superstar' being shot, and that was amazing. Getting to meet and hang out with Armin Shimerman, who played the principal, but who had also played Quark on *Star Trek: Deep Space Nine* . . . that was fantastic. Meeting Danny Strong, whom I already admired, and who became a life-long friend even during his meteoric rise. Watching how the musical came together. The time Joss told me about his idea for *Firefly* and I just could *not* get my head around the fact there were no alien species in it. When I came back from being sick and the staff had bought a slot machine for my office. Oh, and the time that one of the writers ate off a plate on the floor of the lunch room because we dared her to. And all the times we'd get to read a new script or watch a new cut of an episode.

"On more of an everyday basis, I loved hanging out with Doug Petrie in his office during our first couple years on the show. We'd just gab and gab. Then Drew Greenberg joined the club. And Drew Goddard and Rebecca Kirshner . . . oh, the whole staff was really cool."

Everyone says that working on a long-running TV series is a lot like high school, with circles of friends and then those people you wish you'd hung out with more. Who do you wish you'd hung out with more from your *Buffy* days?

JANE: "Tom Lenk and Aly Hannigan—they're such funny and kind people, but I was a little shy to talk with them as much as I'd have liked to."

If you're willing to share . . . what are the best and worst fan moments you can remember?

JANE: "There have been so many great fan interactions that I don't want to slight anyone, so I'll just give you the most recent good interaction. I was at Swancon in Perth earlier this year and there was a little girl, perhaps twelve or so, entered in the costume contest as *Buffy*. It was so nice to see the show continuing to find new fans! The worst fan moment was in the line for the women's bathroom at *Rock of Ages*, during the time when Tom Lenk was in the Broadway cast. The woman in front of me said she was the *biggest* fan of *Buffy*, and she just had one question, 'It's called *Buffy the Vampire*, but when did she become a vampire?'"

DOUGLAS PETRIE (WRITER, SUPERVISING PRODUCER)

Most recently you've been working in a prominent spot in the Marvel Netflix realm, writing and executive producing on both *Daredevil* and *The Defenders*. Are you a comics guy by nature?

DOUGLAS: "Always. Marvel comics in particular provided a seminal kind of storytelling that I carry with me to this day. It was action-based storytelling, certainly, but the team of artists and writers who made up the original 'bull pen' came, largely, from the world of romance comics. So there was always an element of soap opera and heartbreak baked into the larger, more operatic adventures. Nobody else was doing this at the time and the impact was enormous. So when Joss created a character whose calls to adventure were linked like a DNA strand to her interior personal life, it just felt right. All the writers embraced this dual-world approach pretty naturally, I think. We never saw it as a dichotomy. It was all one thing, like life."

As passionate as the fan base was on *Buffy* and *Angel*, those shows faced a constant battle to keep coming back season after season. With the Marvel stuff you're working on, the fan base is just as passionate, but how has the television model changed as far as the working experience?

DOUGLAS: "The Netflix model has changed storytelling in that binge watching is now the norm. Nobody waits a full week for next week's episode anymore (with some exceptions). Even if the episodes of a particular show, be it on network TV, FX, or HBO, are shown week by week, most viewers wait and then do a bingeing weekend. As a result, the threads of plot lines, exposition, and even things like musical cues need to be paced out differently. Showrunners get to be much subtler now, because we're going back-to-back-to-back with story. As for the fear of cancellation, that sword of Damocles still hangs over all our heads! Some things never change. . . ."

Like so many of the *Buffy* writers, you'd written episodes for a handful of series before you came onto *Buffy*, but it certainly seems to have been the launching pad for you. Do you remember what it was like getting hired for the first time? How did that come about?

DOUGLAS: "I remember seeing the show for the first time, and I just lost my mind. It was so good. The emotional build of it—even within a single episode—felt like music. Like a great, well-paced rock concert. The first episode I saw ended with Buffy firing a rocket launcher in a mall with the emergency sprinklers going off, and it felt great. I knew I wanted to be a part of this world and wanted very, very badly to be able to pull it off. It felt important. Still does."

I'm fascinated to see that you wrote episodes of *Rugrats* and *Clarissa Explains It All*, shows that had a certain sophistication but were ostensibly children's TV. Did that help or hinder you when trying to get the *Buffy* gig?

DOUGLAS: "Helped. No doubt. The important thing about shows like the ones Nickelodeon put out in the nineties was that nobody thought of them as kid's shows. *Clarissa* was pretty emotionally legit. So I was trained to work internally from early on. Meaning, you don't judge the material, you just try to make it as real and funny and emotional as you can. Kids are smart and their inner lives are tumultuous and rich, so we spoke to that."

Some of the show's writers engaged regularly with fans and others didn't. It's no exaggeration to say that the *Buffy* fandom—particularly the core fans on posting boards like *The Bronze*—basically invented modern fandom. How much do you still interact with fans of the many shows you've worked on, and what are your thoughts on the relationship between modern TV and its fans?

DOUGLAS: "Oh man. It's such a huge privilege to have a fan, any fan, let alone a bunch. But I stay off social media as much as I can. Sooner or later somebody's going to tell me I suck, and I have the voice in my head for that."

Your *Buffy* episode "Bad Girls" remains one of my favorites. What's your favorite among the episodes you wrote for the series, and why?

DOUGLAS: "I don't know if I have a single favorite. Not of my own, anyway. Surely 'Fool for Love' was a special experience in many ways, and the fans responded nicely. But there is no match for the thrill of seeing your first-ever-produced *Buffy* episode, so I will always associate

'Revelations' with getting into the clubhouse for the first time. I did enjoy channeling the character of Faith and was pleased and still honored to have been trusted with the episodes Joss assigned in season three. Huge fun."

I've heard so many people talk about *Buffy* changing their lives—in many cases *saving* their lives. How do you feel when you hear that sort of thing, and have you had similar reactions to other series you've worked on?

DOUGLAS: "Art's a big deal. Storytelling is a big deal. *Buffy* spoke to a huge population that felt unheard and unseen until Joss unloaded his unique world vision. I think the best thing a show or a movie can do is to make us feel brave. I've had that experience. In 2016 the stakes have gone way, way up. The world needs saving more than ever, so we better pull some special shit out of our hats now."

You directed episodes of *Buffy* and *The 4400*. Any plans to return to the director's chair?

DOUGLAS: "Absolutely. Stay tuned."

So much time has passed. What are your favorite behind-the-scenes memories of your time on the show?

DOUGLAS: "Oh wow. So many. When people ask what it was like working on *Buffy*, I tell them it's like being able to say 'I graduated from Hogwarts.' The writers' rooms, where we'd congregate, could get unbelievably, brutally funny. Funniest group ever. And smart. I remember scouting the school bus with Joss as he was prepping his shoot on the final episode, and I realized that our adventure together was going to end. All things do. But that was hard."

SEASON 4

Hush
Episode 4.10

In the history of the series, there are a handful of episodes that became pop-culture moments in their own right. *Buffy* had done chilling horror before, but "Hush" remains the single most frightening episode. The arrival of The Gentlemen, the "floating" effect of their movement, their hideous grins . . . come on, it's creeping you out just to think about them right now. For an episode with so little dialogue and so full of horror, "Hush" also offers its share of comedic moments. The episode is notable too for its introduction of shy, stammering witch Tara Maclay.

WRITTEN AND DIRECTED BY: Joss Whedon
GUEST STARS: Marc Blucas as Riley, Emma Caulfield as Anya, Leonard Roberts as Forrest, Phina Oruche as Olivia, Amber Benson as Tara, Brooke Bloom as Cheryl, Jessica Townsend as Nicole, Lindsay Crouse as Maggie
CO-STARS: Doug Jones as a Gentleman, Camden Toy as a Gentleman, Don W. Lewis as a Gentleman, Charlie Brumbly as a Gentleman

> "Hush" is considered a groundbreaking piece of television in that it's almost completely silent. Many other directors have dreamed of making silent episodes; Joss Whedon achieved it. It was nominated for an Emmy.

THE PLOT THICKENS:
Buffy dozes off during Professor Walsh's lecture on communication. Her dream is a curious mixture of kissing Riley and of a young girl reciting a strange nursery rhyme about The Gentlemen. The girl is holding a mystical-looking box. Riley wants to analyze the dream, but Buffy shares it with Giles instead. Neither he nor his Weetabix-hogging housemate, Spike, has ever heard of The Gentlemen.

Anya drills Xander about the nature of their relationship, and any resolution is deferred by Giles's request that Xander take care of Spike for a few days while Olivia comes to visit. The campus Wicca group is a major disappointment to Willow, but she does notice a shy young woman there named Tara.

That night, as everyone sleeps, the evil Gentlemen come to town and magically steal all their voices. Confusion reigns. Riley and the Commandos don civvies, intending to help keep order in the Dale. Buffy and Willow walk through the town, stunned by the silence.

That night The Gentlemen glide eerily through the town. Olivia sees them and is able to sketch one of them for Giles the next morning. They take their first victim, a young male college student, who shrieks in silent terror as they slice open his chest and extract his heart.

Giles finally realizes that The Gentlemen are part of a fairy tale. To kill them, the princess must scream. But he has no idea how to give Buffy back her voice.

Tara goes in search of Willow, intending (we later learn) to do a spell with her. She is nearly captured by The Gentlemen. She and Willow escape together and for the first time join forces to create magick. Buffy and Riley also join forces, coming upon each other as they battle The Gentlemen at the clock tower. Riley smashes the box containing all the voices of Sunnydale, and Buffy (the princess) screams. The Gentlemen's heads explode. The horror is over.

In the morning Riley comes to Buffy's dorm room. They have to talk, he tells her. She agrees . . . and they sit facing each other in uncomfortable silence.

> REVELATION 15:1
> A minister and his flock are silently reading from the Bible. This is the verse written on the congregates' signboard: "Then I saw another portent in heaven, great and wonderful, seven angels with seven plagues, which are the last, for with them the wrath of God is ended."

QUOTE OF THE WEEK:
Buffy accidentally makes an obscene gesture as described in the stage directions:

Xander has scribbled on a pad, holds up for all to see: HOW DO YOU KILL THEM?

Buffy snorts contemptuously, then circles her fist around an imaginary stake, plunges it down repeatedly.

Everybody looks at her, a little thrown: the gesture doesn't read the way she intended.

Realizing it, Buffy hurriedly and sheepishly grabs a stake from her purse, repeats the gesture.

The part of the newscaster was played by Carlos Amezcua, then real-life co-anchor of KTLA morning news in Los Angeles. Amezcua produced "Comedy Compadres," the first all-Latino standup comedy program in Los Angeles. It aired on KTLA. Weathercaster Mark Kriski from KTLA was in "Amends."

THE AGONY AND THE ECSTASY:
Despite their soulful first kiss, Riley and Buffy founder just when the moment for honesty arrives. Willow still misses Oz terribly. And Anya is thrilled when Xander attacks Spike when Xander thinks that the vampire has bitten her. Olivia and Rupert must decide if she can handle knowing that the things that go bump in the night are real.

Sign on the Initiative's wall near the elevator:
IN CASE OF EMERGENCY, USE STAIRS.
(The elevator is voice-activated.)

POP-CULTURE IQ:
Riley is not loving keeping his Commando life a secret from Buffy. Forrest gets it, as shown by his Superman reference:

"We have a gig that would inevitably cause any girl living to think we are cool upon cool, yet we must Clark Kent our way through the dating scene and never use this unfair advantage."

Giles mentions this classic British band while confessing to Olivia that while monsters are real, his rock fame is not:

"Well, no, I wasn't actually one of the original members of Pink Floyd."

The Fairy Tale Connection: "Gingerbread" from season three and "Hush" both take their cue from fairy tales. These stories of witches, goblins, and trolls, when first told, were aimed at adults, not children. The original "Sleeping Beauty" has the Princess waking up during labor—she's pregnant with twins!

There is a subgenre of horror literature consisting of traditional fairy tales retold for adults. A representative sample can be found in Snow White, Blood Red, edited by Ellen Datlow and Terri Windling. Buffy costume designer Cynthia Bergstrom searches out old fairy-tale books for their illustrations, which she uses as inspiration to clothe the many demons in the show.

CONTINUITY:

There is an oblique reference to Angel when Buffy dreams of kissing Riley: he tells her he will make the sun go down. Buffy and Riley do kiss, in the street during the silence that has spread all over town. Xander and Giles continue to work together on matters arcane. Willow floated a pencil in "Doppelgangland," and in "Choices" she staked a vampire with a pencil. She mentions she would like to float something bigger than a pencil in "Hush"; then she and Tara together use their powers to slam a soda machine against a door.

FROM THE ORIGINAL TELEPLAY:

The following dialogue was cut for length from the Wicca group scene:

> CHERYL: "Well, you missed last week. We did a healing chant for Chloe's ankle. She said the swelling went right down."
> NICOLE: "What's she doing on a mountain bike, anyway?"
> CHERYL: "She was trying to impress Justin."
> WILLOW: "I was actually talking more about real spells."

Here are descriptions from the shooting script of two scenes:

INT. TARA'S ROOM—CONTINUING

Her room is wicca-y and also painted black and depressed-y.

EXT. CLOCK TOWER—NIGHT

From up here we can see the whole town—or possibly much less than all of it, but I can hope—and the collective breaths snake all across the town heading here.

Description of one of The Gentlemen:

> *He's old, bone white, bald—Nosferatu meets Hellraiser by way of the Joker. Actually, he looks kind of like Mr. Burns, except that he can't stop his rictus-grin, and his teeth are gleaming metal.*

> "Danse Macabre," the classical music Giles plays during his presentation on The Gentlemen, was also used as the theme song for the UK production *Jonathan Creek*, which Anthony Stewart Head also appeared in.

This Year's Girl
Episode 4.15

WRITTEN BY: Douglas Petrie
DIRECTED BY: Michael Gershman
GUEST STARS: Kristine Sutherland as Joyce, Amber Benson as Tara, Leonard Roberts as Forrest, Bailey Chase as Graham, Chet Grissom as Detective Clark, Alastair Duncan as Collins, Harry Groener as Mayor Wilkins, Eliza Dushku as Faith
WITH: Jeff Ricketts as Weatherby, Kevin Owers as Smith

THE PLOT THICKENS:
Faith lies in her hospital bed in the basement of Sunnydale Hospital, dreaming of cold-hearted, murderous Buffy and a warm and caring Mayor Wilkins. When at last she defeats Buffy in one of her nightmares, she awakens from her coma to discover that Graduation Day has come and gone. She beats up a woman and takes her clothes. Her nurse alerts someone by phone and tells him to "send the team." Making her way to the ruins of Sunnydale High, Faith faces the truth: the Mayor is dead.

Riley also rises from his hospital bed and has to pull rank to leave the Initiative complex. He has kicked the meds Maggie Walsh was feeding him, but the wound Adam dealt him is still troublesome. Buffy is filled with joy at the sight of him, and their reunion is tender. She reminds him that he has choices, despite the fact that he's been trained to obey orders.

Someone contacts Buffy (we don't know who) to tell her that Faith has escaped, while Faith seeks Buffy out. Faith is enraged that Buffy seems to have forgotten all about her. She goads Buffy, reminding her rival that Buffy tried to kill her for her Slayer's blood in order to save Angel. And now Buffy's boinking some *other* guy. . . . Their fight is brutal, but inconclusive, as the police arrive and Faith disappears onto the streets.

Meanwhile, "the team" arrives: three nasty-looking men who make themselves at home in Giles's condo and greet him familiarly.

Willow and Tara are more of a couple now, Willow acting protectively toward Tara as she explains to her about Faith. Meanwhile, Faith is moved by the Mayor's love for her—he made a farewell video for her. He also left her a magical device, a Draconian Katra, which will allow her to switch bodies with Buffy. She goes to Buffy's house and terrorizes Joyce, assuming that Buffy will come rescue her mother. Buffy crashes into the bedroom, rescuing her mother, and she and Faith have a battle royal all over the Summerses' home. The police sirens blare in the background—Joyce has called 911—and at the last possible moment, Faith makes the switch, with no one the wiser.

QUOTE OF THE WEEK:
Xander talking strategy with the gang on whom to go after first, Faith or Adam:
"I'd hate to see the pursuit of a homicidal lunatic get in the way of pursuing a homicidal lunatic."

THE AGONY AND THE ECSTASY:
Faith knows how to hurt Buffy—by reminding her of Angel. Buffy hurt Faith by destroying the Mayor. But Buffy and Riley's love appears very strong as they reunite. Tara and Willow are close and affectionate, clearly happy to have each other.

POP-CULTURE IQ:
Wordplay we have known and loved: Trey Parker's film, *Orgaszmo*, which was executive-produced by Fran Rubel Kuzui and Kaz Kuzui. The Kuzuis also executive produced *Buffy*. Woody Allen's 1973 film *Sleeper* and Roger Vadim's *Barbarella* also featured Orgasmatrons. However, Xander is talking about an Initiative blaster:

"Now, if it was called 'The Orgasminator,' I'd be the first to try your basic button-press approach."

Buffy, referring to the character played by Arnold Schwarzenegger in the *Terminator* movie franchise:

"He's the Terminator without the bashful charm."

Buffy's referring to *The Patty Duke Show*, which ran from 1963–1966. It starred Patty Duke as lookalike cousins:

"She's my wacky identical cousin from England, and every time she visits, hijinks ensue."

"Marshal Dillon" Summers wants Faith gone from Sunnydale in this reference to the city in *Gunsmoke*, a popular TV western series:

"If I were her, I'd get out of Dodge post-hasty."

Faith's referring to *The World According to Garp*, a novel by John Irving, made into a film in 1982:

"In *The World According to Joyce*, Buffy's gonna come crashing through that door any minute."

> Faith asks a hospital visitor for the date. In the original script the answer was Tuesday, February eighth. It was changed to Friday, February twenty-fifth.

CONTINUITY:

The blaster Xander is trying to repair is the faulty one Maggie Walsh gave Buffy when she tried to kill her in "The I in Team." The duplicity of Maggie Walsh and the murky ethical status of the Initiative are kept in focus. The past with Faith—"Faith, Hope & Trick," "Revelations," "Bad Girls," "Enemies," and "Consequences"—is partially spelled out. Spike still has the chip in his head, which prevents him from hurting any human being—no matter how much he might like to. Buffy tells Riley about the Watchers Council and about Faith.

FROM THE ORIGINAL TELEPLAY:

Buffy explains what kind of force she plans to use to get into the Initiative, in this line cut for length:
   "Explosives, tear gas, grappling hooks."

Stage directions for one of Faith's dreams:
   [We cut back to the Mayor. He's being horribly, brutally HACKED APART by Buffy with her knife. He's real dead real fast. Finished with this prey, Buffy whips her gaze to Faith, impatient and peeved.]

Who Are You
Episode 4.16

WRITTEN AND DIRECTED BY: Joss Whedon
GUEST STARS: Kristine Sutherland as Joyce, Amber Benson as Tara, Leonard Roberts as Forrest, George Hertzberg as Adam, Chet Grissom as Detective Clark, Alastair Duncan as Collins, Emma Caulfield as Anya, Eliza Dushku as Faith
WITH: Rick Stear as Boone, Jeff Ricketts as Weatherby, Kevin Owers as Smith

THE PLOT THICKENS:
Trapped inside Faith's body, Buffy is strapped to a gurney and loaded into an ambulance as Joyce and Faith, in Buffy's body, observe. Faith is able to fool Joyce as she mimics Buffy's speech patterns and movements, and she extricates herself from an uncomfortable moment of tenderness in which Joyce hugs her, by announcing that she's going to take a bath. Alone, she luxuriates in her new body, and she mocks Buffy's goody-goody attitude in front of the mirror.

Meanwhile, in the hospital, Buffy frantically tries to get free of the doctors, nurses, and cops holding her down long enough to sedate her. She tries to explain that Faith has taken her body and is alone with her mother, but she finally succumbs to unconsciousness.

Willow and Tara are in Tara's room, and Willow is frightened that Faith will come after her. Tara reminds her that since no one knows she, Tara, exists, Willow ought to be safe with her. It's clear she's hurt that Willow hasn't introduced her to her friends. Willow tries to explain that she's being possessive of Tara, rather than ashamed, and Tara glows with understanding.

Faith buys a plane ticket with Joyce's credit card. While Buffy is being transported from the hospital to jail, a van deliberately pulls into the path of the police car, causing a crash. The men of "the team" drag Buffy into the van. They are the Watchers Council operatives. Faith as Buffy goes on over to Giles's house "to kill time" before her flight by chatting with them about the capture of "Faith." Giles informs them all that the Watchers Council team has gotten hold of her. Faith is delighted. She's also having psychotic delusions of gutting Willow, but she manages to keep her psychotic interludes hidden from the others.

Pretending to be the good little soldier, she informs the others that she's going to go patrolling for Adam. Instead, she goes to the Bronze to party. There, she runs into Spike, whom she's never met before. Once she realizes who he is, she baits him mercilessly, coming on to him and then laughing in his face.

Adam has taken over the lair of Boone, a young vampire. He kills one of Boone's lackeys to get the attention of the others, then offers them some interesting perspectives on their existence, and on his own personal mission.

Buffy wakes up shackled in the Watchers Council van. The assassins are not loving her, and they are not believing her story that she's really Buffy Summers inside Faith's body.

Back at the Bronze, Willow brings Tara to the club for the first time. They're holding hands, clearly a couple. Willow spies "Buffy," chugalugging and flirting with a bunch of guys in a most un-Buffy-like way. She introduces Faith to Tara; while she goes off for drinks, Faith verbally savages Tara, making fun of her stammer and making sure poor Tara knows just how much Willow loves Oz.

But Faith begins to experience what it's like to be well regarded: after she dusts a vamp, the girl he was feeding on shakes Faith with the depth of her gratitude. When she seeks out Riley and tries to work her sexual wiles on him, going for the kink, he stops her and makes tender love to her. Believing he's with his Buffy, he tells her for the first time that he loves her.

Buffy manages to escape from the assassins, and Tara tells Willow that Buffy's not herself. Willow and she work intense magick, sending Willow to the nether realms. They conjure a Katra for Buffy, to switch her back into her own body, and find her at Giles's condo. They tell her that for it to work, she must make physical contact with Faith.

Adam has launched his assault against humanity by sending Boone and the other vampires to a church. Faith, still masquerading as Buffy, charges to the rescue. She accidentally meets up with Riley, who's on the scene because he was going to church. The real Buffy and company show up.

Buffy and Faith fight the vampires, and then each other. Buffy manages to clasp hands with her, and they switch back into their own bodies. Buffy is left to deal with the aftermath of Faith's escapades—including Riley's having slept with her—while Faith catches a train out of town, trying to process everything that's happened.

QUOTE OF THE WEEK:
Facing down Adam's vampires, Faith rises to the occasion:
>   FAITH: "You're not gonna kill these people."
>   BOONE: "Why not?"
>   FAITH: "Because it's wrong."

> There were six drafts of the script for "Who Are You," the first draft delivered on January 24, 2000, and the final pages distributed to the cast, staff, and crew on February 2, 2000.

THE AGONY AND THE ECSTASY:
Faith experiences tenderness and kindness for perhaps the first time in her life; her lovemaking with Riley, followed by his declaration of love, throws her into a panic. Willow tries to explain her intense feelings to Tara, who clearly reciprocates. Tara and Willow bond ever closer as they work magick together. Buffy's devastated when she discovers that Riley—unknowingly—slept with Faith.

CONTINUITY:
This is part two of a two-part episode. Faith is unimpressed when the Watchers Council sends someone to retrieve the rogue Slayer "because that worked out so well when Wesley tried it" (in "Consequences"). They discuss Adam, who's still at large. Spike brings Faith up to date on the chip in his head. Boone, the vampire, becomes Adam's mouthpiece in the church confrontation. One of the assassins reminds Faith that Buffy and Giles are no longer part of the Council. Willow tells Tara that she, Xander, and Buffy used to live at the Bronze. Faith has switched bodies with Buffy and goes after Riley, the same as she did with Angel. Willow mentions hyena possession, which occurred to Xander in "The Pack." Riley mentions the drugs Maggie Walsh had been giving him. Buffy's still a bad driver, which has been a recurring joke in many episodes, including "Band Candy." In trying to convince Giles that she's who she insists she is, Buffy makes reference to his being a demon ("A New Man") and Olivia ("Hush"), blowing up Sunnydale High ("Graduation Day, Part Two"), and his having had sex with her mother ("Band Candy").

FROM THE ORIGINAL TELEPLAY:
The following line of Adam's was cut due to length:
> "You are here to be my first. To let them know I'm coming. I am the end of all life, of all magick. I'm the war between man and demon, the war that no one can win. You're a part of that now. You have to show me you're ready."

Superstar
Episode 4.17

WRITTEN BY: Jane Espenson
DIRECTED BY: David Grossman
GUESTS STARS: Danny Strong as Jonathan, Amber Benson as Tara, Bailey Chase as Graham, Robert Patrick Benedict as Jape, John Saint Ryan as Colonel Haviland, George Hertzberg as Adam
WITH: Erica Luttrell as Karen, Adam Clark as Sergeant, Chanie Costello as Inga, Julie Costello as Ilsa

THE PLOT THICKENS:
Who ya gonna call? Jonathan!

Jonathan Levenson, former Sunnydale High classmate of Buffy and company, is the coolest, most important person in the world. Jonathan is stronger and more agile than the Slayer; a computer hacker cleverer than Willow; idolized by everyone, and the inventor of everything.

Buffy and Riley are feeling very awkward around each other; while Riley didn't realize it was Faith he slept with, nevertheless he did sleep with her. The two concentrate on finding Adam, who is still on the loose. Jonathan gets to the heart of the problem for Buffy: when it mattered most, Riley didn't look into her eyes and realize she wasn't looking back at him.

Colonel Haviland, the new head of the Initiative, reviews the troops and explains that he's there while the government conducts a facility review. Their primary mission remains the recovery of Adam. To that end, Colonel Haviland asks the aid of their tactical consultant . . . Jonathan. He has detected Adam's internal power source: a small reservoir of uranium 235 encased in lead.

While Jonathan is briefing Riley and the other Commandos, Karen, a fan of his, is attacked by a hideous monster with a distinctive symbol on its forehead.

Jonathan offers Riley advice on how to get back together with Buffy; at the Bronze, Xander accuses Anya of murmuring "Jonathan" during a critical private moment. All is forgotten as Jonathan takes the stage and begins singing. Then Karen enters, bloodied and weeping.

It seems she was attacked on his property; Buffy, Riley, Jonathan, and Karen go to investigate. When she sketches the symbol that was on the monster, something registers with Jonathan. Buffy notices, but he quickly recovers and insists it was nothing. He assures her that he'll take care of the monster himself.

But Adam knows it's something. He knows that Jonathan has cast some sort of spell, because he himself is impervious to it.

Shortly after that, Tara is attacked by the monster. Buffy's faith in Jonathan is badly shaken. It occurs to her that some of Jonathan's accomplishments don't add up: He's only eighteen, yet he's graduated from medical school. He starred in *The Matrix*, but he never left town.

Then she realizes Jonathan sports the identical mark as the monster, and she pressures him to go on recon with her to find it. While the two of them search, the others research the mark. It turns out that Jonathan did an Augmentation spell on himself to make everyone idolize him. But he also created the monster. Kill the monster, and the spell is broken.

With Jonathan's help, Buffy prevails. The world becomes as it should be, with Jonathan something of a nebbish. However, the advice he gave Buffy and Riley sticks . . . and they reunite.

QUOTE OF THE WEEK:
Controlled by Jonathan's spell, the gang's not used to Buffy's leadership skills:
WILLOW [trying it out]: "Buffy was right. Buffy was right."
ANYA: "Doesn't sound very likely, does it?"

> The Jonathan comic features a brown-eyed super-Jonathan, but his eyes are actually crystal blue.

THE AGONY AND THE ECSTASY:
Buffy and Riley are having a lot of trouble dealing with the fact that Riley slept with Faith. Xander's jealous of Jonathan. In the end Buffy and Riley are able to put the past behind them, and Xander and Anya are solid again. Willow and Tara are still very much in the honeymoon stage.

POP-CULTURE IQ:
Aron Nimzowitsch is one of the pioneers of hypermodern chess. In his magical world, Jonathan is a chess master:
"The Nimzowitsch Defense. Let's see if I remember. . . ."
This famous theorem was not proven for more than 350 years after Fermat first described it; Willow's talking about Jonathan, who solved it, of course:
"He got a perfect score, and then he re-created the original proof of Fermat's last theorem in the margins around the answer bubbles."
Buffy's seeing the illogic in all the things she and others believe about Jonathan. Joss Whedon has said the classic film is one of his favorites:
"He starred in *The Matrix*, but he never left town?"

CONTINUITY:

Spike is still defanged; Adam is still at large. In this reality Buffy gave Jonathan the Class Protector award at the prom. Once the jig is up, Jonathan refers to the events in "Earshot," when Buffy stopped him from committing suicide in the bell tower. Anya's past as a vengeance demon is discussed.

> *"Superstar" author Jane Espenson also wrote "Earshot." She and Danny Strong became friends.*

FROM THE ORIGINAL TELEPLAY:

The following line of Spike's was cut due to length:

> "You're a bleeding idiot, you are, Jonathan. 'Cuz you'll be the first victim and you'll be stone dead before you hit the ground. [then, to himself, proudly] The *worst* kind of scum."

Primeval
Episode 4.21

WRITTEN BY: David Fury
DIRECTED BY: James A. Contner
GUEST STARS: Leonard Roberts as Forrest, Amber Benson as Tara, Bailey Chase as Graham, Jack Stehlin as Dr. Angleman, Conor O'Farrell as Colonel McNamara, George Hertzberg as Adam, Emma Caulfield as Anya, Lindsay Crouse as Professor Maggie Walsh

THE PLOT THICKENS:
Adam reveals to Riley that he has activated a chip in Riley's arm, placed there by Maggie Walsh. He controls Riley's movements and actions now, even to speak or to be silent. He reveals the master plan, to create "demonoids" like himself, amalgams of demons and humans. Spike shows, enjoying watching Riley's frustration, but is frustrated himself when Adam refuses to take out Spike's chip . . . just yet. Spike didn't quite think through his plan to separate the Slayer from her friends—Willow is decrypting the disks he "smuggled" from the Initiative, but she's not speaking to Buffy now, and vice versa.

Willow forgot her laptop at Giles's condo. She and Tara go back for it, and Giles is extremely hungover. They leave awkwardly, with no resolution. Anya tries to cheer up Xander, who is worried that his friends are right and that he is a directionless loser. Adam introduces Riley to the reanimated Maggie Walsh and Dr. Angleman, who will help Adam create demonoid creatures for the new world order. Dead Forrest is there as well. He is sentient and actually quite pleased about his transformation.

Buffy is searching for Adam back at the cave where she last saw him. Spike is there, pretending that he's looking for "a little weekend getaway place." He's awkward in his attempts to encourage Buffy to go down into the Initiative all by herself, and she grows suspicious of his motives. As the disks decrypt themselves, Buffy calls Willow and gets the four—Xander, Giles, Willow, and Buffy herself—to meet and clear the air. Tara and Anya sit out the peace talks.

The four realize that Spike deliberately set them against each other. They also acknowledge that he was able to do so only because they had grown apart. As they talk, they compare notes and figure out Adam's plan to build a new race from dead humans and dead demons in an all-out war between Initiative Commandos and captured Hostile Sub-Terrestrials (HSTs).

Buffy, Xander, Willow, and Giles sneak into the Initiative via the elevator shaft and have a teary make-up session at the bottom, but Colonel McNamara and his men are waiting for them. Buffy demands that he listen to her, but he's already convinced she and the others are anarchists;

his opinion isn't changed when Giles explains that the object he's holding is a magick gourd. The power grid goes down and backup doesn't respond. Adam releases all the demons and the carnage begins.

Buffy tries to get McNamara to let her fight, but he orders two of his men to lock up the lot of them. As soon as McNamara is out of the room, Buffy clocks both of the guards left in charge of them. She leads the way and they battle everything in their paths. Spike is waling on demons as he looks for an escape route.

Willow jacks in, searching for Adam. She discovers evidence of a secret lab behind room 314. That's where Buffy expects to battle Adam. Spike is now fighting the demons (and Adam) because he didn't deliver Buffy alone, so Adam won't take his chip out.

Xander, Willow, and Giles magickally imbue Buffy with supernatural gifts surpassing her current Slayer abilities. Once he digs the chip out of his arm, Riley joins in, battling Maggie, Dr. Angleman, and Forrest. Speaking in Sumerian, Buffy is able to rip the power center—the heart—right out of Adam. The battle rages all around them, and Spike protects the Scooby Gang as they finish up.

Colonel McNamara is killed, but many other Commandos get out, thanks to Buffy, Riley, and the others. After a debriefing about the incident, the military brass decide to "erase" the Initiative: one suit goes so far as to suggest they sow the ground with salt.

QUOTE OF THE WEEK:
Buffy, explaining the way things are to Colonel McNamara:
"This isn't your business. It's mine. You, the Initiative, the suits in the Pentagon . . . you're all messing with primeval forces you can't begin to understand. I'm the Slayer. And you're playing on my turf."

> *Lindsay Crouse was disappointed when she discovered Maggie Walsh was going to be killed before the end of the season. As often happens on Buffy, that didn't prevent her return to the show.*

THE AGONY AND THE ECSTASY:

Anya reassures Xander that no matter what, she loves him; Willow and Buffy tell each other that they love each other, then shower affection on Xander. The four original members of the Slayerettes essentially reunify when they combine to fight Adam. Riley is filled with regret at seeing the zombiefied Forrest.

POP-CULTURE IQ:

Spike, informing Adam that Buffy's in the Initiative, is parodying the phrase "The Eagle has landed," spoken as the lunar module *Eagle* touched down on the moon's surface in 1969:

"The Slayer has landed."

Spike is referring to *Alice in Wonderland,* a nineteenth-century fantasy novel written by Lewis Carroll (Charles Dodgson). He's anticipating that Willow will decrypt the disks for Buffy:

"The little witch gives her the info and—pop—Alice heads down the rabbit hole."

CONTINUITY:

Maggie Walsh's mad plan to merge humanity and demonity is finally revealed. Spike's left with the chip in his head after the destruction of Adam. Forrest, Dr. Angleman, and Maggie Walsh return, though they are reanimated dead. Buffy and company rediscover their original affection for one another after deconstructing their various grievances from "The Yoko Factor." Xander asked Riley in "This Year's Girl" if he had a chip in his brain; turns out it was in his shoulder. The final battle occurs, and as usual, Sunnydale history will not record it.

FROM THE ORIGINAL TELEPLAY:

Willow and Tara discuss Willow's computer hacking skills in this exchange cut due to length:

WILLOW: "I'm scaring you now, huh?"

TARA: "A little. In a good way. It's like a different kind of magick."

Restless
Episode 4.22

WRITTEN AND DIRECTED BY: Joss Whedon
GUEST STARS: Kristine Sutherland as Joyce, Amber Benson as Tara, Mercedes McNab as Harmony, David Welles as The Cheese Man, Michael Harney as Man, George Hertzberg as Adam, Emma Caulfield as Anya, Seth Green as Oz, Armin Shimerman as Principal Snyder
WITH: Sharon Ferguson as the Primitive, Phina Oruche as Olivia, Rob Boltin as Soldier

THE PLOT THICKENS:

After the battle against Adam and his army, Buffy and her friends go to her house to detox by watching movies. Riley's off to testify on "the administration's own Bay of Mutated Pigs," with hopes of getting an honorable discharge.

Xander's vote for cinematic release is *Apocalypse Now*, but he has plenty of "chick-and-English guy" flicks in case it doesn't please. But they all fall asleep before the FBI warning is over, and each has a dream that speaks in some way of their personal condition. Each is attacked by a strange, savage woman, seeking their destruction via the same aspect of themselves that they used to enjoin magickally with Buffy: Willow's spirit, Xander's heart, and Giles's intellect, or brain.

Willow dreams of being safe with Tara, although they appear, at times, to be in a remote desert. She is getting ready for drama class, and she runs into Oz. Despite the fact that this is her first class, Giles is directing their production of *Death of a Salesman*. Harmony is in it, as a vampire. Buffy is a flapper. Riley is a cowboy. Anya and Xander both appear. The theme of the dream seems to be that Willow has been playing a part and that acting is about hiding. Once the truth is known, she will be punished. Buffy rips off Willow's costume, revealing the outfit Willow wore the first time she met Buffy. Said truth appears to be that deep inside, she's still the frightened, insecure Willow she was back then.

While Oz and Tara whisper about her, Willow tries to present her book report. Xander is bored out of his mind, even when the Primitive attacks her and sucks the life right out of her, both in her dream and in reality.

Xander dreams that Joyce comes on to him, but he ends up in his basement instead of her bedroom. Then he's on a playground. Giles and Spike are on swings, and Spike declares that he's going to become a Watcher. Giles says that Spike is like a son to him. Xander acknowledges that these are both notions *he's* considered. Buffy refers to him as her big brother. Then he's in his ice-cream truck. Anya talks about getting back into vengeance while Tara and Willow, tarted up, kiss each other and invite him to come into the back of the truck with them. Everything is mixed up with *Apocalypse Now* and continually being sent back to his basement. Snyder tells him he's a whipping boy, and there are intimations that his time is running out. In his dream his father taunts him with the knowledge that he'll never get out of the basement; he hasn't the heart for it. Then he plunges his hand into Xander's chest; his hand becomes the hand of the Primitive, and he rips out his heart.

Giles, in his dream, faces the notion of the road less traveled, as Olivia appears pushing a baby carriage. Buffy appears in a childish sundress, urging him to let her have fun at a strange carnival. Spike (in black and white) has hired himself out as a sideshow attraction, striking scary vampire poses as the flashbulbs pop at him. Then they're at the Bronze, where Anya is doing standup. Giles performs a rock opera ("The Exposition Song") and pieces together that the spell they cast with Buffy has released some kind of primal evil. He tries to warn Buffy, but the Primitive appears and slices open his head.

Now it's Buffy's turn. She is standing in her bedroom. Anya, in her bed, urges her to wake up, to no avail. Tara appears, talking to Buffy as the Slayer makes the bed at seven-thirty, recalling that she and Faith just made it. Tara informs her that she doesn't know what she's doing. Buffy begins to look for her friends, and finds her mother living in the wall. She moves on, finding Adam, completely human, sitting opposite Riley at a glass conference table inside the Initiative. They seem to be creating a new world order. A loudspeaker announces that the demons have escaped; Buffy begins covering herself in mud as she finds herself facing Tara and the Primitive. Tara translates for the Primitive. The woman is the First Slayer. She and Buffy battle furiously, Buffy insisting that she, unlike the First Slayer, is more than rage. Buffy is not alone and she does not sleep on a pile of bones. And she wants her friends back.

The Primitive stabs her over and over—in the enjoining, Buffy was the Hand, the physical vessel for all the magick—but Buffy does not accept that fate. She wakes up—as do the others, unhurt.

After discussing what happened, Buffy goes upstairs to use the bathroom. She tosses off the comment, "Yeah, well, at least you all didn't dream about the guy with the cheese . . . don't know where the hell that came from. . . ."

Of course, they all dreamed about The Cheese Man.

As Buffy stops on the threshold of her bedroom, Tara, in voice-over, promises Buffy once more that she has no idea what she is, and what's coming.

QUOTE OF THE WEEK:
The Cheese Man, with slices of cheese on his head, addresses Giles during his dream:
"I wear the cheese. It does not wear me."

THE AGONY AND THE ECSTASY:
In the dream, Riley and Buffy may or may not be together; Anya is talking about becoming a demon again, while Xander, who almost sleeps with Joyce, and with Tara and Willow together as well, continues to wind up in the basement. Willow and Tara are together, but Tara reveals that she is not all that she seems. Giles appears to be facing a choice: home and hearth, or something different?

POP-CULTURE IQ:
Discussing the post-battle viewing selections for the evening. *Apocalypse Now* is based on the novella *The Heart of Darkness*, updated to take place during the Vietnam War:
XANDER: "And I'm putting in a preemptive bid for *Apocalypse Now*. Heh?"
WILLOW: "Did you get anything less Heart-of-Darknessy?"

> In the line "Come back before Dawn," Tara is referring to the new character, Dawn, who appears in season five.

CONTINUITY:
Joyce meets Riley "finally." Riley's future will be based on what Graham and the others testify about the Initiative. As dreams often are, this episode is fraught with threads referring back to past episodes and characters. Principal Snyder even makes an appearance, standing in for Marlon Brando during Xander's "Apocalyptic" nightmare. Willow's real-life decision to take drama represents a giant step forward in self-confidence; in "Nightmares," her worst nightmare was performing in front of an audience. But in her dream, she's the shy, unconfident Willow again, making a reference to *Madame Butterfly*, which was the opera that in "Nightmares" she was forced to perform in. She's also dressed exactly the way she was when she first met Buffy. In Giles's dream, Olivia returns, as does Harmony. Buffy reminds us of Faith's strange conversation with her in "Graduation Day, Part Two" about seven-three-oh, and also about making the bed with Faith—which was actually Faith's dream.

FROM THE ORIGINAL TELEPLAY:
Buffy talks a little wacky to her mom, in this line cut due to length:
   "I think they might be in trouble-danger."

From the script, a description of The Cheese Man:
   [A skittish, balding, bespectacled little fellow in an old woolen suit. A voice not unlike Peter Lorre's.]

More stage directions:
   [And at this moment, as Giles continues to speak, he is suddenly DUBBED INTO FRENCH. We can see him talking, but we can't understand a word any more than Xander can, unless we speak French, in which case la-di-da aren't we intellectual, I'm not Joe DICTIONARY, ALL RIGHT?]
   GILES (FRENCH DUBBING OVER): "—the house where we're all sleeping. All your friends are there having a wonderful time and getting on with their lives. The creature can't hurt you there."
   XANDER: "What? Go where? I don't understand."
   GILES (STILL DUBBED): "Oh, for God's sake, this is no time for your idiotic games!"
   [Anya rushes to them, worried. And dubbed.]
   ANYA (WITH THE DUBBING): "Xander! You have to come with us now! Everybody's waiting for you!"
   GILES (DUBLY): "Honey, I don't—I can't hear you. . . ."
   [Anya grabs his arm, starts dragging him.]
   ANYA (DUBBAGE): "It's not important. I'll take you there."

GEORGE HERTZBERG (ADAM)

A lot of time has passed since the days of *Buffy*, but the fandom is still out there and passionate, and new generations are coming into it. What does it feel like to be a part of something so enduring?

GEORGE: "Fantastic and incredible. It's not something I think anyone knew would happen back when the show was shooting, certainly not when I was on, [which was] primarily during season four. It's been an awesome and life-changing experience to meet incredible people from around the world, all of whom have been touched in some way by the show."

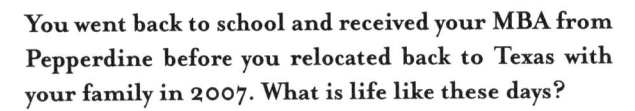

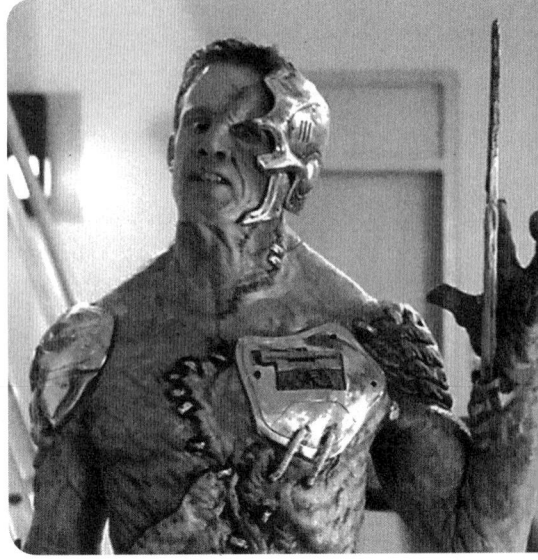

You went back to school and received your MBA from Pepperdine before you relocated back to Texas with your family in 2007. What is life like these days?

GEORGE: "I have been focused on raising three healthy boys (four, if you include me) in the state where I grew up. While I have done a few minor roles on TV since relocating, I transitioned out of acting and into business. That said, now that my boys are getting older, I'm looking at possibly returning to the stage, my first acting love."

Looking back now, what stands out to you about the process of being cast as Adam—about the audition or your first look at the script, or both?

GEORGE: "The audition piece was the monologue from my second episode. 'I'm a kinematically redundant biomechanical demonoid . . .' I remember calling my manager after I received the sides to say, 'WTF?' His response was, 'Just make it your own, man, and make it real.' I went into the audition and a couple of folks I didn't recognize were in the room alongside the casting director. I was fully committed and believing these nonsensical words. I went through it once, and when I finished, a smallish guy that reminded me of my college roommate said thank you and turned to the other guy to say something as I left. I didn't get ten feet from the door when the casting director came out and called me back in. The guy asked me to take a few minutes outside to change a couple things in my delivery and then come back in. I made the adjustments, and the guy, who I later learned was Joss Whedon, was impressed. An hour later my manager called to tell me I booked it and I needed to go to the valley and get a full-body cast . . . the journey had just begun!"

You still do conventions from time to time, and they often come with some pretty strange fan interactions. If you're willing to share . . . what are the best and worst fan moments you can remember?

GEORGE: "Literally upward of 95 percent of interactions have been overwhelmingly positive. The *Buffy* fandom seem to be very smart, very creative, and generally friendly and good. Now, to balance that there was once a gentleman who I believe was a postal worker, judging by his authentic uniform, who came through an autograph line and then proceeded to hide out in a corner and film the guests for the next thirty minutes. That said, the most shocked I've ever been by an interaction was when I saw my character tattooed on a person's back. I was in Europe, and at the prompting of a nice young girl, her father raised up his shirt and *bam*, there was the whole principal cast and selected guest stars, including yours truly."

So much time has passed. What are your favorite behind-the-scenes memories of your time on the show?

GEORGE: "Sarah was always very focused and yet friendly to me on set. Here I was, standing about six feet seven inches with boots on, sweating under lights and heavy makeup, and she asked about getting me cooled off. She was friendly and helpful. Marc Blucas was a good dude—easygoing, friendly. I remember he had a custom van he used to drive with a full queen-size bed in the back and a PS3. Between his scenes he'd go hang out and play games sometimes. Other than those, there's always the common, great story of arriving before everyone to get in makeup, and then getting wrapped before everyone and hitting the craft-service table only to get stares and glares from people who are thinking, *Who's this guy loading up on trail mix and Emergen-C?* It wasn't until my final episode in season four when everyone finally knew what I looked like out of makeup. That was a great time. I only had to arrive an hour early instead of the four and a half for makeup and wardrobe."

I've heard it said that working on a long-running TV series is a lot like high school, with circles of friends and then those people you wish you'd hung out with more. Who do you wish you'd hung out with more?

GEORGE: "Hmm . . . I hung out with James Marsters quite a bit while I was filming. We lived pretty close to one another, and he was pretty down to earth. Other than that, James Leary—whom I never worked with on the show but met doing conventions—is a great friend of mine to this day. He's a great, solid mensch, a very talented guy whom I have incredible respect for and whom, without *Buffy*, I would probably have never met. I certainly wouldn't have all the insane memories."

MARC BLUCAS (RILEY FINN)

You were a basketball star at your alma mater, Wake Forest University, and went on to play in a European league after graduation. How did the transition from court to camera come about?

MARC: "It was an accident. I was a business major at Wake Forest, had a full scholarship to law school, and had started a business with the late NASCAR legend Dale Earnhardt. All was going according to plan, when Wake's sports-information director called me to say a local movie in North Carolina had come to town, and they needed a baby-faced white kid who could play basketball. I auditioned, got the job, and simply caught the bug. It was an interesting conversation with my parents when I said I was turning my back on law school and a successful business to move to California to pursue something I'd never done before."

You had a number of film and TV roles prior to being cast as Riley Finn, but *Buffy* was your first recurring role. Was that a turning point for you as an actor?

MARC: "I hadn't really done much before *Buffy*—a few small gigs—and I frankly had no idea what I was walking into. In hindsight, I wish I was more seasoned and mature back then to appreciate how good the show was—I was just too green to get it."

You've had all sorts of film and TV roles since *Buffy*, including long stints on *Necessary Roughness* and *Underground*, and a major role in the film *Knight and Day*, alongside Tom Cruise and Cameron Diaz. Of the many parts you've played, which role would you hope *Buffy* fans only familiar with you as Riley would track down and watch, if they haven't seen it?

MARC: "I don't watch the things I do, so I certainly wouldn't wish that on anyone else."

Looking back now, what stands out to you about the process of being cast as Riley—about the audition or your first look at the script, or both?

MARC: "The thing that stands out the most is what Joss did for me. The audition process was pretty standard—casting director first, then a callback with a few producers, then a callback to read with Joss. He then narrowed it to two people, who had to read opposite Sarah. The night before that audition I got undercut playing basketball and threw out my back—I couldn't move. I went to the audition in flip-flops and leaned against a wall. After I sucked, I apologized for wasting their time and wished them luck. That night, Joss called me at home and said, 'I know you're the guy; I've seen you do it. Come back when you're better, and I'll tape you and Sarah again.' We did that two weeks later. He gave me a second chance in a town that isn't known for them. I won't ever forget that."

Did you know what was in store for Riley when you were cast, that he would become Buffy's boyfriend and have such a major role to play in the series?

MARC: "Joss kept things pretty close to the vest, especially back then. I knew that Riley and Buffy would have an attempt at romance. I also knew after Angel that would be an insurmountable mountain. I distinctly remember Joss telling me to stay offline. I asked, 'Why?' And he replied, 'Because they're gonna *hate* you!' And he was right."

So much time has passed. What are your favorite behind-the-scenes memories of your time on the show?

MARC: "I loved the crew on that show. I'm still in touch with a handful of those guys. Being so new to the industry, and that show already being a big hit, they were very patient with me. Especially Sarah—I couldn't have asked for a better person to have my first big role alongside. As frustrating as I know it was for her at times, she always knew I was trying and working my ass off, and I think she respected that."

Everyone says that working on a long-running TV series is a lot like high school, with circles of friends and then those people you wish you'd hung out with more. Who do you wish you'd hung out with more?

MARC: "Well, Joss is currently writing and directing some of the biggest movies in the business, so I guess him. Ha! No, it happened at the right time, with the right people for me. I have no regrets, as I made some really good friends during that year and a half."

What are the best and worst fan experiences you've had?

MARC: "Just this year I did my first convention . . . funny how the industry's view of conventions has changed over the years. Early on it was career suicide to go, and now it's career suicide *not* to go. But I had an amazing time—many of the people there were rediscovering *Buffy* again by watching it with their kids. Maybe that nearly twenty-year gap was needed for people to separate the actor from the character—I know it was good for me! No one threw shit at me, at least."

What are you working on now, and what does the future hold for Marc Blucas?

MARC: "I've been really lucky in that I can make a living doing what I love and still be a real father and husband. I'm at my perfect level of celebrity: 99 percent of the world could give a shit, but I get enough recognition to stroke my ego and let me know I at least have some kind of career. I live on a farm in Pennsylvania with my wife and kids and animals and couldn't be happier with the ups and downs that life has delivered. I'm glad *Buffy* was a small part of that."

JAMES C. LEARY (CLEM)

You've done a series of blogs called *Confessions of a G-List Celebrity*, in which you talk about your Hollywood dreams, your time as Clem on *Buffy the Vampire Slayer*, the wonderful and the awful things that resulted, and your retreat from Los Angeles. Folks can go and read the blog for the full story, but what prompted you to be so brutally frank, and how has your honesty been received?

JAMES: "Hmm . . . well, part of it had to do with being in recovery and wanting to own up to the crappy things I had done—when something like that goes out, there is no hiding from that stuff anymore. There is a saying: 'You are only as sick as your secrets,' and most people had this image of me as this 'fun-loving, wacky nice guy,' who maybe liked to party just a little too much—but it felt like a mask. People didn't see the aftermath or that 'wacky nice guy' was just a cover to hide insecurity. People got hurt, jobs lost, relationships ruined because I couldn't be honest. When Clare Kramer (and Brian Keathley) approached me to do something for GeekNation, after talking about ideas, we settled on this concept of me just being brutally honest . . . but you know, in a funny way.

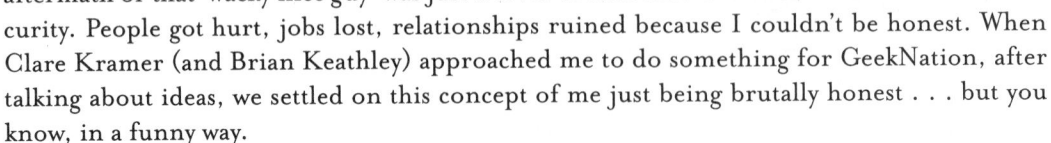

"The other reason is that I think people have this image of Hollywood actors—that it is this glamorous lifestyle full of parties and pampering and piles of cash—and while that may be true for the very, very top percentage of actors, for everyone else it is a daily grind to get work. There aren't a lot of people who talk about the everyday struggles of the rank-and-file actor, and I thought maybe I could shed some light on that.

"And finally, I had hoped that by sharing my story—good, bad, and ugly—that maybe I could help someone else who was struggling through something similar. To show that no matter how far you've fallen or how many mistakes you've made, there is a way back.

"A few people were upset by the revealing of such personal details . . . and I have to take full responsibility for that, but overwhelmingly the response was very positive. It was one of the scariest things I've ever done in my life, putting it out there—and I'm grateful I took the leap."

Looking back now, what stands out to you about the process of being cast as Clem—about the audition or your first look at the script, or both?

JAMES: "The writing. Always the writing. When I got the sides for the audition I was so excited it was a scene with Spike and Buffy. I was a huge fan of the show, so I was super excited to get to audition. I was lucky enough that I knew the casting associate, and she brought me right in to the producers. That can be a double-edged sword, but I like having an audience. I knew the show well and decided to read my lines as if my character were human and for as much humor as I could. Once I got the first laugh in that room I knew in my gut I had the gig. One of the few times I'd ever had that feeling."

Did you have any idea after that first episode that Clem would be back, and at what stage did you start to realize what a fan favorite he'd become?

JAMES: "I really didn't. I mean, I certainly hoped, and I knew the show had a habit of bringing characters back. It's funny: at the end of my day of shooting for that first episode, James Marsters and I were chatting and I expressed how awesome it would be to come back, and he said, 'You're funny. Trust me—you'll be back.' I thought, *Yeah, he says this to all the day players.* But sure enough, when I came back a few months later for 'Older and Far Away,' where I got to shoot for the full week, he came right up to me and said, 'See! Told you you'd be back.'

"I don't think it hit me what a fan favorite Clem was until I started doing conventions the following year. I certainly had no idea while I was shooting. I was just happy to keep coming back, because I was having such a fun time. It still seems surreal to me, even after all these years. I only did eight episodes over two years, but for whatever reason Clem struck a chord, and I'm grateful for it. The role truly changed my life (both good and bad)—I've been all over the world and gotten to meet so many fans to whom the show means so much. As an actor, that is what you do this for—to affect people, to make them laugh or cry or forget about the crappy day they've just had."

A lot of the cast members from *Buffy* still get recognized in public on a regular basis, but you were under makeup the whole time—virtually unrecognizable, except to hardcore fans. Is that a good thing? Do people recognize you outside of convention settings? And is it strange to shift back and forth between ordinary day-to-day life and those convention settings?

JAMES: "I think it was a good thing and a bad thing. Good in the sense that I could and still can go just about anywhere. I never had to deal with what the other actors had to as far as, say, not being able to go to the mall or out to eat without being recognized. (And look, that comes with the territory, it's part of the gig.) So I was able to maintain my privacy and anonymity. Unfortunately, it also meant that casting directors didn't recognize me. Because I was in makeup, they felt like they didn't get a sense of what I could do. I'm not sure why that is, but in talking to other actors who work with makeup I certainly wasn't alone in that thought. I even remember getting called into an agent's office because his assistants loved the show, only to get in to meet him and have him say, 'Oh, you were in makeup. . . . Yeah . . . Sorry, not much I can do for you.'

"Shifting back and forth from cons to regular life proved *very* hard for me. I'm an extrovert in every sense of the word. I love attention. Being the life of the party, and at cons that was the name of the game. Where it was hard for some of the top of show actors to mingle with the fans due to the mayhem that sometimes occurred, I could (and always did) hang out. At home I was a struggling actor waiting tables and auditioning for herpes commercials, but at cons . . . I was a damn rock star. So the transition from that much attention was tough for me."

We've talked about how conventions come with some pretty strange fan interactions. If you're willing to share . . . what are the best and worst fan moments you can remember?

JAMES: "The best moments are always when someone tells a story about how the show helped them through a hard time. From divorces to deaths in the family to just getting them through a deep depression—the show kept them going. As an actor that is what we strive for—we want to affect people. Onstage you get that interaction immediately, but with film and TV it's different—you don't get the instant feedback, so to hear that from people really means a lot.

"Worst fan moments—hmm, I'd say it's like that old *SNL* sketch with William Shatner. Occasionally there are folks that have a hard time distinguishing the character from reality. There have also been the odd inappropriate touch or hug that lasts too long, and people who share a little too much personal information: 'I've written thirty pages of slash fan fiction between Clem and Spike—would you like me to read it to you?' But the majority of interactions are very positive. It's why I love cons so much."

What are your favorite behind-the-scenes memories of your time on the show?

JAMES: "All of them. I certainly loved that Emma and Alyson loved playing with Clem's ears—that didn't suck. Also the first time I showed up on set out of makeup—since I always arrived way before everyone else to start getting into makeup, no one had ever seen what I really looked like. One day I wrapped early and went to go say good-bye to everyone and they had *no clue who I was*. I believe Emma said something to the effect of: 'Oh, wow! You're cute!'—another thing that didn't suck."

Everyone says that working on a long-running TV series is a lot like high school, with circles of friends and then those people you wish you'd hung out with more. Who do you wish you'd hung out with more?

JAMES: "Anthony Stewart Head, for sure. I got to meet him later doing conventions, and he is one of the warmest people I've ever spent time with. I wish we'd had scenes together. Oh . . . and Joss. He was doing *Firefly* for most of season six, so I never got to work with him directly."

You've recently returned to theater. What have you been performing in, and what are your plans for the future?

JAMES: "I've been doing a lot of improv comedy in the Austin area. Austin, Texas, has kind of become the Chicago of the South for improv. I perform mostly at the Institution Theater. In fact, I'm working on the second run of an award-winning show called *Hard-ish Bodies* that is basically *The Full Monty* in a *Magic Mike* world, which has been incredible. I also do as much local film as I can—mostly indie stuff, Web series, shorts, and stuff. Beyond that, I'm not sure what the future holds. There is a part of me that would love to get back into the acting world now that I'm older and wiser, so if anyone needs an average-looking funny white guy, drop me a DM (as the kids say these days)."

TODD McINTOSH (MAKEUP DEPARTMENT HEAD)

You've been doing professional makeup for film and television since 1979 and your heroes were FX [special effects] makeup giants like Rick Baker and Dick Smith, yet judging by your site, you hadn't done a lot of FX makeup—monsters, at least—before your 107 episodes of *Buffy*. Was that part of the attraction of the job, and did you get everything you wanted out of it?

TODD: "If you look at the list of my early projects, I did the films *Clan of the Cave Bear* and *Masters of the Universe*, and TV productions like *Hoover* for Showtime. These were done with Michael Westmore, whom I consider to be my mentor. All of them were heavy prosthetic shows. Perhaps they weren't monster movies, but they were certainly FX character makeups, which is what I was more interested in then, as I still am today. There is a misconception outside the industry that we crew members somehow choose the projects we work on—I wish that were the case! I take what's offered to me. In the case of *Buffy*, I was the right fit and was able to stay with the show and make a spot for myself that allowed what I do best—painting and application, as well as management skills—to shine. It was a serendipitous marriage. I was inspired to get into makeup because of the TV show *Dark Shadows*, which I saw when I was seven years old. Yes, it had monsters, and other people aside from myself have noted that *Buffy* and *Dark Shadows* have a TV lineage in common; so I certainly felt at home on a vampire show, and in a way I felt I had come full circle to the genre that attracted me to my career. But I got the job because I was simply in the right time and place to get it. Did I get from it what I wanted? I got recognition as an artist and a chance to shine at my craft—while earning a living!—I can't think of anything better."

The mind boggles when attempting to tally up the sheer number of hours that must have gone into being the department head for makeup on 107 episodes of *Buffy*, handling both beauty makeup and FX makeup. Did you ever expect the job to last so long? And did it ever get boring or was there always something new to intrigue you?

TODD: "*Buffy* was a hard show. I'm sure any crew member you ask who lived through the show will agree with me. We called it *Buffy the Weekend Slayer* because the hours were so long, and we worked right into Saturday morning most weeks. I did my first twenty-four-hour day on that show, though it hasn't been my last! Most days were fourteen hours, to my recollection. Did I expect the job to last that long? No. We made the pilot and first season in a vacuum—it was a midseason replacement, so we didn't know if it would even be aired when we made season one. When it turned out to be a success, I was just happy to be asked back. TV shows are like any freelance contract—when you finish a season you go home and begin looking for your next job. No one asks if you want to come back for another season. That changed when it seemed that the show would have a seven-year run, and I was thrilled to be asked to return. Bored? Never! It was so fast-paced. And sometimes there were three units filming simultaneously and I was running them all out of the main makeup trailer, so there wasn't time to get bored!"

Many years ago, when I first interviewed you, we talked a lot about your inspirations, but what TV and film makeup—other than your own—would you point to as new inspirations?

TODD: "Frankly, in the years since *Buffy*, the makeup field has simply exploded. There are makeup artists under every rock now! When I was a young artist, there were only a few masters that we looked up to—mine being Dick Smith and Mike Westmore. Today there are so many talented prosthetics and beauty artists working that I cannot keep track of them. Everywhere I look I see beautiful work—out of England, Canada, Europe, as well as at home in every state that films are made. I'm so impressed by the work on the *Star Trek* movies, on the TV show *Westworld*, and the Harry Potter movies, just to name a few. But also—look at the schools! The IMATS makeup competitions are showing the amazing level of creativity and talent coming out of the schools. When I started, there were no schools!"

During your time on *Buffy*, you became a celebrity in your own right within the fandom, doing the occasional convention appearance. How unusual is that, and do you still have contact with *Buffy* fans?

TODD: "Well, I don't know if 'celebrity' is the word. 'Notorious' might be better! Let's say I gained a certain amount of notoriety. I think that was unusual at the time. The Internet and fan sites were new, and it was the first time random crew members could, if they wanted, interact with the fans. I took advantage of that because if I were not in the industry, or I wanted to be a makeup artist, I would have been a fan of the show and beside myself with excitement to talk to someone directly involved with making it. I have always been an educator and have tried to give back to the people who support the shows we make a living from. Now, with the explosion of awareness of the career of makeup, we as a craft are regularly a part of the conventions.

"Yes, I still get the occasional *Buffy* fan contact. More often I'm on set and some actor I'm working on will tell me they watched *Buffy* as a child—or worse, that their big sister watched it when they were a baby and they have only recently discovered it. I guess the years catch up with us all—but it's an odd feeling. Sometimes I get e-mails from girls saying, 'What eye shadow did you use on Buffy in episode [blank]?' Really? That was twenty years ago! I've gone through a lot of eye shadow since those days. The beauty makeups I did on *Buffy* are so old they are considered 'period' makeups now! I also get requests for the actors' phone numbers or addresses . . . funny how people not in the industry imagine that it works . . . or even if I had that information that I would just hand it out."

You've worked on so many fantastic films and TV series—everything from *Memoirs of a Geisha* to *Pushing Daisies*, from *Torchwood* to *True Detective*. What non-*Buffy* project would you point to as your favorite example of your work, and why?

TODD: "There is no doubt in my mind that *Pushing Daisies* stands out as the other prime example of my work on camera. The other makeup artist, David DeLeon, and I are two matched painters. We get it as a team. David and I, with the support and freedom given by Bryan Fuller, and the amazing lighting by Michael Weaver, created a look that every day made my heart soar. Plus, for the first time in my career, I was allowed to design and have constructed all the prosthetic makeups. It was a dream job, and I would have stayed on it until the end of my career if I could have. I won my second Emmy for *Daisies*, and what makes the situation special is that the Emmy for *Buffy* was for prosthetics and the Emmy for *Daisies* was for beauty and character work. That sums up my career—what has always been most important to me is to be a well-rounded and complete makeup artist in the mold of my heroes, those amazing artists that came before me. Many people forget that Dick Smith could do a beauty makeup as well as any prosthetic."

So much time has passed. What are your favorite behind-the-scenes memories of your time on the show?

TODD: "You know, I get asked this question often, and the minute I do, I can't remember a thing. As I said, the work was intense and the hours long. I have flashes of certain moments: One season, Jay Wejebe and I had terrariums with tiny frogs on our stations that we kept and coddled for the whole season; I remember long and deep conversations with James Marsters in the wee small hours of the morning while I put him in vamp-face; I remember the camaraderie of ten makeup artists huddling by a heater in the woods while rubber monsters roamed around in bee-smoke fog; I remember one makeup artist so exhausted that she touched up a dummy of a creature, thinking it was the actor. So many laughs and tender moments. After all, it was six years of my life! Perhaps my favorite memory was of one Halloween night, which we always worked. I hired extra help to cover the set, and my team and I stayed in the trailer and made up anyone who wanted it—actors who had the night off, office staff, producers' kids—anyone. It was a lovely night."

Everyone says that working on a long-running TV series is a lot like high school, with circles of friends and then those people you wish you'd hung out with more. Who do you wish you'd hung out with more from your *Buffy* days?

TODD: "I know this is going to sound like I'm prevaricating, but I did manage to socialize with all the people I liked on the show. To this day I am still friends with Sarah. Recently, I was working on the Fox lot, and a crew van pulled to a stop beside me and David Boreanaz jumped out and gave me a hug—I hadn't seen him in twenty years! James Marsters and I ended up in Vancouver at the same time and had a lovely dinner. I see Juliet Landau quite often and recently was interviewed for her *Undead* documentary. I loved our camera crew, and we had a great sarcastic and joking rapport. I still work with the odd crew member going from show to show. Of course, the makeup artists that were part of my crew are still in my working life, and we socialize when we can. I even had a party in my home for the stuntmen and -women on the show—with so many hours spent in makeup we became friends. I have few regrets for those days."

What does the future hold for Todd McIntosh?

TODD: "I truly wish I knew! As I said earlier, I am not in control of the work that comes my way. As we speak, the show I was on just had its order cut suddenly, so I'm sitting by the phone waiting for the next call that will change the landscape of my career. That is the fun and scary side of being freelance in the film industry—what, indeed, comes next?"

LOOKING BACK: INTERVIEWS OVER THE YEARS

ALYSON HANNIGAN (WILLOW ROSENBERG)

The way Alyson read her lines in her audition has defined Willow ever since.

"I was sitting in the parking lot in my car waiting for the audition," she recalls. "I was reading the lines, and it was just sort of depressing. She was saying, 'Oh, boys don't like me, and this and that, and I can't really speak around guys.' I just didn't want to feel sorry for her. How are [viewers] going to like her if they're saying, 'Oh, look at her feeling sorry for herself'?

"There was a scene between Buffy and Willow, and in the beginning of the scene Willow says, 'Xander and I went out when we were four or five, and then we broke up.' Buffy says, 'Why?' 'Because he stole my Barbie.' It changed once we got to [shoot] the actual scene, but in the [original version] Buffy says, 'Did you ever get your Barbie back?' And Willow's line was: 'Most of it.' And so I thought, you know what, I'm gonna make that a really happy thing. I was so proud that I got most of my Barbie back. And then that clued in how I was going to play the rest of the scene. It defines the character. That was the one line that triggered it. Then I went back and said, 'Okay, now how can I play the whole scene like that?' And it really helped me. And Joss said later, 'Oh, yeah, *most* of it!' It was a funny line, and he didn't even know there was a joke there. I made the right choice."

Were you interested in horror and fantasy growing up?

ALYSON: "Yeah. I mean, I was a chicken. I still pretty much am, you know. I'm the screamer in the theater, but it was always fun to get spooked."

What were you afraid of as a child?

ALYSON: "Tests that I hadn't studied for? I was sort of afraid of my spelling teacher. She was mean. Obviously, you go through the phases of 'Okay, there are monsters moving under my bed,' so I was obviously afraid of anything that could be under there. That's why I kept all of my toys under my bed. You know, my mom thought I was just messy. No, no, it was protection."

NICHOLAS BRENDON (XANDER HARRIS)

Are you expecting Speedo backlash over your performance in "Go Fish"?

NICHOLAS: "I'm not looking for backlash. I'm looking for forward lash."

Do you have any skills or talents you haven't showcased as Xander yet?

NICHOLAS: "I *discover* new talents. Like dancing. Whatever comes up, I'll do it. I've done a lot of pratfalls and stuff like that."

Do you have a favorite moment, on or off camera, from your tenure on the series?

NICHOLAS: "Probably the day I did my Speedo stuff. The crew was so supportive. I was so terrified of it. When we finally did my scene it was four minutes of sheer hell. Walking in, doing my dialogue, then diving into the pool. Then, coming up from the water, I heard this weird smattering, and then I emerged and the whole crew was applauding. It was really nice. Everyone was very supportive."

You've kissed or been in some intimate situation with each of the female cast members. Is this the best job you've ever had?

NICHOLAS: "It's not bad. I'm sure I can get paid to do worse things."

Everyone on the set seems to think that *Buffy*'s success, and the team that came together to make it happen, was almost destiny. Do you share that feeling?

NICHOLAS: "It's one of those things where everything worked. When you're creating a successful show, it's ninety percent luck. Joss has the talent, but when it comes to casting, it's all luck. It was my first pilot season, and I kind of won the lottery."

CHARISMA CARPENTER (CORDELIA CHASE)

Charisma first auditioned for the role of Buffy.

"I was wearing overalls and these bright orange flip-flops and a jacket, and I was just kind of hanging, you know, because I felt that Buffy could really just be herself," she remembers, a wry smile playing at the edges of her mouth. "She could wear the flip-flops, and she could be low-key and still be very—it wasn't about looking as cute as I could to get the part. It was about just being cool, just being fun with your identity. And that's how I felt. The other girls in the room were really dressed up, and they were wearing very high school trendy clothes with knee-high stockings and short skirts."

To Charisma's surprise, however, the producers asked her to audition for the role of Cordelia as well. To say the least, the actress was unprepared. She had, after all, come to read for Buffy.

"I was thinking, *I'm never going to get this part because of the way they're seeing me.* Sometimes you have to show people. Cordelia is definitely a character to dress for. You have to kind of give it to them and let them work on that. It was an interesting experience, because I had about fifteen minutes to go outside and prepare for Cordelia when I had spent all this time on Buffy."

Obviously, it went well. The producers soon had Charisma scheduled for a screen test for Cordelia. All did not go as smoothly as one might imagine, however.

"I was super, super late for the screen test, because I was working all the way down on the beach for *Malibu Shores,* and I had to go to Burbank, which was on the opposite end of the city. I was late, and there was traffic, and it was raining," she remembers. "My agent called me right when I was at the exit, paged me, 911, and I went, 'Oh, gosh, I better answer this.' So I pulled over, even though I was tremendously late. I said, 'What? I'm on the exit right now.' She tells me, 'They're going to leave, you'd better hurry up.'

"I said, 'You tell them that they'd better order a pizza or something, because I did not drive an hour and a half in all this traffic to not go in there and at least audition.' Obviously, I was panicked."

Fortunately, when she finally arrived, the audition went well. The producers were "laughing, really responsive," Charisma recalls. She left with a rush of confidence. "After it was over and they had all left, I called my agent and said, 'I got this part.' She said, 'No, don't say that, you don't know.' But I knew I had the part, I could tell."

She was, of course, absolutely correct. During the first season, the character of Cordelia seemed little more than Buffy's snobby nemesis. But in the season finale, the character learned the truth about Sunnydale. From that point on, Charisma knew that her character was going to be much more involved with the Slayer's posse. Ironically, she admits that this news caused her some anxiety.

"I wasn't sure how I felt about it, because I didn't want to lose my edge. I didn't want her to be nice; I didn't want her to change because that's who she is," she says thoughtfully.

In fact, when discussing a moment of kindness Cordelia exhibits toward Xander in the second-season finale, Carpenter asserts in no uncertain terms that: "We don't want too many of those nice moments." She has often urged the producers to "make her meaner."

"It would be boring if she was too one-dimensional. It's a challenge for me to find that balance. That's why I enjoy playing her so much. She's got to be somewhat tolerable or why would they hang out with her? But I [try] not to lose her edge, her honesty."

Was she Cordelia in high school, or was she more like one of the other characters on the show?

"Well, I wasn't Willowish, I wasn't terribly academic," she says quickly. "I wasn't in the clique, either; I wasn't Cordy. I was kind of a loner, and nobody really is a loner in this cast."

Do you have a favorite moment, either off camera or on, since you've been on the show?

CHARISMA: "I have a lot of favorite moments, most with Xander. A lot of Cordy's conflict, and a lot of who she is, comes out around Xander. Because she is in love with him in spite of herself, or in spite of him. I have my best moments with Nicky [Nicholas Brendon]."

DAVID BOREANAZ (ANGEL)

Which of your character's personae have you most enjoyed portraying?

DAVID: "There are pluses and minuses to each," he points out. "With Angel's good side, I wasn't really exploring as much, as far as his being as outgoing as I wanted to be. But I know when I go back to being good, then I'll have learned from that. I think they both balance each other out pretty well. . . . Yeah, I've done some bad things."

Were you interested in the horror genre at all when you were growing up?

DAVID: "I remember being terrified by *Frankenstein* when I was a kid. The old *Frankenstein*. Boris Karloff. When he came and visited the little girl playing by the lake. Terrible, I couldn't watch it. That, and I like Godzilla movies."

Do you have a favorite moment, either on or off camera, from your work on the series?

DAVID: "There were a couple, actually. When I had the scene in the Factory—just after I had changed—and I was striking the match off the brick table. That was a really cool moment. The whole scene seemed to really gel.

"Also, I work with Sarah a lot and there is good chemistry between the two of us. We are able to grasp each other's insights pretty easily. That's really pleasant. There have been a lot of moments with her that I would walk away and say, 'Wow, that was really great.' And there are moments where you say, 'Wow, that was really bad,' but it comes out great. You can't really judge yourself. You've just got to do it. You learn from your mistakes; you grow from them."

SETH GREEN (DANIEL "OZ" OSBOURNE)

He's the only member of the series cast who was in the movie.

Yes, really.

"I was cut out of the film, but I'm on the back of the video box," he says. (Go on, check it.) "I was awful in it, and I really hope the footage never surfaces, because in retrospect I realize how bad I was in it. At the time, I was very excited. You see me really early on as sort of a geeky guy that Sasha kind of makes fun of in passing, like knocks books out of my hands or something like that. . . . And then he is walking through the woods toward the merry-go-round.

"The way it goes in the movie now, Sasha says, 'I'm going to turn around, and when I do, you are not going to be there.' When he does, it is Paul Reubens on the merry-go-round. There are five minutes cut out of that, where he turns around and I'm standing there and I have the face of a vampire, and I call him by name, and he says, 'What are you doing here?' and he comes over and I just start laughing, and he picks me up. He lifts me up threateningly, gripping my collar, and he lets me go and I stay floating in the air. I start laughing like crazy, and I grab him and I bite him.

"It was terrible. For some reason, I told them I had a thirty-two-inch waist, so the harness they gave me was five sizes too big. I just look like I'm wearing a diaper. . . . It was impressive," Seth concludes with a dry chuckle.

Were you interested in horror and fantasy growing up?

SETH: "Absolutely. There was a time when I was very into vampire mythology and things like that. Then it got a little spoiled for me. It is difficult for it not to be spoiled when there are all these people running around with dyed black hair and Marilyn Manson T-shirts talking about how they suck blood. Quite frankly, when you have something that you take relatively seriously just made so laughable by a few ignorant people, it is difficult to still hold it with the same amount of respect. That is why I am glad there is a show like *Buffy*, where even though the show is a little tongue-in-cheek sometimes, they take their monsters seriously and it is scary. It is not a joke. Like *Buffy* the movie was just on TV a couple of times, and I always get that kind of sadness when I see it."

Do you have a favorite moment from your tenure on the series?

SETH: "There was a day when we were making 'Innocence.' They had built that whole mall in this warehouse in downtown Los Angeles, and we had a kind of mini-revolt, and Aly and Charisma and Nick and Tony and I all went to the mall across the street and we ate lunch there. It was so bad, we were told there was a Chinese place and they wouldn't serve us. They were like, 'We're only doing lunch orders now.' We said, 'Yeah, we want lunch.' 'No, no bulk orders for delivery,' and they wouldn't give us food. So we wound up eating at McDonald's or something, and then we started scouring the mall for board games, and we wound up buying TVopoly, which is like TV Monopoly. It was just like a long time between setups. Juliet and David and Sarah were all on set; they were working. We didn't have anything to do, so we just sat in Charisma's trailer playing board games. It was so much fun."

ROBIA LAMORTE (JENNY CALENDAR)

Robia came to the series through the usual audition process. But she knew right off that this was something different.

"Sometimes you get scripts, and you just know," she says. "The words just fit in your mouth a different way when you know you're supposed to speak them. And I kind of knew I was going to get it. I came in and auditioned, and they liked me, and I came back and met with everybody, and Tony [Head] came in to read with me. I think it was me and one other girl, so they wanted to see the chemistry. But I didn't know who he was. I thought he was a producer, so he was talking with me, and I was joking with him, and we walked into the room, and I was chewing gum, and I gave it to him, and said, 'Here, hold this.' I didn't even know. I was just playing around with him. They hired me, I think, the next day."

Do you have a favorite moment, on or off screen, from your time on the show?

ROBIA: "The moment I loved, loved, loved, is in the very first episode I did. As soon as I saw it on tape, I said, 'Praise God that I get to say this kind of line, because you don't get the chance to do it very often.' It's when Giles is returning her earring. I loved it on the page; I loved the way it came off. 'No, that's not where I dangle it.' Yeah, that's a classic."

Unlike many of the other characters, you didn't get much chance to kick butt. Are you disappointed?

ROBIA: "I have not gotten to kick as much butt as I would have liked, but I did get to do a little bit of stuff in my demon episode. I jump out the window, and I throw Giles. I got to slam his head into the table and throw him and do some stuff like that. That was a fun episode."

ARMIN SHIMERMAN (PRINCIPAL SNYDER)

Armin admits that there are certain traits he shares with the youth-hating Snyder.

"Principal Snyder bristles much more so than I, of course, but I am not particularly easy around children. I have a lack of communicative skills with people that age and younger. So that is what I draw upon. Some of the principals that I remember growing up were major authoritarian figures who had a disdainful aura about them. . . . And I draw upon that as well."

In fact, Armin believes that, to a point, Snyder is more threatening to the teen characters on the series than the vampires.

"He really holds power over their future," he explains. "If they get expelled from the school, then they'll really be screwed over. They can attack a vampire, but they can't attack a school record. To our younger viewers, that's a real threat."

What were you afraid of as a child?

ARMIN: "I was afraid of snakes, which I just had to recently deal with in *Buffy*—not as close as Charisma did, but close enough. I was afraid of chickens, because I grew up on a chicken farm and they constantly pecked at me, and that was pretty unnerving. And certainly, as far as the show is concerned, I was certainly afraid of not being liked. That is probably what endears the show to me the most. Here are teenagers who are desperately dealing with the angst of growing up amidst a group of people that they are not a part of."

Do you have a favorite moment, on or off screen, from your tenure on *Buffy*?

ARMIN: "It happened the very first day. I knew that I wanted my new character to be something totally different from Quark [on *Star Trek: Deep Space Nine*] and I wanted it to be serious and comic at the same time. I was blessed from the very start. It is the scene where Tony and I are walking down an aisle of the school auditorium. As it went on, I remember thinking, *This is exactly the character; this is exactly right; right off the bat this is working exactly right.* I was elated. When I did *Deep Space Nine*, it took six full episodes before I realized, *Ah, this is who Quark is!* But when I walked down that aisle with Tony in that first scene and talked with the four of them on my first day, I thought, *This is it.* It was a great feeling of achievement. Sometimes I try to re-create that specialness. Sadly, my acting moments aren't always as good as that first encounter. But that first meeting was just something magical for me; when I worked with those people for the first time and slipped flawlessly into character the first time. It was perfect."

KRISTINE SUTHERLAND (JOYCE SUMMERS)

"As a mother, I can't help but be concerned about Buffy not having a father figure and not having a father around. My parents were divorced, so I have some sense of what it is like to grow up in a divorced household. The dynamic, at least from my experience, was very different, because for me, when my parents got divorced, it was such an admission of failure on their part somehow, that they lost a tremendous amount of authority in the household. They both had their own emotional problems, which I suppose contributed to that, but as an adolescent you take that and you wedge it wide open: 'What would you know? You screwed up in such a big way, and *you* are going to tell me what to do?'

"That makes it difficult for a single parent to wield authority over an adolescent. Actually, I have gotten a number of letters from parents in their early thirties who write to me about their empathy with Joyce as a single mother and the struggles involved.

"I think everybody was sort of finding their way, and there were other things to establish the first season," she notes. "I have been really, really thrilled with the writing and some of the stuff we have to do [during season two]. It has been really nice. I think one of my favorite scenes was the one at the end of her birthday, that two-party story ["Surprise" and "Innocence."]. When [Joyce and Buffy are sitting] on the couch. I thought Joss did something so wonderful in that scene with Joyce being her mother and *knowing* that something is going on that is very hard for her. Just being there and not asking what it is. Knowing that. You just have to be there and hope for the best for them. You can't say, 'Oh, let me be your best friend and tell me everything that is going on.' That's not your place; you're a mother.

"I get very caught up in the story," she says happily. "I remember so much of what it was like to be an adolescent, and it just rings so true in so many ways." And as for the second-season finale, she reports having been "stunned" by it.

"I read it in my car," she says incredulously. "I couldn't wait to read it and I had picked it up, but then I had to go to this morning voice-over thing. Well, the first free moment I had, I am sitting in my car, baking without air-conditioning, parked somewhere in Hollywood. I just had to find out what happens and I just sat there and read it. I was in shock. I mean, when she gets on the bus and leaves. I was just sobbing in the car."

Were you a fan of horror or fantasy growing up?

KRISTINE: "I loved fantasy and science fiction, but I could never stomach horror. In fact, when I rented the movie *Buffy the Vampire Slayer*, I had to have my husband sit and watch it with me. I know it is funny and everything, but I am so terrified of horror films. I am waiting for Sarah to do a film that isn't a horror film so I can go see it. I don't know if I could even watch the show if I wasn't in it. I'm terrible. I get scared watching the show even when I'm in the episode and have seen most of it being shot."

Do you have a favorite moment, on or off the screen, from your work on the series?

KRISTINE: "It has been really fun for me [during season two], because last season almost all my work was just with Sarah, and I felt I didn't know the rest of the cast that well. So this year has been really fun, getting to know everybody else and feeling much more a part of the group. But my favorite day this year was Halloween. I was working Halloween day—which was a slight bummer because I didn't get to go trick-or-treating with my daughter—but what better place to be on Halloween than on the set of *Buffy the Vampire Slayer* with vampires running around? A lot of us came in costume, which was really fun. We were shooting the episode 'Ted' that week. I came in a whole '50's garb as Ted's first wife. Sarah was Dorothy from *The Wizard of Oz*, and [her dog] Thor was Toto."

Does Joyce think that Giles is sexy?

KRISTINE: "Yeah, I think she does."

In "Band Candy," when you were sixteen, was that how you were at sixteen, or did you just sort of create a composite of what sixteen-year-olds were like?

KRISTINE: "It was sort of a composite, although I have to say that I was not into Burt Reynolds when I was sixteen.

"That was a really interesting episode. I always think that I remember very clearly what it was like to be a teenager, but to actually walk it, talk it, and inhabit it, it was so much more intense than just sitting around remembering what you were like. And it was interesting because I have to say some of it was really fun, and some of it was painful. It brought up feelings that I hadn't even thought about in so long.

"Like the scene with the music, it was that thing of being a teenage girl and wanting to make a connection with the guy and he's into the music, and he's into cigarettes, and he's into the scene, and you want to make a connection with him but you don't quite know how. You're just going along with him because he's leading you into that place. I hadn't even really thought about that so much until we started doing that scene and suddenly all those feelings came back to me of what it was like to be in that given circumstance. But it wasn't until we sat down to really do it that it hit me."

Do you have any mythology you've created about how Joyce gave birth to a Slayer? Do you believe there is anything about Joyce that made that be what happened to her? Because we don't really know how the Slayers are picked.

KRISTINE: "No, I've actually always sort of seen it as the opposite. That the way I as Joyce see Buffy as the Slayer is sort of symbolic, when you look at your child and realize that they are a totally different person than you are and that they have different gifts and a different calling. It's a separation thing. In this case it's just more extreme and because it isn't just that she's an incredible pianist.

"It's something that has a moral cause behind it and so it brings dual feelings. 'I'm your mother and I'm older and I'm wiser but yet you're my daughter and you're this really spectacular person who's going places and wrestling with things that are beyond what I'll ever have to do in my lifetime.'"

How was it different when Joyce didn't know that Buffy was a Slayer versus now that she knows? Has it made it harder to play her or is it just something that's built into the way you approach your role?

KRISTINE: "It's been much easier, although it was never hard for me as an actress to play that I didn't know that she was the Vampire Slayer. And a lot of people used to say to me, 'Oh, that must be so hard for you,' and I didn't find it hard at all because I think we have a natural built-in mechanism that allows us to deny the things that it's not the right time to see. And I think a mother, a good mother, needs a good healthy dose of that!

"So I didn't find it difficult as an actress to do that, but at the same time, in terms of my relationship with Sarah, it just became so much richer, it opened up so many more possibilities and experiences for my character to move beyond that."

What about if you were a vampire? What if they made Joyce a vampire? Have you ever wanted them to vamp you out?

KRISTINE: "No, I've never wanted to be a vampire! I'm a little claustrophobic. I just have to say I've never wanted to endure the makeup."

EMMA CAULFIELD (ANYA JENKINS)

Tell us how you auditioned for the role of Anya. How did you find out about the role?

EMMA: "Brian Meyers, who is no longer casting the show. Brian called up my representation and said that there was a part on the show, and would I come in and meet Joss. I of course did, I love the show. I found out the same day that I got it. I mean I went in and got it. I was working pretty immediately.

"The role wasn't designed to be anything more than a one-time guest shot and then just sort of evolved from there. I think we got a call like a month later asking if I wanted to come back again. And of course I did, I went back and about halfway through filming that episode it was made kind of clear that they wanted me to come back again, and it just kept evolving from that point.

"By the end of season three, the whole vibe was pretty much, 'Well, we'll see you next year,' but without anything formalized. And then I guess when they started up production again in July, I got the call and they asked if I'd come back for sort of an indefinite amount of episodes. They wanted to work me in. They worked me in and about hallway through this season, which is season four, they made me a regular. It's been quite an evolution, to say the least."

Do you think the psychology classes you took in college play any part in the way you interpret Anya? Because she's trying so hard to figure out relationships and people?

EMMA: "Well, having a background in psychology, having taken those classes and trying to basically dissect the human psyche, I don't see how that wouldn't help with any character analysis. The process is very similar.

"But Anya, I gotta say, just comes very easy for me. There's just not a lot of guesswork with her. The most difficult part is not knowing what they want to do with her, and not having that to work with. I wouldn't say I identified with her really, we're pretty different people, but when they humanized her was when I really started to have fun with the character, and there's been nice synchronicity between my take on her and what the writers and Joss want to do with her. Just sort of a nice melding of the minds.

"It's just such a fun character to play. So much of it is in the dialogue, and how can it not come easy to you when someone is writing such great words! Joss created a character that is just so much fun. I don't have to sit and go, 'Oh, what am I gonna do with her this week?' She's pretty much out there already."

Who do you think would win a tactless contest, Anya or Cordelia?

EMMA: "Anya! Without any question. Oh, God! Not even a question. 'Orgasm friend.' I mean, who says that? Who talks like that? That's what's great about her. Because it's everything you want to say, but usually don't. She appeals to your base impulses. She is just sort of the id personified for me, and it's fun to play. It's great. She says things I only wish I could say!"

Having been on several teen shows now, how do you feel *Buffy* compares with other teen shows?

EMMA: "I don't think of it as a teen show at all. I think it's been a complete misconception. I think *Buffy* is the ultimate case in irony. I really do. I think even the name, it's sort of like Joss Whedon has the last laugh on everyone. It's a wink and a nod and I really do think that. It got me, too. I mean, when it first aired, I thought, *I'm not gonna watch* Buffy the Vampire Slayer. *I mean, how ridiculous is that! This must be so stupid.* And then of course you watch it and it's so smart and clever and understated, and I think the beauty of it is that it doesn't talk down to its audience. It assumes you're smart enough to get it.

"And they leave it alone. I mean, the disclaimer at the beginning of the show . . . I don't know that that's a strong enough disclaimer. Because if I had a twelve- or thirteen-year-old, I wouldn't want my child watching, especially now. I'm surprised. I'm shocked at some of the things that we get past the censors.

"I don't think it's a teen show at all. Obviously it appeals to teens, and if I were a teenager, I'd be watching it. But the people who make a point to come up to me and say something about the show, they're not teenagers. They're people in their forties.

"I said this before, I do think it's sort of a modern allegory, I really do, and I think the show works so well because they don't treat the situation like it's abnormal. Everything that comes their way is very normal, and that's just life, and they don't camp out the show at all.

"They just play it for straight, and I think that's what makes it so smart. Really, I think ultimately all the characters are good role models for teens. It's a great show, and it bums me out that the Emmy board refuses to acknowledge it every year. It's on every critic's top ten, and so every year they do the plea to the Academy, and they refuse.

"I don't know what their problem is. It's frustrating. I think 'Hush' was some of the best TV I've seen any show do ever. It was a great piece of TV. You don't have to follow the show to understand it. You can just turn it on, and it's complete in and of itself. So smart, so original, it's like, if that doesn't get the show its Emmy nod, I don't know what would. It's very frustrating."

ALEXIS DENISOF (WESLEY WYNDAM-PRYCE)

How did you get *Buffy*, and then how did you end up on *Angel*?

ALEXIS: "I had come over to LA, I had been living in England, where I had trained as an actor at the London Academy of Music and Dramatic Arts, and came over here on vacation, actually, for ten days with two friends, and we promised ourselves—they were actors, too—we promised we wouldn't look for work.

"Which, of course, is when work comes your way. I got a pilot during that time and stayed on to do the pilot and then that led to more auditions in LA. I was intending to go back to London—six months had gone by and I had only expected to be gone a couple weeks—and was anxious to go back, and an audition came up for a show called *Buffy*. I knew nothing about it because it had not aired in Britain. I had no idea that I was going up for this cult, culturally extraordinary show. And really, Wesley was just going to be for a couple of weeks.

"Tony was an old pal from England. We had worked together years ago, and so in fact, he is the one who suggested me. I had called him when I was in town just to hang out socially, and they had approached him from the office and said, 'We're looking for such and such a type part, of Wesley, a Watcher.' And he said, 'I might know a guy who could do it,' and so he called up and said would I be interested, and I said of course I was.

"And so then I met Joss and the team and we had a meeting and Wesley was invented. Really, he was meant to come in, irritate and annoy Giles and Buffy for a couple of shows, and then be gloriously terminated. That was the original thought behind the character. He was sort of a bookish academic, out of the Training Academy, and was here to shake things up and to get them back onto the straight and narrow.

"But then we found this kind of curious humor in this guy, and it was just too hard to kill him off. Suddenly half the season had gone by and they didn't have the heart to kill him off—which I'm delighted that they didn't—so we broke up for the summer hiatus of season three of *Buffy*, and Wesley was kind of hanging in the air. Joss said, 'Well, we really want to keep him here, it's just how and when to make him part of the community.'

"It was tricky. They already have a very successful and loved and adored Watcher in Giles, so they needed to go to the drawing board and figure out what to do with Wesley. And then I went away and did another movie, *Beyond the City Limits*, which actually Alyson did as well.

"I went to England and did a TV show there, and then when I got back from that, there was a call from Joss saying, 'I think we found a place for you. How do you feel about joining the team on *Angel*?' And of course I was thrilled. So we met and we talked about his ideas, and it's just been a wild ride ever since. Demons, fighting and cruising LA, and darker elements, and here we are looking at season two. That's sort of what happened.

"He's obviously been reshaped. Retooled a little. The summer off gave Joss a chance to figure out how to use him in the long-term because the originally conceived character, you know, although lovable in a way, was probably not sympathetic enough to be a long-term character. So we needed to give him a little history and a little experience in the world during that break between *Buffy* and *Angel* so that when he came back he could be used to expand the show."

On *Angel*, we're dying to know if it's hard to kiss badly on purpose.

ALEXIS: "Well, I have to say when that script arrived and we'd been having all this fun playing with the chemistry between Wesley and Cordelia, I read that and I kinda laughed hysterically, but then also was struck with terror. Because so often you're asked to create the most magnetic kiss in screen history, but I had never been asked to create a dud. So when we came to it, that was one of the most fun days we had playing around with it. It's obviously a very funny scene to play. These two highly charged people kind of coming together and it falls flat."

Do you have any funny, interesting, or creepy stories, especially from season three?

ALEXIS: "On Wesley's first episode, I was very anxious to make a good impression, and was working very hard, and we had this fantastic monster who was just the size of a bloated walrus, some kind of demon. Giles and I are handcuffed and surrounded by his henchmen, and this superb actor playing that role, which is scaring the hell out of us, and in the middle of the take the little door of the tub that he's in swung open. And this is how the actor gets in and out of the tub and gets into the fat suit, and there before us is from the waist up, this great, enormous, horrific, slimy, bloated demon and from the waist down is this little actor's legs in a pair of shorts. The poor guy was roasting alive in there underneath the rubber suit, but it sort of dashed the moment."

How did you create your character? Did you draw from personal experience? Was there somebody you thought of to hang him on?

ALEXIS: "You take a lot from the way a person behaves and their interaction with the people in the scene. It was important to use Giles as the model, because it was important that he be close enough to Giles that it be irritating. That he be irritating. That he be similar but not, at the same time. Obviously when he was first brought in, he was there to kind of get tough with Giles and Buffy, so he thought about what type of personality and behavior would be most loathsome to them.

"And then used the whole Council training as a background. He probably wished himself the head of the class kind of guy, the one who did his homework and kind of was a little bit snotty about it to the other kids, and so just a sort of superficially rather irritating person, who was, underneath, this soft, fuzzy guy that just really wanted to be liked.

"So now as time goes on we get a chance to shed some of those outer layers and see more of the kid who, like everybody else, wanted to have good friends in school and wanted to clown around and have fun and do well. So that's how I sort of came about making him. And then in the early days Joss was very clear with notes and saying, 'Well, that's a little too stuffy' or 'Soften that up' or 'Get tough here with that,' so in that way together you start to mold the person. But a lot of it is just from the ground up. You start creating things, things that work you keep, things that don't work get left behind."

Tony said that he is so, so sorry that he ever had Giles stammer 'cause when he does it's so hard to re-create, to follow. Is there anything that you think, "Oh, thank God I did X" or "Jeez, I wish I hadn't done Y"? Or something that is hard to remember that he does, or any kind of a quirk or eccentricity or little point that either you're glad you put it in or you're sorry you ever thought of in the first place?

ALEXIS: "Well, sometimes I'm sorry I made him so intelligent and clever and able to understand these various demons and historical references that he rattles off with such confidence, because now scripts arrive with paragraphs and paragraphs of stuff I have no idea what they're talking about.

"And I think, 'Oh, God, I've got to somehow make sense of it.' Not only that, learn it. And then I see Angel's response is a grunt and I think, 'Oh, God, if only we could switch once in a while.' But I'm only kidding, it's great fun to play him, and he really just exists now. I don't worry about him too much. Wesley's waiting for me when I get to work. Put on the clothes, there he is."

ELIZABETH ANNE ALLEN (AMY MADISON)

Everybody wants to know how you feel about cheese.

ELIZABETH ANNE: "Do you want to know what the funniest thing is? I'm allergic to dairy. That's my standard joke. I love cheese, but I can't eat cheese because it gives me hives."

How do you feel about rodents?

ELIZABETH ANNE: "I used to have mice, and gerbils, and all those little animals in my house. Which I'm sure was to my mother's dismay. But I loved them. I had tons of hamsters and gerbils and guinea pigs. It was like a zoo at my house."

How did you get the part of Amy, and who did you tell first?

ELIZABETH ANNE: "I had originally tested for the role of Buffy, and I didn't end up getting that role, obviously. And they brought me back in for the role of Amy.

"And it was really funny because I went back in four times, because the director of this particular episode just thought, *Well, I just don't think she could be mean.* I kept saying to Joss, 'I don't think he knows what he's talking about.' But he had a hard time. After my fourth audition for that character, they finally gave it to me. And the director was great. He said, 'You've proven me wrong.'"

Can you tell us any stories you'd like to share about any of the episodes?

ELIZABETH ANNE: "Well, 'Gingerbread' was kind of funny, because the day that they put me on the pyre was my birthday. So they said I was a human candle, and when they lit the candle everybody sang 'Happy Birthday' to me."

What is your birthday?

ELIZABETH ANNE: "November eighteenth. It was a very funny episode. I thought, *Somebody's sick and twisted out there.*"

How close did you get to actual flames?

ELIZABETH ANNE: "Pretty close. They have to surround us in it, and it's strange. It's not something that you have a great deal of control over. They always have a guy with fire extinguishers, and there's actually a fireman on the set any time there's fire."

We thought it must have been CGI.

ELIZABETH ANNE: "Well, they do to some extent. But it's a few inches from you, at times. It's kind of scary. Some of your reactions are completely genuine."

Could you feel the heat?

ELIZABETH ANNE: "Oh, definitely. I mean, they make sure you're okay. There's somebody standing next to you who appears to be an extra but who really is a fire person."

Do you think Amy is aware that she's a rat?

ELIZABETH ANNE: "I'd like to think that rats have some capacity to process thoughts. Rather than wake up in a complete stupor two years later, and still think I'm that guy on *That '70s Show* or something. I'd like to think I know some of the things that are going on. But then again, I don't know. I think some of the things I could have possibly seen . . . maybe I don't want to hold on to those. I had a couple of people send me letters and ask me if I remember anything from the night Willow spent with Oz."

Do you know anything about Wicca in your real life?

ELIZABETH ANNE: "I actually did quite a bit of research originally, because I didn't want to falsify what Wicca's about. And Wicca is actually pretty much about the Earth, and what you put out there you bring back. Be careful what you say, because it comes back to you. If you call for judgment, be prepared to receive judgment on yourself. I don't think those are things that people into Wicca would use as lightly as some of the things that we use. It's very serious. They take a lot of responsibility for their actions because it directly affects them. Sort of like instant karma."

MARCIA SHULMAN (CASTING)

What about the famous "David Boreanaz was walking his dog" story?

MARCIA: "[Angel] was supposed to be in just the first episode. Sort of like a vision. . . . The character was supposed to start working the next day. I said to Joss, 'Just give me one more day. I don't feel like he is there yet.'

"[The person who became David's manager] was looking out the window as David was walking his dog. He's a friend of mine, and he called me and he said, 'I am telling you, I just saw Angel. I can send him.' David walked in and I ran down the hall [to Joss]."

She flips through her casting book. "9-9-96. I wrote, 'He is the guy.'"

How did you know Sarah Michelle Gellar was Buffy?

MARCIA: "We didn't know she was Buffy. I knew Sarah from New York, when she was a kid, as I knew Seth Green from when they were eight years old. At the time we were all trying to find our way to make the show something, its own thing apart from the film. Sometimes it's sort of hard to get a new vision going. So we didn't think of Sarah as Buffy because we thought she [Sarah] was too smart and too grounded and not enough of a misfit in a sense, because Buffy was this outsider. How could Sarah be an outsider? She's so lovely.

"So we brought her in as Cordelia, and she was fantastic as Cordelia. We still kept looking for Buffy. Then when we went to the network, they [knew] that Sarah was a star [from her previous work], and that she could be a Buffy, and that we could do that Buffy. It was a different Buffy. It was a great Buffy."

Then how did you cast a new Cordelia?

MARCIA: "I had met Charisma before, and I brought her in and she just nailed it. She was hysterically funny. . . . She was just great and beautiful and she brought so much to it."

What about Willow?

MARCIA: "Willow was really hard. Because when you think about it, the kind of character Willow is—a sort of shy, insecure person—is the exact opposite of what somebody has to be as an actress. So it was like working against who came in and had the nerve to audition.

"When Alyson came in, we all got her immediately. I had pre-read her first and then brought her to everyone else and we felt good. She just brings so much vulnerability. She makes me cry all the time and she is also funny. She is an 'everygirl.' I think Willow is the kind of character that there is someone like her in high school . . . or most of the girls in high school are like her."

What about casting Nicholas Brendon as Xander?

MARCIA: "Nicky also came in [via the pre-reading process]. I read him and then I brought him to the guys and every time he came for a callback, he brought more and more to it. When we went to the network for everybody to see him, he improvised a line, which was, 'Let's go get some schwarma.' And now we have used it in the show. I think that gave him the part. We all just died and so the part was his."

Tell us about Tony Head as Giles.

MARCIA: "I had brought him in the first day and we all just completely fell in love with him. I was so happy because when you start working for somebody new, you always want the first day of casting to be good. Because you want [your boss] to say, 'Good,' so you can stay for the second day. When everybody responded to Tony the first day, I said to Gail, 'I'm so happy Joss is happy today.' Tony was a no-brainer. Like David [as Angel]."

And the newest regular, Seth Green.

MARCIA: [smiling] "Seth and I . . . we get each other. When I knew Sarah Michelle Gellar and Seth [in New York], you brought them in on everything. They were really star kids. And now they are star adults, and no surprise."

What about some guest stars?

MARCIA: "James Marsters came in on the pre-read process. But I am always partial to theatrical training on a résumé [which James had]. In New York, it's not even a question. Out here it is very different. With Juliet Landau, I knew her. I got a tape of her and I went in to Joss. Same with Armin Shimerman. Merrick is Richard Riehle, a really wonderful actor I know from New York."

Do you have a special moment?

MARCIA: "Well, the David moment, because it was so hard to find [Angel] and he walked in the day before we were shooting, but there are so many moments. This is a really special group.

"Joss has such a complete vision and you sort of come not to expect in your career that [working on a show] is going to be such a cohesive thing. It is crazy to produce this number of shows on this schedule. That goes with the territory. I am always amazed that a group of people can carry out a vision that it is somehow communicated through the writing, and through who Joss is as a person. It is a very unique situation. It is why I want to do *Buffy*."

JOSS WHEDON

Joss has said that *Buffy* "is the most personal work I've ever done. Which is funny. The opportunity to mythologize my crappy high school experience makes it extremely personal, but also sort of exorcises it. It isn't just reliving it, it's sort of reinventing it, so it moves me more than anything I've ever done. The opportunity to keep developing the characters and finding out what's going to happen to them and how they're going to grow apart or together is . . . the more it goes on, the more personal it gets."

With all that soul-searching, one would think that Joss would begin to change his feelings about his high school years. Joss disagrees. He also notes that, contrary to popular opinion, "my high school years were not all terrible. There was that Thursday. . . ." He laughs.

"No, I did have a couple of friends, and I had a lot of good times, but all the bad high school stuff definitely went down. This lets me come to peace with that. But really, I'm at enough of a distance, and it's not like 'That girl, and I'll get her. . . .' There's nobody I harbor any particular malice toward from high school.

"I think that's part of why I like doing the show so much. I'm able to look at high school and say, 'There's the dumb jock who was mean to me. Well, what's his perspective? He's going through something too. There's the teacher who flunked me.' I suppose in that sense, it is sort of revelatory. It's nice because I can go to the pain, but at the same time, I have a much more pleasant view of it, because I am seeing it from a bit of a distance."

That pain, in fact, has become almost more important to the series than the horror or the humor of the characters.

"When we realized how much we could really live these characters' lives, we found that we could go to that dark place," Joss says. "I made a joke that, 'The key to the show is to make Buffy suffer.' Sarah said, 'Why do you do this to me? Another crying scene? Do you know what I go through here?' and I said, 'America needs to see you suffer, because you do it really well.'"

Joss laughs, but he isn't really joking.

"We're doing these sort of mythic-hero journeys in our minds," he says. "A lot of times, the story doesn't make sense until we figure out who's suffering and why. Including the bad guy. If the bad guy's not hurting, not relating to her, then it's just a cardboard guy to knock down. And the same thing goes for the audience. If they're not feeling it, if her relationship to what's going on isn't personal, and if ours isn't, then it's just guys with horns running around and some good jokes, but it's not going to resonate."

It's amazing, given how personal a project this is, that Joss ever got to do it at all. The film was not what he had originally envisioned, and he thought he'd had his chance. Then Gail Berman and Fran Kuzui came to him to ask if he wanted to do the TV series.

"I had never thought of doing it myself, but I was like, 'Oh, wow, that's sort of neat!' And I thought about it, and the more I thought about it, the more I realized how many stories there were to tell and how excited I was," he recalls. "I was pretty much out of TV completely at that point, and my agent asked me, 'Now, come on, really, what do you want to do?' I said, 'I'm already writing scenes for this in my head,' and he said, 'Fine, I'll make the deal.' I did not expect it to take over my life like this. I did not expect it to move me as much as it did."

And, though he loves horror and always has, it isn't really the horror that moves him.

"I love invoking all those [old horror] movies, but at the same time, the core of this series, emotionally, is a very safe place. These are people who care about one another and when their world is upset, *you* care about it. Whatever horror is out there is not as black and terrible as what is already within and between us."

Still, horror has and will always have a special place in Joss's heart. His knowledge of films, comic books, and movies is encyclopedic, and his influences are many and varied.

"I have a lot of influences," Joss says. "So many, in fact, that I can't even think of them all. I've sort of hodge-podged together my favorite bits of everything. I take what I need for the series. For example, vampires look like vampires part of the time, because I want to see demons so you don't have a high school girl just stabbing people. At the same time, I want her to see people that [the viewer] doesn't know if they're vampires or not. They turn to dust because it's cool, but also so we don't have to have twenty minutes of body-cleaning-up at the end of every show."

Do you have a favorite moment, on or off the screen, from the series?

JOSS: "At the end of 'I Robot, You Jane,' when they're all sitting there realizing how pathetic their love lives are, that was my favorite ending. That was very nice. For me, there have been a bunch of things. I think one of them was definitely when I shot 'Innocence.' Things came together for me. That's when everything just completely fell into place. And I thought we had created something that is more than the sum of its parts. And I'd always been proud of its parts, but that was the first time the thing really just completely talked back to me.

"That was really neat, and then everyone was like, 'You must be so happy you did well?' And I would say, 'Oh, yeah, but I was so happy before.' I didn't even notice the ratings because I was already on such a high.

"There was a moment when we were shooting that scene in 'Innocence' with the rocket launcher: the guys are flying, a big explosion, and I was quite literally jumping up and down. I was so happy. And the next day, we shot the last scene with Buffy and her mom, and I was watching the two shots of Kristine and Sarah, and I thought, *Yesterday, I had the rocket launcher, and this is better.* They were so good in that, and it looked so beautiful, and it felt so right, and that to me was just . . . we had everything. We had the kitchen sink on this show, but it's still the small stuff that holds it together."

Has the cast ever inspired the evolution of their characters?

JOSS: "Oh, absolutely. They certainly inform the way the characters behave and the way they talk. They can't help but bring some of themselves to it. Although I'm still pretty strict about what they have to do. But the more we write the characters, the more Willow becomes like Aly . . . all of them. As I get to know them more as people. They bring so much more depth to it. They all become the heroes to their own stories because I know them as people."

Are the vampires in the *Buffy* mythology organized as clans?

JOSS: "I don't really think of them as clans. I think of them more like people. There are religions, there are religious leaders, different sects. What do they say in C. S. Lewis books, 'We all worship the same god, we just call it different names'? Well, they all worship evil, they just call it different names. It's not so much clans where different vampires have different appearances or powers. What you have are certain charismatic figures who find themselves surrounded by stuntmen."

Is there a Council of Watchers?

JOSS: "There is an actual little Watcher Bureaucracy based in England that Giles works for. But they're very loose and pretty incredibly inefficient. Since nobody ever seems to know what anybody else is doing. But so much of finding the Slayer and training her and figuring out who's going to be next is magic and luck. And nowadays, people are just not that dedicated. Giles tried to get out of it. It's a little bit muddy. Things get balled up at the head office."

Are you prepping Willow to be a Watcher?

JOSS: "No, I'm not. I've never thought of Willow as a Watcher. I've got something else in store for Willow."

Everyone involved with this show seems to think of it as some kind of destiny. Does that spook you?

JOSS: "It's only spooky when I think, *Jeez, I'm going to work on other shows where this doesn't happen.* It does feel like Manifest Destiny. It's such luck and chance that everybody from our DP to David Greenwalt to the entire cast just happened upon this project. And if they hadn't . . . I break into a cold sweat thinking about what I would do without any of them. Let alone Sarah. It does have a kind of inevitability to it. It seems like it just flowed into being."

SEASON 5

No Place Like Home
Episode 5.5

WRITTEN BY: Douglas Petrie
DIRECTED BY: David Solomon
GUEST STARS: Clare Kramer as Glory, Charlie Weber as Ben, Ravil Isyanov as Monk, Kristine Sutherland as Joyce Summers
CO-STARS: James Wellington as Nightwatchman, Paul Hayes as Older Nighwatchman, Staci Lawrence as Customer, John Sarkisian as Old Monk, Pasha Lychnikoff as Young Monk

THE PLOT THICKENS:

Two months ago: A trio of monks bolt themselves into a chamber of their monastery to perform a ritual over an unseen glowing object they refer to as the "Key." Outside the room, a powerful force pounds on the heavy wooden door trying to get in. The glow intensifies and then disappears just before the doors explode.

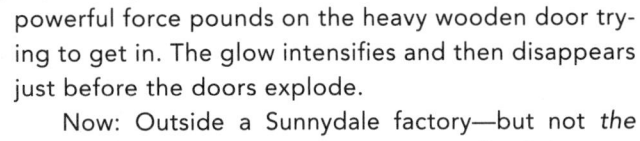

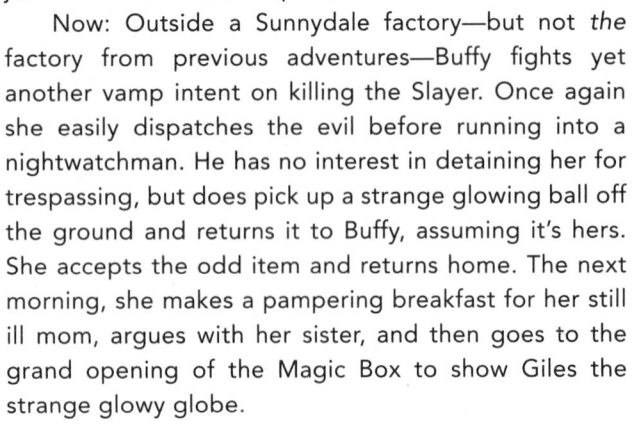

Now: Outside a Sunnydale factory—but not *the* factory from previous adventures—Buffy fights yet another vamp intent on killing the Slayer. Once again she easily dispatches the evil before running into a nightwatchman. He has no interest in detaining her for trespassing, but does pick up a strange glowing ball off the ground and returns it to Buffy, assuming it's hers. She accepts the odd item and returns home. The next morning, she makes a pampering breakfast for her still ill mom, argues with her sister, and then goes to the grand opening of the Magic Box to show Giles the strange glowy globe.

All the Scoobies research the presumably mystical device, Buffy returns home with her new sister, Dawn, to find Joyce all icky feeling on the couch. Although Buffy wants to take her mom back to the hospital, Joyce insists that she just needs her prescription refilled. Buffy goes on the errand to the hospital pharmacy, where she runs into intern Ben trying to subdue a patient. Buffy uses her Slayer strength to lend a hand and is surprised to find that the rambling man is the nightwatchman from the previous evening. The suddenly crazy man warns her that "they come to you through your family." Suddenly her mom's mysterious illness doesn't seem as mysterious.

Back in the factory the surviving monk from two months earlier is still being pursued by the hideous beast in the form of a perky yet intense young woman. She begins a fun game of "torture the monk" to get him to reveal the location of The Key. When that doesn't work, she moves on to another nightwatchman and gives the guy a serious brain drain.

Buffy reports to the orb researchers on her assumption regarding Mom's illness: something or someone is attacking her through her mom. While helping customers in the packed Magic Box, Anya suggests a spell to "pull the curtain back" and reveal the source of the magick affecting Joyce. So Buffy goes all trancelike and is disappointed to find that nothing seems to be affecting her mom, but her sister begins to zone in and out of reality. Finally Buffy realizes that Dawn is not her sister.

As Buffy struggles with the realization, unable to accept the news, Giles calls to report that he and the team have identified the orb as the Dagon's Sphere, created to repel "that which cannot be named."

Buffy goes back to the factory where she found the item and finds the monk, as well as *she* which cannot be named. A fight ensues and Buffy pretty much gets the crap beat out of her, but she does manage to escape with the monk. However, the torture and fight were too much for the man. As he lies dying, he reveals that he had sent The Key to the Slayer in the form of a human . . . namely, Dawn. He and his fellow monks created false memories in the Slayer's family and friends so that they would accept Dawn as real. With his last breath, the monk explains that Dawn is not aware that she is anything other than Dawn Summers, and that she must be protected. With that news, Buffy returns home to her sister and puts aside their petty fights . . . for now.

> Clare Kramer starred in the cheerleading movie Bring It On with Eliza Dushku.

QUOTE OF THE WEEK:
BUFFY: "What are you doing here?"
Spike starts gesturing. Long answer alert.
BUFFY: "Five words or less."
Spike starts to count them off on his fingers.
SPIKE: "Out. For. A. Walk. . . . Bitch."

LOVE IN VEIN:
The Buffy/Riley weirdness continues. Yet another strain is added to things when Dawn blurts out that Buffy's been talking about him in a "weak and kitteny" sort of way. Spike is caught stalking the Slayer, and not in the usual vampy way, either.

POP-CULTURE IQ:
Dawn likens her sister's control of the kitchen to that of the participants in the cult hit cooking "game show" imported from Japan that pits restaurant cooks against a selection of Iron Chefs to make the best meal featuring one surprise ingredient:

"Who died and made you the Iron Chef?"

Buffy's prescription for relaxation for Joyce includes watching the queen of daytime television:

"Feet up, plenty of Oprah."

Riley compares the Slayer training room to the Danger Room from Marvel's line of X-Men comic books:

"Giles, you got that danger room set up out back?"

Ben falls into Popeye speak when impressed by Buffy's buffness. The Paramount Pictures/Famous Studios cartoons from the 1940s starred a sailor man with a penchant for spinach:

"You've got some serious mus-kles for a girl."

Ben jokes that Buffy's mus-kles might have the same origin as Marvel Comics' Spider-Man:

"Radioactive spider bite?"

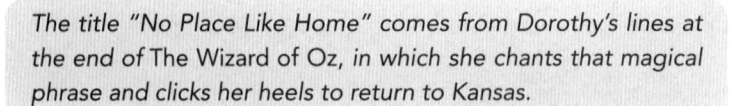

> The title "No Place Like Home" comes from Dorothy's lines at the end of The Wizard of Oz, in which she chants that magical phrase and clicks her heels to return to Kansas.

> "Somebody's gotta sit down on their tuffet."
> The beast (later known as Glory) makes a reference to the nursery rhyme "Little Miss Muffet," continuing the curious theme started by Faith in the dream sequence in "Graduation Day, Part Two."

CONTINUITY:
Dawn's mysterious arrival is explained, along with the arrival of the new Big Bad for season five. Joyce's headache is back and it brought friends. For a time Buffy suspects it is supernatural in origin, but her spell confirms that it is an earthly malady, as we will later learn.

DRAMATIS PERSONAE:
Anya's interest in money truly blossoms as Giles hires her to work at the Magic Box.

Glory complains that she doesn't want to be in this state, or on this planet, and that she finds this whole "mortal coil" thing disgusting.

FROM THE ORIGINAL TELEPLAY:
The script for this episode is very specific in describing the monk who arrives in Sunnydale:
   A monk (not the old one, not the young one, but the surviving one) hastily resets a fallen candle. . . .

Glory's first entrance is described as follows in the teleplay:
   BOOM! The door comes BLASTING off its hinges and lands, intact, ten feet from the doorway, revealing not some hulking monstrous demon, but a GIRL. Real hottie, too. About Buffy's age. Whoever she is, she's a star and she knows it. Curly blond tendrils fall all around her shoulder, highlighting her sharp red business dress and killer pumps.

Family
Episode 5.6

WRITTEN AND DIRECTED BY: Joss Whedon
GUEST STARS: Mercedes McNab as Harmony, Clare Kramer as Glory, Charlie Weber as Ben, Amy Adams as Beth, Steve Rankin as Mr. Maclay, Amber Benson as Tara
CO-STARS: Ezra Buzzington as Bartender, Peggy Goss as Crazy Person, Tory Pendergrass as Demon, Megan Gray as Sandy, Brian Tee as Intern, Kevin Rankin as Donny

THE PLOT THICKENS:
Buffy tells Giles what she's learned about Dawn being The Key, which isn't all that much. They decide not to tell anyone else for the time being to keep Dawn safe. In the meantime, Willow's plans for Tara's twentieth birthday celebration are under way, even though the rest of the Scoobies aren't entirely on the bandwagon since they don't feel that they know Tara all that well. The plans, however, hit a considerable snag when Tara's father, brother, and cousin show up unexpectedly.

As Buffy tries to figure out more about the new threat to Sunnydale and, more importantly, what to get Tara for her birthday, she kicks the overprotective up a few notches around Dawn. Tara's family seems just as overprotective when they insist that Tara come home with them simply because her birthday is nearing. As it turns out, the women in the Maclay family have a nasty habit of turning full demon on that wondrous occasion.

Tara refuses to leave Sunnydale and casts a spell so that her friends won't see her demon half. Sadly, the spell goes awry and Buffy et al. are unable to see the demons that the Big Bad sent to kill the Slayer. They aren't even able to see Spike when he arrives and suddenly finds himself in the middle of the fight to save the Slayer's life.

Tara enters the Magic Box mid-battle and reveals the demons and then the truth. Her family comes to take her away, but the gang stands by their friend in spite of her supposed demon leanings, which, considering the demons they know. . . . Tara's father insists that she's evil and it's for her own good. That's when Spike decides to test Tara by punching her in the face to prove she's not a demon. As his violence-blocker kicks in, he realizes that her father is just trying to exercise his control over the women in the Maclay clan. A joyous Tara—bloody nose and all—sends her family home and celebrates a fully human birthday with her friends, who have grown closer to her than family.

QUOTE OF THE WEEK:
Willow worries that her tardiness may have kept her from hearing the important information so helpful for demon slaying and, more importantly, telling the audience at home just what's going on.

"Am I late? Did I miss any exposition?"

LOVE IN VEIN:
Buffy's dad is living in cliché off in Spain with his secretary. Hank hasn't even gotten in touch with his daughters since Joyce got sick, but this is only the beginning of his absent-father act. Spike continues to dream of Buffy, and his rush to kill her becomes more of a life-saving thing. To combat his romantic ennui, Riley frequents Willy's demon bar, where he's hit on by a vampire.

POP-CULTURE IQ:
Xander notes one of the highlights of Buffy's now "former" dorm room is that it can be used to re-create comic plays known for their high-energy pacing with characters making many entrances and exits:

"Got two entrances, lotta opportunities for bawdy French farce."

Buffy compares the perky evil being to a beauty pageant title awarded to the nicest contestant by the other pageant participants:

"Any breakthrough on the identity of Miss Congeniality?"

Buffy tries to mask the seriousness of the "demon's" incredible power by using descriptive phrasing taken from the theme song from the Aaron Spelling hit that premiered in the seventies, *The Love Boat*:

"This demon chick is exciting and new."

CONTINUITY:
The events of this episode start on the same night as "No Place Like Home" ended. Five cases of sudden insanity have hit the local hospital in the past month—presumably all people touched by the as yet unnamed evil one. Harmony mentions that she went "shopping" at April Fool's, which is the store where Cordelia worked at the end of her senior year (following her father's bankruptcy). A possible reason Tara

messed up the demon locator spell in "Goodbye Iowa" is revealed. She was probably afraid it would locate *her*. Tara's mother is mentioned in the past tense. More about her will be revealed when she bonds with Buffy in "The Body."

DRAMATIS PERSONAE:
Buffy begins to grasp the weight of the fact that her memories of Dawn's life are entirely false. After complaining that Dawn needs to grow up ("Real Me"), Buffy now sees her sister as someone who needs to be protected, even sheltered. She moves back home temporarily.

Willow is surprised to learn that Tara has a brother.

Tara apparently didn't have many friends in high school—according to her brother. Tara's father indicates that she used to hide her magick.

Glory is embarrassed to learn that she had been fighting with something as common as a Vampire Slayer.

FROM THE ORIGINAL TELEPLAY:
The following stage direction is written into the scene where the team is moving Buffy out of her dorm room:

Tara is in the closet (no jokes, please).

Fool for Love
Episode 5.7

WRITTEN BY: Douglas Petrie
DIRECTED BY: Nick Marck
GUEST STARS: David Boreanaz as Angel, Mercedes McNab as Harmony, Juliet Landau as Drusilla, Julie Benz as Darla, Kristine Sutherland as Joyce Summers
CO-STARS: Kali Rocha as Cecily Addams, Edward Fletcher as Male Partygoer, Katharine Leonard as Female Partygoer, Matthew Lang as 2nd Male Partygoer, Chris Daniels as Stabbing Vampire, Kenneth Feinberg as Chaos Demon, Steve Heinze as Vampire #1, Ming Liu as Chinese Slayer, April Weeden-Washington as Subway Slayer

THE PLOT THICKENS:
When Buffy gets beaten by a regular ol' average vamp, she feels the full weight of her mortality bearing down and develops a sudden interest in finding out why her many predecessors became predecessors. Finding a dearth of information in the Watcher's Diaries on the actual death of Slayers, Buffy consults the only person she knows who actually bore witness to such notable events: Spike.

As Buffy picks the brain of the killer of two Vampire Slayers, Riley leads the Slayerettes on a less-than-stealthy recon for the vamp that nearly did in the Slayer. They stumble across a nest of vampires, causing Riley to revise the plan so the gang will come back in the morning. But he returns alone to do in the entire nest and take out some aggression.

Out of the goodness of Spike's heart, and more than a smattering of greed, the neutered vampire recounts his personal history to Buffy. Starting in the year of our lord eighteen hundred and eighty, he tells of his birth into the darkness while glossing over his priggish prevampire life and briefly touching on a story of an unrequited love. Along with Angel, Darla, and his beloved Drusilla, Spike trips through time, taking out one Slayer in China during the Boxer Rebellion and another in a New York City subway in the seventies. After a night of lessons, he finally imparts to Buffy the reason why the Slayers died. He claims that death is what every Slayer truly longs for.

Buffy does not want to admit that she understands the feeling, nor does she want to admit that she has any feelings for Spike other than hate. Instead she echoes the words of his long-lost unrequited love by telling Spike that he is beneath her.

Feeling the full weight of Spike's lesson, Buffy returns home to find her mom packing to go to the hospital. The "nothing to worry about" that Joyce had been experiencing over the past few weeks has turned into something worthy of further exploration. Buffy goes out to the backyard to be alone when Spike comes to put an end to his pain by putting an end to the Slayer. But when she looks up at him in tears, the vampire softens and sits beside her to lend his silent support.

QUOTE OF THE WEEK:
Harmony kindly reminds Spike of his powerlessness over the Slayer:
> "The second you even point that thing at her you're gonna be all . . . 'Ahhh!' and then you'll get bitch-slapped up and down Main Street."

LOVE IN VEIN:
Spike's revisionist history shows great glimpses into his romantic life, starting with an infatuation from his human days for the refined Cecily Addams. He also glosses over his relationship with Drusilla from their meeting in England in 1880 to their most recent breakup in South America in 1998 (under the watchful eye of a Chaos Demon). It is also implied that his infatuation with the Slayer was evident to Drusilla at that time. Buffy reiterates Cecily's words when she tells Spike that he is "beneath her." Spike continues his discourse on love and blood as he first told Buffy and Angel in "Lovers Walk."

POP-CULTURE IQ:
Buffy hopes to experience the same power of preservatives as in the puffed cheese snacks Cheetos, made by Frito-Lay:
> "I know every Slayer comes with an expiration mark on the package, but I want mine to be a long time from now. Like a Cheeto."

Spike protests that his siring was far more intriguing an event than the hunting and gathering rituals of animals in programs routinely seen on the cable channel devoted to science and nature:
> ". . . don't make it sound like something you'd flip past on the Discovery Channel."

CONTINUITY:
Spike's history is on display as numerous life moments are revealed, including the truth behind both his "William the Bloody" moniker and his nickname, "Spike." (Because his poetry was so

"bloody" awful one would rather have a railroad spike driven through one's head than listen to it.) The audience gets to see Spike from his siring and through the killings of two Slayers as well as learn about his prevampire life and a brief mention of his close ties to his mother. These will be further examined in the sequel-like seventh season episode "Lies My Parents Told Me." Spike reiterates Faith's comment earlier in the series that death is something he gets off on and suspects that Buffy does too. His lessons for Buffy on the subject of her search to know more about death are major foreshadowing, including the fact that he will be there for her final swan dive just as he promises—although he won't be celebrating. The New York Slayer from the seventies is shown, as killed by Spike, and her long leather trench coat is snagged by him as a prize. More about this particular Slayer will be revealed in the seventh season episode "First Date."

> *The episode was the first in a two-part crossover event with the second season* Angel *episode "Darla," which showed more of Angel and Darla's history in the time periods seen here.*

> *The actress playing Cecily, Kali Rocha, returns in the sixth season as Anya's demon friend Halfrek.*

DRAMATIS PERSONAE:
Buffy realizes that death is all around her, a point that will echo through the rest of the series, as various characters—good and bad—will point this out to her.

Giles suspects that the reason Watchers never chronicled the deaths of their Slayers is that, if the Watchers were anything like Giles, they would find the whole thing too painful.

Spike considers his siring to be a very profound and powerful experience and that getting killed made him feel really alive for the first time. Once Angel told him about Slayers, he became obsessed with them because he was looking for fun and death. If Spike does not *intend* to hurt someone, he can get away with a limited form of violence without the chip in his brain activating to cause him pain.

FROM THE ORIGINAL TELEPLAY:
The following stage direction for a bit not seen in the episode explains one of the Spike life mysteries.

We are in a Buddhist Temple. We hear a punch and Spike comes staggering back into frame, sporting a bloody nose. Before he can regain his footing a sword comes slicing into frame, just nicking the top of his eyebrow, cutting it open (the eyebrow where he's got his scar today).

> *The title of this episode, "Fool for Love," comes from a play written by Sam Shepard.*

The Body
Episode 5.16

One of the series's most pivotal episodes—and certainly one of its best—"The Body" is often misremembered as the one in which Buffy's mom, Joyce Summers, dies. In reality, Joyce was discovered lying dead on the living room sofa at the end of the previous episode. "The Body" picks up in that same moment and carries on from there. The characters have dealt with death many times, but this is a real, human death—a reminder of mortality and the fragility of being human. The grief on-screen feels real and relatable, and when Buffy goes to Sunnydale High to share the news with her sister, Dawn, the seen-but-not-heard conversation is shattering. The minutiae of dealing with the death of their mother, of handling burial arrangements and a funeral, both brings the grief into sharper focus and brings the group closer together. Joyce's death changes the series and its characters forever afterward, including their relationships to one another. In the midst of this comes another moment that was pivotal for *Buffy the Vampire Slayer*: comforting a mourning Willow, Tara kisses her. It wasn't the first lesbian kiss on American television, but it was the first between two female characters involved in a committed, long-term, loving relationship.

WRITTEN AND DIRECTED BY: Joss Whedon
GUEST STARS: Randy Thompson as Dr. Kriegel, Amber Benson as Tara, Kristine Sutherland as Joyce Summers
CO-STARS: Kevin Cristaldi as First Paramedic, Stefan Umstead as Second Paramedic, Loanne Bishop as 911 Operator, J. Evan Bonifant as Kevin, Kelli Garner as Kirstie, Rae'ven Larrymore Kelly as Lisa, Tia Matza as Teacher, John Michael Herndon as Vampire

THE PLOT THICKENS:
Buffy comes home to find her mom on the couch sprawled out in a way that doesn't quite look like sleep. Flashback to Christmas and a happier time: the family of Scoobies is together at the Summers house, celebrating good food and a slightly singed pie. Jump cut back to Joyce lying on the couch, eyes open.

Buffy shakes her mom to wake her, but the jolt does no good. She calls 911 and the operator talks Buffy through CPR, but her Slayer strength cracks a rib. The operator is not concerned by the snap, but her tone does shift when she hears that Joyce is cold. She switches from referring to her as "your mother" to "the body." Buffy hangs up on the operator and calls Giles, telling him only that he has to come. When the paramedics arrive, they try to revive Joyce, but fail.

Buffy is instructed to wait for the coroner to come and not to move the body. She becomes sick.

Thinking that Glory has attacked, Giles rushes into the nearly empty house and, seeing Joyce, tries to revive her as well. Buffy yells at him to stop, citing that she is not supposed to disturb "the body." She is horrified that she too has now distanced Joyce from what is happening here.

In the meantime, Dawn is suffering the tortures of being a teenager at school, but just when things start to look up for her, Buffy interrupts her art class with the devastating news. Her class—including a hot guy she was hoping to impress—looks on as Dawn collapses in the hallway.

The rest of the Scoobies gather in Willow's dorm room to present a united front for their friend. Tara tries to calm Willow who can't stop crying or changing clothes so she doesn't make the wrong statement. Anya keeps asking inappropriate questions, because the thousand-year-old ex-demon doesn't know how to handle death. And Xander feels the need to take out his aggression on a defenseless and shoddily made wall. They head over to the hospital, not knowing that—in an instance of the mundane—Xander has just been issued a parking ticket for parking his car illegally in front of the dorm.

After they arrive at the hospital, Buffy is informed that her mom suffered an aneurysm due to post-surgery complications. Even if Buffy had been around at the time, it is doubtful that anything could have been done to help Joyce. She wants to know if her mother suffered. The doctor assures her that Joyce didn't, but Buffy hears something different in his pat answer.

While Tara, who's also dealt with the death of a mother, talks with Buffy, Dawn sneaks down to the morgue to see her mother one last time. As she approaches the body that is hidden under a sheet, another sheet begins to move behind her. A vampire rises and attacks. Buffy realizes where her sister has gone and comes in just in time to stop the vampire. During the course of their struggle, the sheet comes off Joyce's face. Once the vampire is dust, Dawn gets up to look at her mother and reaches out to touch the body. . . .

> Joyce is called "the body" eight times in the dialogue from this episode.

QUOTE OF THE WEEK:
Anya tries to cope with her grief:

> "But I don't *understand*! I don't understand how this all happens, how we go through this, I mean I knew her and then she's, there's just a body, and I don't understand why she just can't get back in it and not be dead. It's stupid, it's mortal and stupid, and, and Xander's crying and not talking and I was having fruit punch and I thought, well, Joyce would never have fruit punch ever and she'd never have eggs, or yawn or brush her hair, not ever and no one will explain to me why."

LOVE IN VEIN:
This episode contains Willow and Tara's first on-screen kiss, which Tara instigates at an emotional moment to calm her lover's outburst.

> This episode is very different from traditional episodes in some very distinct ways:
> - There was no "Previously on Buffy the Vampire Slayer" clip package at the opening of the episode.
> - There is no musical underscore.
> - Each act is essentially constructed as one scene in one location. (Teaser: Buffy in the house with her mom. Act 1: Buffy in the house with her mom, the paramedics, and Giles. Act 2: Dawn at school with her friends and Buffy. Act 3: Willow, Tara, Xander, and Anya in Willow's dorm room. Act 4: The entire group at the hospital.)

CONTINUITY:
The episode picks up at the moment "I Was Made to Love You" left off. The flashback to Christmas would have been following the events of "Into the Woods." Buffy's warning to Joyce and Giles to "stay off the band candy" is a reference to the time the pair shared an interesting evening in "Band Candy." Word has spread through Dawn's school about her cutting incident in "Blood Ties."

DRAMATIS PERSONAE:
Anya uses the advantage of her thousand-year-old demon knowledge to explain that the myth about the myth of Santa Claus is a myth. In fact, Santa Claus does exist and has been around since the 1500s. He wasn't always called Santa, but the part about Christmas night, flying reindeer, and coming down chimneys is all true, although "he doesn't traditionally bring presents so much as, you know, disembowel children."

Tara tells Buffy about her own mom's death—which was both expected and sudden—when she was seventeen.

FROM THE ORIGINAL TELEPLAY:

When the scene shifts to Dawn's art class watching her and Buffy in the hall, this is what's being said between the sisters, according to the script:

BUFFY: "Mom died this morning. While we were both at school, she—"

DAWN: "No . . ."

BUFFY: "I don't know exactly what happened, but, she's dead. . . ."

DAWN: "No, NO NO no no you're lying you're lying she fine she's FINE and you're lying oh no no please please no you're lying she's fine, she's fine . . ."

BUFFY: "Dawnie . . ."

DAWN: "It's not true it's not real it's not real ohhhhh noooooo . . . no . . ."

The Weight of the World
Episode 5.21

WRITTEN BY: Douglas Petrie
DIRECTED BY: David Solomon
GUEST STARS: Clare Kramer as Glory, Charlie Weber as Ben, Dean Butler as Hank Summers, Lily Knight as Gronx, Bob Morrisey as Crazy #1, Amber Benson as Tara
SPECIAL GUEST STARS: Joel Grey as Doc, Kristine Sutherland as Joyce Summers
CO-STARS: Todd Duffey as Murk, Alexandra Lee as Young Buffy, Paul Bates as Crazy #2, Carl J. Johnson as Crazy #3, Matthew Lang as High Priest Minion

THE PLOT THICKENS:
It's been over a half hour since Glory took Dawn. Buffy is still in her catatonic state, Giles is still in his weakened condition, Xander and Spike are about to come to blows, and no one seems to remember that Ben and Glory are one and the same. Suddenly a calm and controlled Willow takes charge, ordering the team back to Sunnydale, where Xander will take Giles to the hospital, Anya will look after Tara, Spike will check in on Glory, and Willow will try to help bring Buffy back.

Work is taking place at a construction site where minions and the people Glory has "touched" have gathered. The god is beginning to feel her mortal half fighting for control of their body as the veil between the two sides begins to weaken.

Willow takes a trip into Buffy's mind, where she is met by a six-year-old version of Buffy waiting at home for her parents to return from the hospital with her new sister, Dawn. The dream images continue as Willow follows to find a grown-up Buffy replacing a book on a shelf at the Magic Box. Then Willow is thrust out to the desert, where she learns of Buffy's recent discovery that "death is her gift."

After helping Giles get patched up at the hospital, Xander goes along with Spike to see if the demon who helped Dawn with the spell to reawaken her mom knows anything about Glory. As it turns out, the demon, Doc, is aware of Glorificus and fights against Spike and Xander to protect a wooden box. The guys manage to take out the demon and take the box. Meanwhile, Willow continues her head trip, visiting Joyce's bedroom, where the bed has been replaced by her grave, and then on to Dawn's room to watch Buffy smother her sister, citing that "death is her gift."

Glory and Ben continue to battle for control of their body, with the god finally gaining the upper hand when she convinces Ben to realize that either he dies or Dawn does. Willow continues round and round through Buffy's mind until she pieces together the puzzle with the help of the Slayer's dream selves. In a brief moment of past weakness while putting away a book in the Magic Box, Buffy realized that Glory was going to win. In that moment, Buffy wanted Glory to win so it could all be over. And that moment of giving up is the reason she blames herself for Dawn's death.

Willow reminds the Slayer that her sister isn't dead yet, and all this wallowing is only going to make her fear come true. This snaps Buffy out of her state, and she and Willow go to rally the troops, where Giles informs them of what he has learned of Glory's plan based on scrolls found in the mystery box. The god intends to enact a ritual bloodletting using Dawn's blood to open the demon dimensions, but the only way to stop it once the gate is open is to kill Dawn.

QUOTE OF THE WEEK:
  GLORY: "Funny, 'cause I look around at this world you're so eager to be a part of, and all I see's six billion lunatics looking for the fastest ride out. Who's not crazy? Look around—everyone's drinkin', smokin', shootin' up, shootin' each other, or just plain screwing their brains out because they don't want 'em anymore. *I'm* crazy? Honey, I am the original one-eyed chicklet in the kingdom of the blind 'cause at least I admit the world makes me nuts. Name one person who can take it here. That's all I'm asking. Name one."
  DAWN: "Buffy."

POP-CULTURE IQ:
Spike is likely drawing a parallel to *The Patty Duke Show*, a TV series from the sixties in which the main characters were identical cousins played by the same actress:
  "Ben. Glory. He's a doctor. She's the beast. Two entirely separate entities, sharing one body. It's like a bloody sitcom!"

> *The script refers to the three Buffys as "Buffy," "Young Buffy," and "Bookshelf Buffy."*

CONTINUITY:
The events of this episode begin a half hour following the end of "Spiral." However, no one except Spike seems to remember that Ben and Glory are the same person, because of some mojo that makes them forget, just like Dawn forgot about it in "Blood Ties." Doc was first seen in "Forever." Willow visits the vision Buffy had during her quest in "Intervention." The moment in the Magic Box where Buffy briefly wanted it all to be over is just the type of thing Spike had been talking about during his lesson on the deaths of Slayers in "Fool for Love."

DRAMATIS PERSONAE:
Buffy's state is the almost natural conclusion to all of the grief she has endured this season, from finding out she didn't really have a sister to losing Riley, from her mother's death to her father being effectively missing, and from dropping out of school to finally having Dawn stolen away (and believing it's her fault).

FROM THE ORIGINAL TELEPLAY:
Buffy's intro in this episode reads as follows in the script:
   We cut to see Buffy. Sitting, staring off into dead space, not hearing her friends, eyes open but deaf, dumb, and blind to the world around her.

The Gift
Episode 5.22

WRITTEN AND DIRECTED BY: Joss Whedon
GUEST STARS: Clare Kramer as Glory, Charlie Weber as Ben, Amber Benson as Tara
SPECIAL GUEST STAR: Joel Grey as Doc
CO-STARS: Todd Duffey as Murk, Craig Zimmerman as Minion #1, Josh Jacobson as Teen, Tom Keische as Vampire

THE PLOT THICKENS:
It could be just another night in Sunnydale. A random vamp attacks a random teen and the Slayer comes to the rescue. However, this slay is especially odd since the vamp has never heard of the Vampire Slayer. The teen remarks that she's "just a girl," which is what Buffy keeps saying! But she's not "just a girl," and this is not just a regular night—it could be the end of the world. Then again, that does happen fairly often in Sunnydale. Buffy goes back inside.

The mood is tense in the Magic Box because this apocalypse is just a little worse than the ones that have almost come before. Dawn is still being held by Glory, Tara is still babbling incoherently, and the team doesn't know what to do about any of it. Giles reviews the facts: if Dawn's blood is spilled, it will break down the walls between dimensions and all manner of Hell will be unleashed on Earth.

Giles tries to get Buffy to see the cold, hard reality that Dawn may have to be killed for the world to survive. But the Slayer will not hear of it and refuses to let anyone even try to harm her sister. The team is still lacking for ideas when the biggest surprise of the night comes: Anya suggests two pretty helpful thoughts: using the Dagon's Sphere and Olaf the troll's big, powerful hammer.

Tara has been mildly sedated up until now, content to mutter about the time and how she has places to be. Buffy and Willow realize that Tara is responding to some unheard call from Glory for help.

The Ben and Glory show continues to freak Dawn out as they prepare for the ritual bloodletting, which will involve putting Dawn atop rather tall scaffolding. In the meantime, Xander tries to calm Anya down with a little lovin' in the Magic Box basement and then an oddly timed marriage proposal. She accepts, and then they go upstairs to share another idea, but not the good news.

Buffy and Giles prepare for the coming fight, aware that his insistence on the possibility that Dawn might have to die to save everyone else has put some distance between them. Buffy admits to being tired and wishing her mom was there. Then she tells Giles that if they make it through this, she quits. She doesn't know how to live in this world anymore if this is the price that is asked of her.

Buffy heads home with Spike to get some supplies. She has to let the vampire back inside to do that, and then she asks him to look after Dawn for her while she fights.

The team regroups at the Magic Box and finally lets Tara go where she's been feeling a pull to go all night: to join the rest of those infected by Glory. Before she departs, Tara looks at Giles and calls him a killer.

The Scoobies follow her to the construction site. When Tara and Glory are in close proximity to each other, Willow works the mojo to return her girlfriend's mind and weaken Glory slightly. Then Buffy comes in using the Dagon's Sphere to further weaken the god while Giles, Anya, and Spike handle her minions and crazies. The plan is to keep Glory busy so that she misses her window of opportunity to perform the bloodletting on Dawn. The plan goes well, until the Slayer is decapitated.

It turns out that they were using the Buffybot (requisitioned by Spike in "I Was Made to Love You") as a diversion, and now the real Slayer steps up with the troll hammer to continue the beating up and down the scaffolding. When she loses the hammer, Xander comes in with a good blow from a wrecking ball. The battle continues as someone new seems to be atop the scaffolding with Dawn. Willow sees this and telepathically instructs Spike to go up, and she clears the way for him with her magick. When he gets there, he finds Doc prepared to fill in for Glory. The two fight and Spike is thrown for a big fall.

Buffy manages to pummel Glory back into Ben but doesn't finish the job. As she goes off to help Dawn, Giles comes in quietly and puts an end to Glory by ending Ben's mortal life. Atop the scaffolding, Buffy takes out Doc, but it's too late—he's already started cutting Dawn. Dawn's blood has spilled, creating a ball of energy that is mixing other dimensions with Sunnydale. All around the world beneath them they can see hell dimensions bleeding into Sunnydale: the town hall, Main Street—everywhere demons are beginning to run loose.

A resigned Dawn goes to stop it, but Buffy prevents her. The Slayer realizes that all the messages she has been receiving over the past several months have led to this moment, this gift.

Knowing that she and her "sister" are linked by blood, Buffy bids farewell to Dawn and throws herself into the ball of energy, shutting it down for good and joining her mom in the afterlife.

QUOTE OF THE WEEK:
>BUFFY ANNE SUMMERS
>1981–2001
>BELOVED SISTER
>DEVOTED FRIEND
>SHE SAVED THE WORLD A LOT

LOVE IN VEIN:
Willow has been focusing on spells to reverse Tara's madness rather than working specifically on the Glory problem. Luckily, she finds a way to help with both issues.

At first Anya refuses Xander's proposal, afraid that he's only asking her to marry because he thinks the world is going to end. He tells her that the world *isn't* going to end and that he does want to marry her when it doesn't end. She accepts, although she refuses to wear the ring until the world doesn't end. She later sacrifices herself to injury by pushing Xander out of the way of falling debris. When they are alone in Buffy's house gathering weapons, Spike tells Buffy he knows she will never love him, but she treats him like a man, not a monster, and that's enough for him. Buffy does not respond. As the gang gathers around Buffy's body on the wreckage of the site, an injured Spike collapses to his knees, crying.

POP-CULTURE IQ:
Spike makes reference to an address given by the king to his troops in Shakespeare's *Henry V*:
>"Not exactly the St. Crispin's day speech, was it?"

The actual quote from Henry V's speech was "we band of brothers":
>"We band of buggered."

CONTINUITY:
So much of the fifth season led to this episode that it would be ridiculous to try to list them all here. Okay, let's try: Dawn was introduced in "Dracula vs. Buffy" and we learned that she was a little . . . different . . . in "No Place Like Home." However, the team did not learn the majority of their information about The Key and the bloodletting ritual until "Tough Love" and "The Weight of the World." We discovered that Ben and Glory were one and the same in "Blood Ties," although the gang didn't realize it until "Spiral" (or, actually "The Weight of the World"). Buffy first dealt with the concept of killing a loved one to save the world in "Becoming, Part Two," when she thrust a sword into Angel's chest and dumped him into Hell. This will come up again in season six with Willow, and season seven with Anya. Xander suggests joining essences like they did in "Primeval." Anya suggests the

Dagon's Sphere that Buffy found in "No Place Like Home" and the mighty troll hammer they took from Olaf in "Triangle." They also use the Buffybot created for Spike in "Intervention." With all the stress on her, Buffy wishes her mom were there, but she passed away in "The Body." (Well, technically in "I Was Made to Love You.") Xander and Anya's engagement follows their love affair that began when she asked him out in "The Prom." Anya takes a stuffed bunny as a bad omen, since her fear of the little furry creatures was established in "Fear, Itself." Buffy reminds Willow that she was able to use magick to hold Glory off in "Blood Ties," "Tough Love," and "Spiral." Willow enacted the de-invite spell against Spike in "Crush." Tara was brain-sucked in "Tough Love." Doc made his first appearance in "Forever." And those references are really just the tip of the iceberg. Moving on . . . it's the end of the world and they know it: Buffy and Giles note that this is at least the sixth apocalypse for them. As of this episode they've faced the potential end of the world in "Prophecy Girl," "Innocence," "Becoming, Parts One and Two," "The Zeppo" (although we never really know what's going on in that one), "Graduation Day, Parts One and Two," and "Doomed."

> The "Previously on Buffy the Vampire Slayer" preview to the episode features an explosion of clips from the show's history.

DRAMATIS PERSONAE:

Though she told Giles she didn't know how to live in this world, **Buffy**'s good-bye speech goes as follows: "Dawn, listen to me, listen. I love you. I will always love you. This is the work I have to do. Tell Giles . . . tell Giles I figured it out . . . and I'm okay. And give my love to my friends. You have to take care of them now. You have to take care of each other. You have to be strong. But Dawn, the hardest thing in this world is to live in it. Be brave. Live. For me."

Xander credits any remotely heroic act that he may do to what he's learned from being Buffy's friend.

Willow is uncomfortable with the fact that Buffy considers her the "big gun." But the Slayer reminds the witch that she is the only one who has been able to hold Glory off.

Giles argues with Buffy over the need for Dawn to die. He later explains to Ben what makes Buffy different from the two of them, then kills him.

Anya reminds Xander that historically, in case of apocalypse, she usually skedaddled out of town. But now she loves him so much that she has inappropriately timed sex and tries to think of ways to fight a god and then does a lot of worrying.

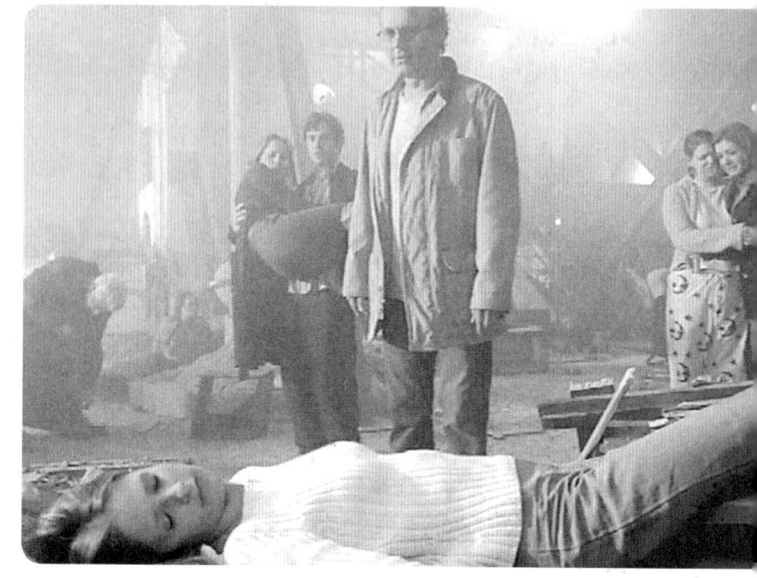

Dawn, as The Key, needs to be "poured" into a specific place at a specific time to break down the walls between dimensions. If it stops, the energy is depleted and the walls come back up. Buffy notes—this is important—that the monks made Dawn out of her. Dawn is a part of her.

> "The Gift" is the one hundredth episode of the series. It was also the last episode to air on the WB, since the show moved to UPN the following season.

FROM THE ORIGINAL TELEPLAY:
Joss Whedon has a little fun with preconceived expectations for Giles (and Anthony Stewart Head) in the following stage direction:

He looks up at her. It's possible—I'm not saying it'll definitely happen, but it's POSSIBLE—he may take off his glasses. Play with them somehow. Could happen.

Joss Whedon has a little more fun with stage directions, this time at the expense of supervising producer David Fury:

And Spike jumps over the whole defensive crazy line to land in the thick of minions, just fists and fury. (Fists, in fact, OF fury.) (Not David Fury.) (Though his fists are formidable.) (What, no I'm not sleepy! Hey, I'm in CHARGE here!)

In the interest of keeping the true ending of this episode from leaking, there were several different scripts, all with slightly different endings, circulated. Here is how the script for one alternate episode ends:

ANGLE: IN THE SKY
A rift opens and a huge dragon flies out, screaming as it sails past the girls.
DAWN (CONT'D): "Buffy—"
BUFFY: "I don't care! Dawn, I won't lose you—"
DAWN: "You have to! You have to let me go! Blood starts it, and until the blood stops flowing, it'll never stop. You know you have to let me. . . ."
ON BUFFY
As she takes in Dawn's words, knowing it's true.
ON DAWN
As, slowly at first, she takes a few steps away from her sister, toward the end of the platform.

ON BUFFY

Who does nothing to stop her.

ON DAWN AGAIN

A few more steps, faster this time, gaining speed until she is running toward the edge of the platform.

ANGLE: ABOVE THE END as Dawn reaches it and SWAN DIVES right out and down toward the ball of energy.

CLOSE ON: DAWN

As she starts down.

CLOSE ON: BUFFY

As she watches, crying. . . .

ANGLE: THE BALL OF ENERGY

As Dawn's body sails down into and disappears in a white light, causing the energy to go even wilder.

CLOSE ON: The group, as they look in vain to see what has happened.

CLOSE ON: DAWN'S FACE

As she floats in the center of the maelstrom, being hit with the equivalent of a million jolts of electricity—

BUFFY—unable to leave the platform. . . .

DAWN—her eyes slowly closing. . . .

THE ENERGY BALL—exploding and suddenly contracting out of existence . . .

Dawn disappearing with it.

CLOSE ON BUFFY'S FACE

BLACK OUT.

END OF SHOW.

CLARE KRAMER (GLORY)

You were one of the founders of GeekNation, one of the best geek-culture sites on the Web. How did GeekNation come about, and what is its mission going forward?

CLARE: "Our original thought was to not just be a voice for someone inside the industry or a voice of a fan—[who] normally is outside of the industry—but [for] both. We're all filmmakers and work in TV, but we're also fans, so we sought to deliver a voice from both perspectives. That's been our mission and that is what we'll continue to do as long as we have people listening.

"As for moving forward, we hope to continue spreading our voice, while at the same time adding new sectors to our company that provide completely different offerings to the user, yet accompany one another. One of those new offerings to our users will be our new ticketing platform, called FanFix (fanfix.com), which specializes in ticket sales for conventions and film fests. We're also launching an app that we started building last year that could completely change the ways in which people attend events. We're *very* excited about the trajectory of the company and where things are moving forward.

"We also just sold our first show to [the network] Decades. *Then Again* with Herbie J. Pilato, which basically interviews classic TV stars. We also have several other shows in development."

As part of your work with GeekNation, you've executive produced a number of Web series. How do you decide what you think is going to work?

CLARE: "It's not easy—you certainly gain a newfound respect for studio execs. Luckily for me, a bad decision won't cost me my job, so I have more freedom to what we're willing to take a risk on. If I make a bad decision—which I never look at that way anyway—I can only blame myself, and it's always a risk and potential loss of revenue that I'm willing to take.

"You're always asking yourself, 'What's everyone going to like?' and unfortunately, it's not always the choice you'd make yourself. It's like choosing a pie for a party, hoping everyone will like the same flavor, with the caveat that there's a good chance that not every pie will taste good. Luckily, we're surrounded by an abundance of crazy-talented people that help make our decisions for us."

Original series for the Web continue to be influential, but where do you see Web-original entertainment going in the future?

CLARE: "For a long while, even up to as little as five years ago, many in the industry were preaching 'the death of TV.' Most people believed that the advent of online content would be the end for TV. . . . It was popular, inexpensive, and effective, not to mention for the first time in history (aside from theater) a fan could engage with the creator. Then came shows like *Game of Thrones* and *The Walking Dead* that completely changed the game. Ad dollars rose, budgets increased, and now you have film-quality television. TV is amazing now! Then Netflix, Hulu, Amazon, HBO Go, Shudder, and others alike proved you can have both.

"Now I think seeing the future is simple: TV and Web content are one and the same, starting with *House of Cards, Marco Polo* . . . It is an amazing time we're living in. We have without question found ourselves in an entertainment revolution, and I'm loving every minute of it!"

You shared the screen with fellow *Buffy* alum Eliza Dushku in the cheerleading classic *Bring It On*, which has gone on to have its own dedicated fandom and a long life. Any thoughts on the experience of making that film and its continued popularity?

CLARE: "*Bring It On* is without a doubt the most fun I've had making a movie! We were all hired to play sixteen-year-olds, so we made sure we stayed in character throughout the filming process. (That was a joke.) Two of my best friends in the world, Eliza and actress Bianca Kajlich, I met on that movie. This may be some fun news for some, but Eliza ended up being best friends with my sister while staying in my apartment in New York. Not to mention, Huntley Ritter is now one of my husband's buddies. We all gained a lot from that film, including some great memories, some we can't share!"

You got to be the Big Bad for all of season five of *Buffy*—and Glory was the one who managed to kill Buffy, even though loads of villains had tried. Does that make Glory the Biggest Bad of all?

CLARE: "Of course, I may be a bit biased here, but *yes* . . . I am the Biggest Bad of all! Ha-ha-ha!

"Seriously, though, I've caught bits of the show since, and it really was lightning in a bottle; it was perfect! From Joss's creation, to the writers, and to the choices all those fabulous actors made were just perfect . . . across the board perfect! Nothing makes an artist or actor happier than to be a part of something that touches so many people in so many ways. At the end of the day, we're only on this marble for a certain amount of time, and it feels good to know you'll be remembered for something amazing. It really does make you grateful to everyone, especially the fans!"

What stands out to you about the process of being cast as Glory—about the audition or your first look at the script, or both?

CLARE: "Trust other artists and sometimes great things happen! That's really it. It was my first time delving into TV, and for someone who likes to control their environment and surroundings, especially when I had reps telling me not to do the show and to stick with only film, I had to trust, and I'm glad I did."

So much time has passed. What are your favorite behind-the-scenes memories of your time on *Buffy*?

CLARE: "As I've stated before, it was my first time filming a TV show. Not that it's much different than filming a movie, other than getting to know your crew a lot better, so that was fun. I stay in touch with my stunt double, and I've also gotten to know so many other actors that I didn't even work with, just by having that connection to a show—having those people in my life has made it all the more special for me.

"My favorite memory would be [accidentally] punching my stunt double straight in the forehead and knocking her out. It was terrifying at the time, but now we both find it hysterical; I'd never punched any more than a punching bag prior to that! It was a late-night filming; we were all exhausted, and I pushed when I should have pulled."

Everyone says that working on a long-running TV series is a lot like high school, with circles of friends and then those people you wish you'd hung out with more. Who do you wish you'd hung out with more while working on *Buffy*?

CLARE: "This may seem like an obvious answer, but maybe Sarah. I think we both really liked one another, worked really well together, and we definitely respected one another. By the time I came in, it was definitely important to me to keep things as professional as possible—I feel like that's what she needed from me at the time so that's what I wanted to give.

"Acting is give and take, knowing your place, and knowing what your co-actors need from you. In hindsight, I probably could have been more personable, and we probably would have become the best of friends. I really like her. With that said, I have zero regrets. It was a 100 percent amazing experience from the beginning—even to now."

As a child, you were Wendy in a series of TV commercials for Wendy's. What's the best burger you've ever had?

CLARE: "Since we're talking fast food, I'm going to have to go with what I've learned from my Texas side of the family, since I married a Texan, and say Whataburger. Early in our relationship his family would pick us up at the airport and we'd head straight to their lake house, and on the way that was always our first stop. Those are fond memories . . . and great burgers!"

What are you working on now, and what does the future hold for Clare Kramer?

CLARE: "Directing! I truly feel that I've matured enough in my career that I can focus on directing—I've done a lot of Web directing in preparation for narrative, and I'm ready to make the jump. I've been offered some nonscripted [projects], but I'm not sure I want to begin my directing career that way. Sometimes you can start in a direction and it gets difficult to break away, so I just want to be cautious and focus mainly on what interests me—for now, anyway.

"I also have a little passion project, which is a feature film that I want to shoot in Texas. I'm also developing a few things with Roddenberry (the *Star Trek* franchise), and as I stated earlier, we're pitching shows we've developed to TV networks. Furthermore, we have a product that we are currently developing that distributes a certain type of content, and it's so secretive right now that I can't even say more than that. It is *very* exciting!

"The future is bright career-wise, but mainly, I'm enjoying life with my family and kids."

AMBER BENSON (TARA MACLAY)

You've written, directed, produced, and edited your own independent films in the past, but you've recently segued into writing for television. How much can you say about the TV projects you're writing?

AMBER: "All I can say at the moment is that I'm working on a true-crime project for Lifetime, and I just sold my first pilot about a female serial killer."

You're a screenwriter, a director, a novelist, and many other things. A Renaissance woman philosophy. How do you decide what projects you want to work on?

AMBER: "It's just whatever moves me and is entertaining and interesting. As I've gotten older, I've decided I only want to work with nice people. Life is too short, so if a project isn't interesting to me and the people aren't nice, I'm not going to do it. I only want to work on stuff that gets me excited creatively and projects that will mean working with people with whom I can enjoy collaborating."

That philosophy has never seemed strategic, but more instinctive. Has that changed? Is there a strategy involved now?

AMBER: "There has never been a strategy to how I do business, I just go by my gut. If my intuition tells me I'm going to have fun doing something, or if I'm scared of something, I'll do it. I'm one of those people who runs toward things that frighten me. I think that was the thing with *Ghosts of Albion*, the original BBC Web series that you and I did. That was terrifying. To think that we were going to go to the UK, and that you and I were basically going to make this thing kind of on our own with the help of people at the BBC we'd never met before . . . that was absolutely terrifying. I could've walked away and said that I'm not doing it, but I run toward those scary projects. Plus, I was doing that stuff with you, so at least I knew I would have one person who would have my back, and that even if it turned out to be a disaster, at least we would have a good time doing it."

You've been narrating audiobooks for a while too, and I know that you enjoy that work. Is that just fun in its own right, or does that come from you being such a voracious reader?

AMBER: "It partly comes from being an audiobook listener. I'm a big reader, but I definitely inhale audiobooks because I do a lot of driving. If you live in Los Angeles, you're in the car a lot. Of course, the other motive is my health insurance. It's the only acting I do these days, so it's how I keep my health insurance up through SAG and AFTRA. It's really fun. It's a good way to be creative without having to get dressed in anything other than your scuzzy clothes, and you don't have to take a shower if you don't want to, because you're sitting in a little booth by yourself."

Looking back now, what stands out to you about the process of being cast as Tara, the audition or the script, or both?

AMBER: "I had these pants—I think they were my sister's pants. I cut them off and they were too big, so I belted them and they kind of were hanging. They were weird, and I don't know why I decided 'I'm wearing *this* to the audition.' I just wore that and a T-shirt. I just did not dress up for it. I didn't do anything specifically makeup-wise. I just went as me. I think I'd just hit a point where I was thinking, *I hate this business, chasing auditions and trying to be an actor. I don't care anymore, so I'm just going to be myself.* I went in, and I did not look like any of the other girls in the waiting area. They were all dressed nice and I was sort of a bum, and I think maybe there was something to that. The 'not caring.' The older I get, the more I think that if you don't give a crap about what other people think, people are more interested in working with you. They think you know something they don't, and they're willing to go on the journey with you.

"And I know that [executive producer] Marti Noxon was instrumental in me getting the part. I think Joss had seen someone who was a little more sylphlike, very tiny and sort of puckish and fairylike. And I am none of those things. So I know Marti basically said, 'We like the one in the weird pants. The one wearing cutoff pants that are three sizes too big for her and hanging around her butt.' That was me."

Tara and Willow's relationship was what I consider an earthquake in pop culture, a truly groundbreaking LGBT relationship on television. Did you know the relationship with Willow was in the cards when you auditioned?

AMBER: "Not at all. I was just supposed to be [in] one or two episodes to play her friend from Wicca group and that was it. And then they just kept adding episodes. The crew kept saying, 'You guys have such great chemistry,' and I had no idea what they were talking about. Then the producers took us aside, each of us separately, and said, 'Okay, you guys are going to be a couple,' and I realized what the crew had meant about our chemistry."

I have seen so many people cry when meeting you—I've heard people tell you that you saved their lives.

AMBER: "I've definitely had a lot of people who've reached out because of Tara. A big part of it is the writing. I'm only a piece of the puzzle. She's had that impact because of who she was, how she was written, how she was shot and put together. I have the face—she's my face, and I guess my empathy, because I guess that comes across—but it was a group effort. There wasn't a character like her around in the world until she was brought into life in the Buffyverse. It was an honor to get to walk in Tara's shoes."

Yes, it's a collaborative effort—creating a character—but when you have all of these personal one-on-one experiences with people who have poured themselves out to you, it has to have an impact on you.

AMBER: "Yeah, of course. It makes you feel very responsible to people and makes you think about how you approach things. It's part of the reason I've kind of pulled away from social media. It makes you feel very vulnerable to know how easily things you can say can be taken out of context, and because there are people who feel very strongly about this character, I started to feel like maybe it's better to take a step back and not make myself so open to both the good and the bad. But there are those moments when I meet somebody face-to-face and they tell me, 'I didn't kill myself, because I saw a couple fall in love who were like me. And there's nobody like me in this small town in the Midwest where I grew up, so I felt like it was okay to be me.' Then I'm reminded that playing Tara is the greatest thing that I've done as an actor. It's the most powerful and will probably be the thing that will go with me to the grave. It will be on my tombstone, you know? So it makes you feel responsible, but it's a wonderful responsibility."

I know you get recognized in public often, even so many years later. Have those encounters changed?

AMBER: "It waxes and wanes. Yes, people always look at me, because they think they know me from somewhere and they can't quite place it. But it's actually become more common recently. I was at the mall, and a girl came over to ask me if I was 'that girl from *Buffy*.' We talked a little and she showed me that she'd looked me up on her phone, just making sure, confirming. I think Netflix and cable have created a new wave of *Buffy* fans."

Many years have passed, but when you think back, what are your favorite behind-the-scenes memories of working on the show?

AMBER: "Um . . . gosh. For me, just making the musical was so amazing. Getting to sing with Tony Head, who is wonderful. You don't get to do something like that very often. It was really magical and truly was like being part of a family. A seventeen-hour day was not out of the norm—and that's a long-ass day—but we went to work and we were just happy to see everybody. You really got to know people well. For me, the saddest part of not being on the show anymore was not getting to hang out with the crew and the cast and the writers and no longer being part of that Stewart Street family. In fact, the Stewart Street studio doesn't really exist anymore. The place where we shot all of those episodes doesn't exist anymore, which is really sad."

Everyone says working on a long-running TV series is a lot like high school. There are circles of friends and then there are always those people you wish you'd hung out with more. Who do you wish you'd hung out with more?

AMBER: "I have a great relationship with Emma Caulfield now. Creatively, we've toyed around with working together on stuff, and she's brilliant and just so much fun, but I didn't really spend a ton of time with her on the set. So I wish I'd had more time with Emma."

You've written two successful urban fantasy novel series, but you've got so much on your plate at the moment. Do you have plans for more novels in the not-so-distant future?

AMBER: "*The End of Magic*—the third novel in my Witches of Echo Park series—came out in May 2017, and now I'm taking a little sabbatical. I got burnt out. A novel is a hundred thousand words. A hundred thousand words is a lot of words. I'm not taking my toe out of the water, but I'm taking a break."

Somehow, no matter how long the line is, or how exhausted you are, you always seem to make every single fan at a convention feel like they got to share a moment with you. What's the secret?

AMBER: "I've been at the end of the line. I know what it's like to want to have a moment with somebody and them not be amenable to that, and it's shitty. I don't want to make anyone else feel that way. I'm sure there are people who have walked away unhappy, because how could there not be? But I would say ninety percent of the people who come to say hello have a positive experience and walk away feeling pretty good. And I think that's a big win. It's why I'm there."

You don't do a lot of conventions, but you've done your share over the years. What are the best fan moments you can recall?

AMBER: "There have been so many nice ones, people coming up and saying thank you for being part of the show, and for playing that character, and for being part of the LGBTQ world and being an ally in that world . . . that's the best stuff. When someone brings their kid up and their kid says, 'I'm trans and I feel like it's okay to be me because of your show,' that is amazing. You have someone who wasn't even born who is comfortable with gender fluidity because of an openness that we offered fifteen or sixteen years before, and that makes me happy."

You've worked in all sorts of film and TV projects in the years since *Buffy*, including guest spots on major network shows, including *Supernatural* and *Grey's Anatomy*, and lead roles in Lifetime movies that we love in our house, like *Holiday Wishes* and *7 Things to Do Before I'm 30*. Then there are the indies like *The Killing Jar*, *Strictly Sexual*, and the unforgettably weird *Dust Up*. What's your favorite post-*Buffy* acting role?

AMBER: "Post-*Buffy* is hard. . . . It's easy to pick something pre-*Buffy*, because that would be *King of the Hill*. That's my favorite. This is tough. *7 Things to Do Before I'm 30* was actually really fun and really good. That was a lovely experience. And *Latter Days* is great. It is a love story between two guys that is super positive and important. It transcended what the genre had been doing until then. When I read the script, my reaction was just: 'Wow. I would do craft service on this; it's really important.' But probably the weirdest one—it makes me laugh every time and people seem to really connect to it—is *One-Eyed Monster*. When I had Ron Jeremy's fake, animatronic penis on my shoulder looking at me . . . I mean, come on. I'm the big winner. You can climb no higher."

DAVID FURY (WRITER AND CO-EXECUTIVE PRODUCER)

You've written for and/or produced some of the biggest series on TV, including *Lost* and *24*, and some of the most popular shows in pop culture and the geek community, including *Buffy*, *Angel*, *Fringe*, *Hannibal*, *Homeland*, and the short-lived *Terra Nova*, which was a favorite in my house. Do you come from a love of TV in general, a love of genre, or both (and give us some of that history)? What brought you to writing, and to writing these particular series?

DAVID: "I spent *way* too much time watching television in my youth, mostly comedy and sci-fi/fantasy. But I wouldn't say I 'loved' TV—I saved that love for movies—but there were a couple of shows that easily inspired me: *Twilight Zone* and *Star Trek*. Both could be funny, scary, touching . . . and, even at a very young age, I recognized them as allegories for the human condition. The former got me reading Bradbury, Matheson, Asimov, and others whose work later informed a different phase of my creative life. While working sporadically as an actor, I tried my hand for a few years as a stand-up and improvisational comedy performer.

"When I first started writing sketches, they were often rooted in allegorical storytelling: an in-denial Frosty the Snowman learning from his agent that he's melting; three mermen bemoaning the fact that all of their women keep dumping them for humans (or 'leg-boys' as they derisively refer to them); an existential fruit fly trying to fathom the meaning of a less-than-twenty-four-hour life span . . . comedy, fantasy, sci-fi allegory. That was my sweet spot. When people encouraged me to write for television, I partnered with my then girlfriend, Elin Hampton, on several comedy shows. But it wasn't until we met Joss at his office while he was developing *BTVS* that I found a project that was everything I was looking for, with a genius at the helm who would let me do my thing.

"*Buffy* led to simultaneously consulting on *Angel*, where I met Howard Gordon, who would later bring me into the 24 franchise. The final season of *Angel* brought Ben Edlund into my life, leading to my partnership with him on the new Amazon incarnation of *The Tick*. After *Angel*, I was fortunate enough to be hired by J. J. Abrams and Damon Lindelof (who were fans of several Whedonverse writers) to come onto the first season of *Lost*. I always tried to be discerning when it came to the shows I wanted to work on, but my experience on *Buffy* opened up far more possibilities and gave me the confidence to say no more often than yes."

Like so many of the *Buffy* writers, you'd written episodes for a handful of series before you came onto *Buffy*, but it certainly seems to have been the launching pad for you. Do you remember what it was like getting hired for the first time? How did that come about?

DAVID: "My writing experience before *Buffy* was exclusively in the comedy world. Sitcom scripts are largely group-written with entire staffs, regardless of what the final credits say. But in an hour show like *Buffy*, I discovered that we each have ownership over our scripts. Others might sometimes contribute or a showrunner may take a pass at a few scenes at first, but ultimately, the voice largely belongs to the credited writer. I think that may be the main reason my name came to be more recognized.

"At the time Elin and I met with Joss, we were just finishing up our stint on a short-lived attempt to bring *Pinky and the Brain* to prime time. Joss was looking for comedy writers and pitched us what the series was going to be. We'd also just had a meeting for another potential job on a more conventional sitcom at ABC, scheduled between *Roseanne* and *Home Improvement*. But after meeting with Joss, we knew his was the show we wanted to do. Our agent told us we were crazy—*Buffy*'s initial order was for only six episodes, airing mid-season on a fledgling network called The WB. There was no future in it. Trusting his judgment, we took the job on the ABC sitcom. . . . It was canceled after eighteen episodes. Meanwhile, *Buffy*'s now twelve-episode season was an almost instant cult hit. So we fired our agent and landed at another agency, which coincidentally represented Joss. When our new agents asked what we'd like to do, our first request was to try to get a second chance with him.

"Near the start of season two, we went in to see Joss and David Greenwalt, and pitched them a few ideas for a possible freelance stand-alone story. They bought the first one, which eventually became the episode 'Go Fish.' Joss and David were so happy with the first draft that came in that an offer was made for us to come on as producers the following season. We were elated by their effusive response and offer. Only problem was, my partner and wife, who didn't share my affinity for horror and occult fantasy, wanted to remain in the sitcom world. So she accepted a writer/producer position on *Mad About You*, while I had to settle for writing a new freelance *Buffy* episode by myself to convince Joss that I was capable. That episode became season three's 'Helpless.' Again, they were so happy with the draft, more freelance gigs followed. Wheels were already spinning for me to officially come onto the staff in season four, as well as help develop and write the second episode of *Angel*, which was slated to begin concurrently. It was a long, winding road. . . . But Joss once graciously said that he thinks of me as being there from the very beginning of both series. It's a sentiment I share and could not feel more grateful for."

I'm fascinated to see that you wrote episodes of *Pinky and the Brain* and *The Wild Thornberrys*. Do you think about animation when you're considering future projects? Is there something you'd like to do as an animated series?

DAVID: "I don't generally think about animation projects, largely because I see it as a medium for real artists to expand the boundaries of their imaginations and budgets. I feel like the best comic-book writers can actually draw, themselves. And I couldn't draw a stick figure. In truth, I'm more a product of the theater in that my stories tend to be more character-based . . . my ideas are more contained—quirky, but hopefully smart—rather than big and epic. In the scripts we wrote for *Pinky and the Brain* and *The Wild Thornberrys*, there was almost no reason to animate them, except that they concerned talking lab mice and wild safari animals. Strip that out and the stories still work.

"That said, there was a book I found a long time ago that I thought I'd like to one day write and direct as an animated film. It's called *Freaks' Amour* by Tom DeHaven, a love story set in a post-apocalyptic world where people have developed strange physical mutations. Just lent the book to one of my sons, who is in film school. Maybe someday I'll produce and he'll direct, or vice versa."

Some of the show's writers engaged regularly with fans and others didn't. It's no exaggeration to say that the *Buffy* fandom—particularly the core fans on posting boards like *The Bronze*—basically invented modern fandom. How much do you still interact with fans of the many shows you've worked on, and what are your thoughts on the relationship between modern TV and its fans?

DAVID: "*The Bronze* was really amazing. Joss told me about it when I came aboard and encouraged me to go on after my first episode. You have to remember this was before 'live tweeting' or any social media. . . . To be able to interact with fans in real time, answer questions, have debates . . . it was the first time a lot of us felt like a part of the ever-enlarging geek community. And unlike the kind of fan interaction that's done now, this wasn't about pimping and promoting shows. These were like pen pal relationships. Then, of course, every year there'd be a *Bronze* party in LA, and we'd get to meet so many people we'd been conversing with all season long. I loved the experience so much, I arranged for the site operators of *The Bronze* to bring the same thing to *Lost*. It was called *The Fuselage*. I imagine it continued on after I left the series, but I don't really know. The fact is, I never found any site as warm and comforting as *The Bronze*, so I don't have much fan interaction anymore—with the exception of occasional nice notes on Facebook or Twitter."

You were a big part of the original 24 and now you're involved with the continuation, 24: Legacy, which seems to be both a straight continuation of the series but with a different main character and sort of a reboot as well. Do you think such a thing would ever be possible for Buffy, and what other shows you've worked on would you love to see return, either as a reboot or a continuation (and which would you prefer)?

DAVID: "My involvement with *24: Legacy* is minimal at best. The executive producers just asked me to write a couple of freelance episodes to help them keep pace with production and I was happy to do it. As for reboots and multiseason runs, I have kind of a minority opinion on that—I don't believe any series should go beyond five seasons. (Six or seven if it's really exceptional and episode count is minimal.) I fall in love with shows too, but I'd rather see them end in their prime than drag out with diminishing returns. I miss *Buffy*, but to try to revive it or reboot it will only lead to disappointment. Like that recent attempt with *The X-Files*.

"I believe every new film set in the *Star Wars* universe will diminish the specialness of that series. I get it, no matter how much we get, we want more. Which is why J. K. Rowling is putting out new books in the Harry Potter universe. I wish she wouldn't. I wish limited series and movies could be allowed to harden into cherished jewels of memory, untarnished by futile efforts to re-create the magic. But then, I'm only a capitalist up to a point."

Your Halloween episode "Fear, Itself" remains one of my favorites. What's your favorite among the episodes you wrote for the series, and why?

DAVID: "Thanks for that. I'm always a little surprised how often people tell me that's one of their favorite episodes, when I find season two's 'Halloween' episode so perfect. As for my favorite, I guess it will always be 'Helpless,' if only because it was my first solo effort. It was unique and disturbing writing Buffy as a terrified, powerless girl. And I'm responsible for getting Giles fired, which set the stage for Wesley and everything else that followed. That still blows my mind."

177

I've heard so many people talk about *Buffy* changing their lives—in many cases *saving* their lives. How do you feel when you hear that sort of thing, and have you had similar reactions to other series you've worked on?

DAVID: "I'm always incredibly humbled and moved when fans tell me how much *Buffy* meant to them. Their stories are sometimes staggering, telling me how bullied or abused they were as children . . . how difficult it was when their parents split up . . . and how *Buffy* made them feel somehow empowered, or just took them away from their lives for an hour every week. We, the writers and actors, all came to realize the responsibility we had to say something hopeful about relationships, about life. I also meet so many people who became inspired to become writers from the work we did . . . not unlike how the writers of *Twilight Zone* and *Star Trek* inspired me."

I've heard it said that working on a long-running TV series is a lot like high school, with circles of friends and then those people you wish you'd hung out with more. Who do you wish you'd hung out with more from your *Buffy* days?

DAVID: "I can't think of anyone on *Buffy* that I missed getting to hang with. We were a pretty tight group, going to movie matinees, playing office golf . . . I enjoyed each and everyone's company from time to time, but I suppose I'll always wish I got to hang more with Joss. All the cool kids in show business gravitated toward him and you always wanted to be included. Fortunately, he was generous and included us more often than not."

You're incredibly busy, always, but what do you have coming up that we don't know about yet?

DAVID: "Well, in addition to writing two episodes of *24: Legacy*, as I mentioned, I'm executive producer with Ben Edlund on his newest and bestest series of *The Tick* for Amazon Prime."

SEASON 6

Bargaining, Part One
Episode 6.1

WRITTEN BY: Marti Noxon
DIRECTED BY: David Grossman
SPECIAL GUEST STAR: Anthony Stewart Head as Rupert Giles
GUEST STAR: Franc Ross as Razor
CO-STARS: Geoff Meed as Mag, Mike Grief as Klyed, Paul Greenberg as Shempy Vamp, Joy DeMichelle Moore as Ms. Leftcort, Robert D. Vito as Cute Boy, Harry Johnson as Parent #1, Kelly Lynn Warren as Parent #2, Hila Levy as Pretty Girl

THE PLOT THICKENS:

In a Slayer-less Sunnydale, the Slayerettes manage to do an impressive job filling in for their dearly departed friend. It's been months since Buffy sacrificed herself to save her sister and the world. Willow is the new leader, by unanimous decision, and she's using her magick to guide the team through battle with demons. They've enlisted the rebuilt Buffybot to keep word from spreading that Sunnydale is now Slayer-free. It's also beginning to look like it's going to be Watcher-free, as Giles plans to move home to England.

The Buffybot manages to maintain the human facade for parent/teacher day at Dawn's school, but she's still not the old Buffster. While Spike looks after Dawn and continues to lament the fact that he watched Buffy die, plans are being hatched to alter that reality. Willow, Xander, Tara, and Anya are collecting ingredients for a spell to bring the Slayer back to life. Things are coming together just in time, because the Buffybot gets a little beating from a littler vamp and her circuits are exposed to him. The demon world at large is about to learn that the Slayer is not what she used to be.

Willow's not her old self either. Blinded by the need to bring back her friend, the witch keeps a few things secret from even Xander and the others about the resurrection spell, like the fact that she is off in the woods sacrificing a fawn for the necessary blood. When she returns to the Magic Box with the last ingredient, the gang is surprised to find that Giles is gone and has only left a note of good-bye, but the Scoobies know that's not going to fly and hurry for a farewell scene at the airport.

The gang is a bit wary of reviving the Slayer with the Watcher gone, but they go ahead anyway. Although Willow indicated that she would be "tested" while performing the spell, she failed to prepare her lover and friends for just the extremeness of those tests.

In the meantime, a demon biker gang comes to Sunnydale in search of the faux Slayer, and they easily inflict some damage on the bot.

As Dawn and Spike watch the demons take over the town, Buffybot takes her damaged self to the cemetery to find Willow. Unfortunately, the demons follow and crash the spell-casting party. The gang is forced to scatter as Xander takes a semiconscious Willow to safety. As she comes around, Willow is upset that the spell didn't work. But that's not quite true.

Trapped in her coffin, under layers of dirt, the Slayer has come back to life.

QUOTE OF THE WEEK:
Spike pokes fun at Giles's life, or lack thereof:
"Oooh. Poor Watcher. Did your life pass before your eyes? 'Cuppa tea, cuppa tea, almost got shagged, cuppa tea . . .'"

LOVE IN VEIN:
Tara and Willow have moved into the Summers home and taken over Joyce's old bedroom to look after Dawn. Spike is still torn up over Buffy's death. He is now extremely uncomfortable when the Buffybot makes with the flattering that she was originally programmed to do around him. Xander and Anya still have not announced their engagement. Xander wants to put it off until things settle down, which frustrates Anya, because, really, when does life in Sunnydale ever settle down?

> **TODAY'S LESSON:**
> Dawn's class is reading Henry David Thoreau's Walden.

POP-CULTURE IQ:
Xander refers to the 1978 Brian DePalma movie in which children with paranormal abilities are trained to become killers in war conditions:
"But I saw *The Fury* and that way lies spooky carnival death."
Upon hearing the Buffybot's weird way with words, Spike compares her to the artistic movement in which artists playfully worked to shock their audience in protest of the traditional forms of expression:
"What's with the Dadaism, Red?"
Anya made a deal for the important spell ingredient on the online auction site:
"You found the last known Urn of Osiris on eBay?"
The master negotiator also added a collectible from the bubblegum boy band to the deal:
"I finally got him to throw in a limited edition Backstreet Boys lunch box for—"
Anya makes reference to the oft-mentioned science and nature cable channel, indicating that this group is really into the educational television:
"Discovery Channel has monkeys."
The loserlike vampire is described only with the name of the least capable Stooge in *The Three Stooges*, a comedy television series based on a series of movies that began airing in 1959:
Shempy Vamp
The Shempy Vamp tries to play it cool with the biker demons by referencing the 1993 film *Menace II Society*:
"She's a menace to our society."

> *Among the parting gifts for Giles, Tara gives him a little monster finger puppet and says, "Grrr, arrgh!" echoing the lines of the Mutant Enemy logo from the show's end credits.*

CONTINUITY:
Willow's powers continue to grow and she now communicates with the entire gang telepathically as she had done with Spike in "The Gift." Even Tara is unaware of the power Willow wields over the forces necessary to resurrect someone. The Buffybot was built in "Intervention" and Willow's rebuilt her twice now (following "Intervention" and "The Gift," in which the bot was decapitated). Dawn's father has apparently been located since his disappearing act last season, although it's clear that he still hasn't made a trip to Sunnydale to check in on his daughters since Joyce's death. Giles first mentioned possibly leaving at the beginning of the fifth season in "Buffy vs. Dracula." Tara reminds everyone that reviving the dead *is* wrong, however, since Buffy died an unnatural death, it might work, in comparison to Dawn's use of magick to revive Joyce in "Forever" (and, later, Willow's attempt to bring back someone else at the end of the season). Anya clarifies that zombies only eat brains when instructed by their zombie master, as the gang had sort of found out in "Dead Man's Party." Willow assumes that Buffy could be trapped in some hell dimension like Angel had been between seasons two and three. She'll later learn that's incorrect.

> *The Shempy Vampire, in what's likely an effort to show his absolute "Shempiness," wears a T-shirt from the "MMMBop" pop group Hanson.*

DRAMATIS PERSONAE:
Giles is still coming to terms with the fact that he did "what any good Watcher would do" and got his Slayer killed in the line of duty. But now that his job is over, he finds it hard to leave Sunnydale. He also finds it difficult to depart for fear of making a very un-British-like scene.
Willow was elected head of the Scoobies following Buffy's death when Xander nominated her

and suggested a vote. The choice was unanimous. She programmed the Buffybot with a homing device so it could locate Willow whenever it was in need of repair.

Anya is placed in charge of the Magic Box in Giles's absence, but she has a difficult time waiting to assume her new role when he continually puts off leaving.

Dawn reminds Spike that she's no longer The Key—or at least, if she is, she doesn't open anything anymore. She and Spike are thrown together more often as the Scoobies become secretive about their resurrection plans.

Spike is just an accepted part of the gang's world now, even though Buffy's gone.

FROM THE ORIGINAL TELEPLAY:
The script ends with the following description:

Now, we are inside Buffy's coffin. We can see Buffy's corpse. Suddenly, its eyes snap open and the corpse morphs back into live Buffy. Then her breath starts to come fast, horrified. . . .

Bargaining, Part Two
Episode 6.2

WRITTEN BY: David Fury
DIRECTED BY: David Grossman
GUEST STAR: Franc Ross as Razor
CO-STARS: Geoff Meed as Mag, Mike Grief as Klyed, Richard Wharton as Homeowner

THE PLOT THICKENS:
The Scoobies scatter when they come under attack by the biker gang literally from Hell, unaware that Buffy has risen from the dead, trapped in her grave. Buffy claws her way out of the ground while the demon bikers lay waste to Sunnydale.

Spike realizes that it's not safe in the Summers home with the demons about, so he takes Dawn and hits the streets of town on a stolen demon bike. At the same time, a shell-shocked Buffy wanders through the streets, looking quite confused.

Anya and Tara make it to the Magic Box and are worried for their respective loves, so Tara sends a locator light to guide Willow and Xander home. The little light finds them as Xander tries to get Willow to stop avoiding his talk about the seriously dark magick she was using.

The demons grab the Buffybot and bring her into town too. Just before they chain their bikes to the robot and pull her apart, she sees the real Buffy has come home. The Scoobies also run into the Slayer reborn, but the conversation is limited. Obviously they're thrilled to see their friend, until Xander realizes that they brought her back from death but didn't dig her out of the ground. The demons attack, forcing Buffy into fight then flight.

Dawn and Spike come across bits of Buffybot. The robot is still talking and reveals that she saw the "other" Buffy, which sends Dawn off to search. She eventually finds her sister atop the scaffolding where Buffy was last seen alive. Buffy wants to jump again and wonders if this is Hell. Dawn tries to convince Buffy to stay, but only when the scaffolding starts to fall and Dawn's life is in peril does Buffy snap out of it in time to save her sister. The scaffolding collapses as Dawn weeps in a stoic Buffy's arms.

QUOTE OF THE WEEK:
Anya does what she can to keep her store and her money safe as the demons terrorize Sunnydale:
> "Already been looted! Sorry! Try the appliance store down the block! They've got great toasters!"

LOVE IN VEIN:
Tara notes that she and Anya would both know if anything had happened to their respective loves.

POP-CULTURE IQ:
Xander does a riff off a line of the song "Ya Got Trouble" from the musical *The Music Man*:
> "Yep. We got trouble. Right here in Hellmouth City."

Xander likens the robotic form of Buffy to Robo-Cop, the central character in the similarly titled movie, television, and animated series:
> "And our very own Robo-Buffy led them right to us."

Xander suggests using one of the strongest adhesives known to man to fix the Urn of Osiris:
> "A little tape . . . a dab o' Krazy Glue . . ."

Xander mistakes a little light for the fairy with an attitude from *Peter Pan*:
> "And how long have you known your girlfriend was Tinker Bell?"

Xander kicks up the testosterone when comparing the Magic Box to the North American Aerospace Defense Command Center and alludes to the national Defense Condition's highest alert status:
> "I mean, this place is NORAD when we're at DefCon One."

Xander accidentally calls himself by a name more familiar as a brand of sauce used in sloppy joes:
> "I happen to be a very powerful man-witch myself."

CONTINUITY:
Tara conjures up a light to guide Willow that's rather similar to the one that Willow conjured up in "Fear, Itself." The tower was last seen in the climactic battle scenes of "The Gift." Buffy flashes back to scenes from that battle, specifically the final moments of her life. Buffy wonders if she is in Hell. The reason for that confusion will come out in "After Life."

DRAMATIS PERSONAE:
Willow, fearing the spell was a failure, finally breaks down and mourns the loss of her best friend.

Tara fears that the demons showed up when they did because Willow and the gang should never have been messing with such dark magicks in the first place and invoking forces they had no right to call. Her caution is well-founded, but too late. This tension will only grow as the season progresses.

> Both parts of "Bargaining" aired as a two-hour premiere for *Buffy* on its new home, UPN.

FROM THE ORIGINAL TELEPLAY:
The Buffybot meets her untimely demise as portrayed in the stage directions:

The Buffybot opens its mouth to say something to Buffy when the chains go taut and the robot is suddenly (as described) really REALLY violently torn apart. Drawn and quartered. The crowd howls with delight.

On Buffy, her anguish and terror at seeing her own horrific death wells up inside her and explodes into a scream . . .

Once More, with Feeling
Episode 6.7

Do we really need to spell this out for you? (Maybe we should sing it.) "Once More, with Feeling" is the musical episode, featuring songs written by Joss Whedon and performed—for better or worse—by the entire cast. By turns funny, adorable, scary, silly, sexy, and heartbreaking, "Once More, with Feeling" is in many ways the ultimate distillation of what makes *Buffy the Vampire Slayer* one of the greatest shows in TV history. After the overlong episode made its debut on November 6, 2001, the soundtrack for the musical became a hit on the Billboard charts and could be heard playing from half the booths and stalls at various pop culture conventions around the world for several years thereafter. The episode also spawned a host of imitations, as other series attempted musical episodes with mostly disappointing results. Though mainly remembered for its music, the episode also features a dramatic reveal, when Buffy finally tells her friends that after she died—and they resurrected her—she'd been *in Heaven*, and they'd pulled her out. Heady stuff, but it sets the stage for everything that comes after.

WRITTEN AND DIRECTED BY: Joss Whedon
SPECIAL GUEST STAR: Anthony Stewart Head as Rupert Giles
GUEST STAR: Hinton Battle as Sweet
CO-STARS: David Fury as Mustard Man, Marti Noxon as Parking Ticket Woman, Daniel Weaver as Handsome Young Man, Scot Zeller as Henchman, Zachary Woodilee as Demon/Henchman, Timothy Anderson as Henchman, Alex Estronel as Henchman, Matt Sims as College Guy #1, Hunter Cochran as College Guy #2

THE PLOT THICKENS:
It looks like an atypically calm Sunnydale morning in the Summers home as the girls get up and start their day. Tara even finds a little sprig of flower under her pillow. But that night, things take an even more atypical little

twist when Buffy starts singing about how her life seems empty and she's just going through the motions. The next morning she finds that she was not the only one to burst into song.

The choral group gets to work trying to find out who is behind the song stylings that only Tara and Willow seem to be enjoying. The power of the music forces Xander and Anya to admit things that normally they'd never tell each other, but it would seem that forced honesty is just the peskier side effect of the spell. Giles informs them that a man apparently got so worked up in a dancing frenzy the previous night that he literally burst into song and spontaneously combusted.

Truth continues to come out in lyrics as Spike asks Buffy to let him rest in peace. But it's truth of a different form that comes out when Tara learns that she had a fight with Willow that she doesn't remember. Tara leaves Dawn alone as the witch confirms her suspicion that Willow's got her under a spell.

Dawn is abducted and taken to Sweet, the demon behind the music who intends to make her his bride. When the demon learns that his sister-in-law-to-be is the Slayer, he sends a henchman to inform her of the coming nuptials. The Slayer tries to rally the troops, but Giles feels that he's standing in her way so she must face the demon alone. As Buffy walks through the fire to get to her sister, the gang does rally to her side just in time to learn the one awful truth.

Buffy admits in song that they did not save her from a hell dimension, but ripped her from Heaven. She follows up the admission with a dance of death that Spike ends by physically stopping her. Dawn echoes her sister's words from before her death: "The hardest thing in this world is to live in it."

Yet another truth comes out when it's revealed that Dawn hadn't summoned the demon; it was actually Xander because he just wanted to find out if he and Anya would have a happy ending. The deal is nullified as the gang is left to wonder where they go from here. Buffy ditches the finale as she goes out to thank Spike. Admitting that she knows it's not real, Buffy just wants to feel and expresses that by kissing the soulless vampire.

QUOTE OF THE WEEK:
Another Tuesday in Sunnydale. . . .
    DAWN: "Oh my God, you will never believe what happened at school today."
    BUFFY: "Everybody started singing and dancing."
    DAWN: "I gave birth to a pterodactyl."
    ANYA: "Oh my God! Did it sing?"

LOVE IN VEIN:
Xander and Anya open up to each other about their fears, although it's entirely against their will. Anya worries that Xander will not love her when she gets old, since she really didn't have to deal with aging issues as a demon. While on the subject, her history as a vengeance demon gives her understandable trust issues with her man. Xander, meanwhile, worries that he'll be too boring for her and she's just a bit too greedy. Tara learns how deeply Willow betrayed her by using a spell on her mind.

POP-CULTURE IQ:
Xander does a riff off the philosophy of Tom Cruise's character in the film *Magnolia*:
   "Respect the cruller. And tame the donut!"
Anya's probably referring to Carmen Miranda–style tropical dance numbers popularized in the Twentieth Century Fox musicals of the 1940s:
   ". . . and a dance with coconuts."
The demon known as Sweet refers to a song from the musical *The Band Wagon*:
   "That's entertainment!"
Anya is referring to the practice in which most plays and television shows are set up so the audience is watching the action through a nonexistent "fourth wall":
   "I felt like we were being watched, like a wall was missing from our apartment, like there were only three walls, no fourth wall."
Michael Flatley, famous Irish dancer whose stage show was titled *Lord of the Dance*, became an international sensation in the nineties. Apparently he frightens Tara (and probably more than a few others):
   ". . . some Lord of the Dance—but not the scary one, just a demon."
The Beatles originally released the song "Twist and Shout" in 1963:
   "I'm the Twist and Shout!"
Spike compares one of the demon's wooden puppet henchmen to Pinocchio:
   "Someday he'll be a real boy."
Buffy echoes a line from the Stephen Sondheim musical *Into the Woods* (Joss Whedon admits to being a huge fan of the famous Broadway composer):
   "Wishes can come true."

Buffy also repeats a line from one of the most popular Disney songs from the movie *Snow White and the Seven Dwarfs*:

"Whistle while you work."

Spike does a bit off the famous folk song often sung round campfires and the Rolling Stones record *Get Yer Ya-Ya's Out*:

". . . get your KoombaYa-Ya's out."

Spike refers to the most well-known march song from the musical *The Music Man*:

". . . there'll probably be a parade. Seventy-six bloody trombones."

> The man singing about the dry cleaner getting the mustard out of his suit was co-executive producer David Fury. The woman trying to sing her way out of the parking ticket was executive producer Marti Noxon.

> The behind-the-scenes footage used in UPN's promos for this episode were taken from David Fury's tapes of the rehearsal process.

CONTINUITY:

Lethe's Bramble, the weedlike flower Tara finds under her pillow, is from Willow's spell to make Tara forget the argument they had in "All the Way." Anya sings about the time Xander's "penis got diseases from a Chumash tribe," that happened during "Pangs." Dawn keeps her stolen items in a jewelry box in her room, which will come into play in "Older and Far Away." Buffy originally told Dawn about "the hardest thing in this world" in "The Gift."

> Aside from all that singing and dancing, this episode was also different because it was eight minutes longer than traditional episodes, it was shown in letterbox format, the opening credits were changed as well as the theme song, and the monster in the Mutant Enemy logo sang its "Grrr, arrgh!" (For more information on the making of this episode, including all of the song lyrics, see Buffy the Vampire Slayer: Musical Scriptbook, "Once More, with Feeling." Also, the complete soundtrack is available.)

DRAMATIS PERSONAE:

Buffy still has not spoken with her sister regarding the incident at Halloween, because the Slayer expected Giles to deal with it entirely.

Giles acknowledges to himself in song why he needs to leave Buffy so she can grow into an adult without leaning on him.

Dawn's kleptomania continues as she steals the necklace Xander used to summon the demon and later covers up the theft by saying she had put it on while cleaning and forgot to take it off.

FROM THE ORIGINAL TELEPLAY:
In a line cut due to length, Sweet's henchman reveals that Buffy is not the only thing the demon wants:

>GILES: "What does he want?"
>HENCHMAN: "Her . . . plus chaos and insanity and people burning up, but that's more big-picture stuff."

Tabula Rasa
Episode 6.8

WRITTEN BY: Rebecca Rand Kirshner
DIRECTED BY: David Grossman
SPECIAL GUEST STAR: Anthony Stewart Head as Rupert Giles
GUEST STAR: Raymond O'Connor as Teeth
CO-STARS: Geordi White as Vamp #1, Stephen Triplett as Vamp #2, David Franco as Vamp #3

THE PLOT THICKENS:
Buffy runs into Spike in one of Sunnydale's many cemeteries. He wants to talk about their kiss, but she would rather just forget about the whole thing. Luckily, a very literal loan shark interferes, searching for a kitty collection from Spike.

The Slayer's friends don't know how to deal with finding out that Buffy was in a heaven dimension and Willow thinks it would be a great idea to make the Slayer simply forget. This doesn't sit well with Tara, who tells her girl that she knows Willow used the same spell on her. Tara thinks they need some time apart, but Willow promises to take a week off from magick. Giles also tells Buffy that it's time for some time apart, as he's going back to England so she can learn to live life on her own.

Willow's promise lasts until the next morning when she works the memory mojo on both Tara and Buffy, but the spell misfires and spreads to all the Scoobies, knocking them unconscious at the Magic Box. One by one the gang awakens with mass amnesia, trying to figure out just who they are. Xander, Willow, Giles, Anya, Tara, and Dawn figure out their names, more or less, but since Buffy doesn't have a name she calls herself

Joan. Spike, dressed incognito in a tweed suit to hide from the loan shark, thinks his name is Randy and believes himself to be Giles's son. Although the others know their names, they don't really know their identities, as Willow and "Alexander" think they're dating and Giles and Anya think they're engaged to one another.

As the gang heads to the hospital for help, a gang of vamps comes looking for Spike. Of course, the clueless ones don't know what the vampires want, nor do they know what to do with the evil creature. They try to hide in the Magic Box while their personalities start to reassert themselves, but not their memories.

Joan takes charge, sending Willow, Alex, Tara, and Dawn down through the tunnels to the hospital while Giles and Anya try to work some magick. Joan and Randy plan to distract the vamps by leading them away from the Magic Box, but the plan shifts when Joan, who thinks she's a superhero, runs from Randy after finding out he's a vamp too.

Things start to look good for the forgotten few as their lives are beginning to take very positive turns. Willow and Tara grow closer and Joan is happy with herself for the first time in a while. But then Willow's spell is broken, and reality floods back into their lives. Tara packs her things and leaves the house and Willow. Giles hops a plane for England again, and Buffy tries to wallow alone in her misery but winds up making out with Spike.

QUOTE OF THE WEEK:
Spike (soon to be Randy) makes a horrifying realization:
"He's got his crust all stiff and upper with that Nancy-boy accent. You Englishmen are all so . . . bloody hell . . . sodding, blimey, shagging, knickers, bullocks . . . oh no. I'm English!"

LOVE IN VEIN:
Tara gives Willow an ultimatum in their relationship, but the powerful witch ignores it and the relationship comes to an end. Buffy first tells Spike that she will never ever touch him again, but fails to hold true to that promise, much to the vampire's relief.

POP-CULTURE IQ:
Spike likens his kiss with Buffy to being of the level of the famous 1939 film based on Margaret Mitchell's book of the same name:
"We kissed, you and me, all *Gone with the Wind* with the rising music and the rising . . . music."
Anya refers to the host of *Candid Camera*, who often put people in strange situations to film their reactions:
". . . and I don't see Alan Funt."

Spike compares Giles to the famous nanny from the similarly titled book and movie:
"Oh, listen to Mary Poppins."
Spike quotes *The Book of Common Prayer*:
"From dust . . . to dust."

CONTINUITY:
"Tabula Rasa" deals with the truths learned in "Once More, with Feeling." Buffy and Spike officially begin their fling that was merely a kiss in the previous episode, Giles makes good on his desire to return to England, and Tara finally reaches her limit with Willow's abuse of magick. Spike owes the loan shark Teeth "forty Siamese" from gambling debts incurred in kitten poker. Spike correctly assumes that Giles has (or had) a "classic midlife crisis transport: something red, shiny, shaped like a penis." There is a trapdoor in the basement to the Magic Box that leads to the sewers and is most likely the way Spike gets in and out of the shop during the day as he did in "Life Serial." Willow unknowingly echoes her line about her double in "Doppelgangland" when she says, "I think I'm kind of gay."

> Tabula rasa *is Latin for "Clean Slate" and is the name of a philosophy introduced by John Locke stating that at birth the human mind is blank and awaiting information gained through life experience.*

DRAMATIS PERSONAE:
Buffy immediately starts looking after Dawn when they lose their identities, even though she doesn't know the youngest victim is her sister. She also takes charge fairly quickly and enjoys being Joan the Vampire Slayer until the weight of her world comes crashing back into her mind.

Willow is taking Buffy's admission of being ripped from Heaven the hardest, blaming her own selfishness. She knows that she messed up and wants to be the one to fix it by using magick. Willow and Tara instinctively reach for each other a couple of times when they don't remember who they are.

Xander continues to be his normal manic self during the amnesia-fest. His relationship with Anya is the one relationship that does not really seem to exert itself through the amnesia.

Anya may forget who she is, but she does not forget her fear of bunnies, or her need to "protect the cash register" during their emergency, or her desire to "take vengeance" on Giles when he upsets her.

Tara compares Willow's actions to Glory violating her mind in the previous season, explaining what she referred to as being "through hell" during her song reprise in "Once More, with Feeling."

Spike unknowingly compares himself to Angel, assuming that he too is a vampire with a soul on a "mission of redemption." It's also a bit of foreshadowing for the journey he takes in the seventh season.

FROM THE ORIGINAL TELEPLAY:
The demon Teeth gets the following intro in the stage directions:

The demon has the head of a shark; smooth, pale flesh split by an unctuous smile. Several rows of teeth glisten. He wears a tight sharkskin suit and stacked heel boots which bring him up to about 5'2". He never stops moving, ever; he's always pacing, always smiling. Smooth and dangerous, somewhere between Christopher Walken, Truman Capote, and, well, a shark.

Normal Again
Episode 6.17

WRITTEN BY: Diego Gutierrez
DIRECTED BY: Rick Rosenthal
GUEST STARS: Danny Strong as Jonathan, Adam Busch as Warren, Tom Lenk as Andrew, Dean Butler as Hank, Michael Warren as Doctor, Kirsten Nelson as Lorraine, Kristine Sutherland as Joyce
CO-STARS: Sarah Scivier as Nurse, Rodney Charles as Orderly, April Dion as Kissing Girl

THE PLOT THICKENS:
With a list of recent Sunnydale rentals in hand, Buffy goes door to door in search of Warren, Jonathan, and Andrew's new lair. The trio sees the Slayer's approach through their video surveillance system and summons a demon to defend their home. The demon attacks and sticks the Slayer with a long needle protruding from its hand. Moments later, Buffy is in a mental hospital being strapped down.

As Willow sees Tara at school with another girl, Buffy sleepwalks her way through work, glimpsing flashes of herself in the mental ward. Buffy eventually gets home and comforts Willow over what may or may not have been a misunderstood Tara sighting. In the midst of their general gabber, Xander returns from his post-wedding fleeing, in search of the now missing Anya.

That night the gang of three goes on patrol, where they run into Spike. A fight between the boys takes place, but it's stopped when they see Buffy doubled over in another flash. This time she isn't alone in the hospital. She's with her mom and dad.

Buffy tells Xander, Willow, and Dawn about her mind trips. She is going into an alternate reality in which she was in a hospital for the past six years and never came to Sunnydale. In her dream world, vampires, demons, her friends, and Dawn don't really exist. In the real world, the gang swings into research mode to figure out what the demon with the long needle did to her.

Willow finds out about the demon with the name as long as its needle: Glarghk Guhl Kashma'nik. The stinger also carries an antidote, so Xander and Spike reluctantly team up to bring the demon home for some experiments and chain it up in the basement. In the meantime, Buffy's fictional world starts to take on more and more of a pleasant outlook and she doesn't take her friends' antidote. Then the doctor in her mind instructs her that the only way to be free for good is to break down the safeholds in her reality, namely her friends.

In a daze Buffy rounds up Willow, Xander, and Dawn and ties them up in the basement. Then she lets loose the demon to rid her of her ties to this reality. Xander manages to break free of his binds, but he's no match for the demon. In the midst of the battle, Tara comes looking for Willow and uses magick to free her and Dawn, but they still cannot overwhelm the demon.

Back in the altered state, Joyce gives her daughter words of encouragement hoping that it will free her mind. The talk helps, but not in the way Joyce had hoped. The real side of Buffy asserts herself and she comes to her friends' defense, killing the demon. Buffy apologizes to her friends and asks for another batch of antidote. Until then, she flashes back one more time to the mental hospital where the doctor announces that they've lost her.

QUOTE OF THE WEEK:
  JONATHAN: "We rented the whole house. Can't we at least sleep upstairs?"
  ANDREW: "We're on the lam. We have to lay low. Underground."
  JONATHAN: "That's figurative, doofus."

LOVE IN VEIN:
When Xander returns, he finds that Anya's suitcase is gone and the Magic Box is closed, which chills him to the bone. Apparently she left a couple of days ago but didn't tell Willow or Buffy where she was going. Anya had spent most of her time crying since the canceled wedding. Xander reveals that he still loves Anya, but it was the concept of marriage that overwhelmed him. Willow sees Tara kiss another girl, but can't be sure if it's just a friendly smooch or something more. Spike tells Buffy that he knows she's addicted to the misery because otherwise she would tell her friends about having been with Spike so, one way or another, she would have to deal with it publicly rather than suffer privately.

POP-CULTURE IQ:
The doctor unintentionally makes an allusion to the 1998 film *Gods and Monsters*:
  "Not gods or monsters."
Spike is narrating his and Xander's hunt by recapping recent events, much like sports announcers do when hosting a game:
  "Spike, we need muscle here, not color commentary."
Willow references the book turned movie *One Flew Over the Cuckoo's Nest* in comparison to Buffy's mental ward mental state:
  "No more cuckoo's nest?"

CONTINUITY:
In the real world, it's been "weeks" since Jonathan and the guys were forced to move out of their former underground lair following "Dead Things." In the fantasy world, Buffy's doctor explains that in her schizophrenia she believes herself to be some type of hero and has created an "intricate latticework to support her primary delusion." She has made herself the central character in a fantastic world and surrounded herself with friends, many of whom have their own supernatural powers. "Together they face grand, overblown conflicts against an assortment of monsters, both imaginary and rooted in actual myth." Buffy later inserted Dawn into her delusion, "actually rewriting the entire history of it to accommodate her need for a familial bond." Of course, the doctor notes, that action created inconsistencies in her world. Previously she used to create "grand villains to battle against," but the doctor takes it as a sign that she's ready to give up the fantasy because her latest evil is "just three pathetic little men who like to play with toys." The doctor also mentions that she had a momentary reawakening last summer, but her friends pulled her back in.

DRAMATIS PERSONAE:
Buffy likes to have a little ice put on the back of her neck, according to Spike. She admits to Willow that back when she saw her first vampires she got so scared that she freaked out and told her parents. They thought there was something wrong with their daughter so they sent her to a clinic for a couple of weeks. Buffy stopped talking about the vampires and was released. Eventually her parents just forgot.

Dawn tries to cover up the fact that Willow's been doing her chores when Buffy calls her on it.

Jonathan is growing more and more paranoid over Warren and Andrew's duolike attitude.

FROM THE ORIGINAL TELEPLAY:
The episode ends with the following haunting stage directions, leaving one to wonder whether it was all a dream:

The camera pulls back slowly, down the hall. Leaving the doctor and Buffy's parents helpless, and Buffy lost in a distant delusion.

Villains
Episode 6.20

WRITTEN BY: Marti Noxon
DIRECTED BY: David Solomon
GUEST STARS: Danny Strong as Jonathan, Adam Busch as Warren, Tom Lenk as Andrew, Jeff Kober as Rack, Amelinda Embry as Katrina
CO-STARS: James C. Leary as Clem, Steven W. Bailey as Cave Demon, Tim Hodgin as Coroner, Michael Matthys as Paramedic, Julie Hermelin as Clerk, Alan Henry Brown as Demon Bartender, Mueen J. Ahmad as Doctor, Jane Cho as Nurse #1, Meredith Cross as Nurse #2, David Adefeso as Paramedic #2, Jeffrey Nicholas Brown as Vampire, Nelson Frederick as Villager

THE PLOT THICKENS:
Following a shocking conclusion to the previous episode, this one opens with the paramedics arriving at Buffy's house. Xander rushes them to Buffy in the backyard to treat her bullet wound, totally unaware that Tara was also shot inside the house. Willow's cries for Tara to live go unheard, so she calls on the powers of Osiris to bring back her love. There is a reply in the form of an imposing demon that tells Willow she cannot undo a death by mortal hands, as opposed to her reincarnation of Buffy. Unwilling to believe that, she destroys the powerful entity and goes in search of more power and revenge.

Warren couldn't care less that his former partners are currently in jail as he goes to a demon bar to celebrate the death of the Slayer. There he learns that he's getting his party on a little too soon, because the news has shown that the report of her death has been slightly exaggerated.

Willow stops by the Magic Box and Anya is powerless to stop her as the witch drains all the books on dark magicks and her hair turns as black as her eyes. Willow then goes to the hospital to remove the bullet from her friend and get the Slayer back on her feet.

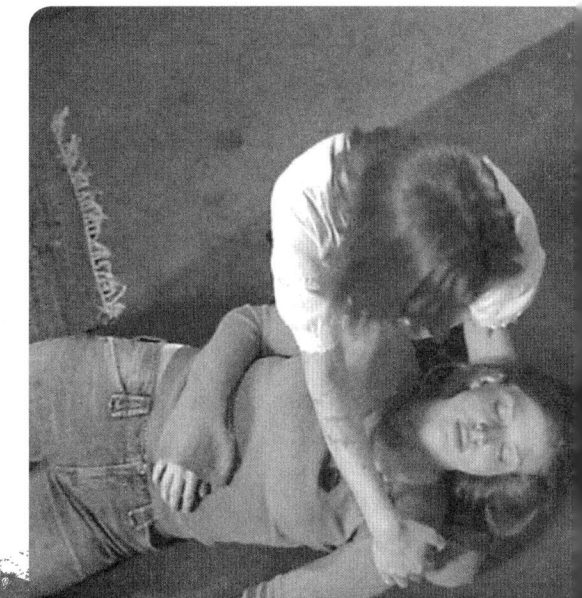

At the den of the magick dealer, Warren learns that he has made a powerful enemy in Willow. He pays Rack for some magickal aid and flees town on a bus. Willow traces his essence and takes her increasingly concerned friends out to the desert to stop him, but it turns out it was a robot mixed with magick that had led her astray. Thinking Willow is distraught over the shooting of Buffy, Xander and Buffy take the moment to try to calm Willow, who finally tells them that Tara is dead.

After Willow disappears, Buffy and Xander return home to find Dawn watching over Tara's body. Buffy tries to calm her sister, who would also like to see Warren dead. Xander, having presided over the removal of Tara's body by the authorities, notes that he's had the blood of his friends on his hands all day. His concern for Warren's well-being is waning too. The Slayer explains why they can't kill a human and then goes to take Dawn to Spike, but has to leave her with Clem since the vampire has surprisingly left town for parts unknown.

Those unknown parts turn out to be halfway around the world as Spike arrives in an African village in search of a cave-dwelling demon with the request to restore him to the way that he was. The demon chides Spike for letting the Slayer get to him in such a way, but agrees to help so long as the vampire passes a series of tests.

Buffy and Xander meet up with Anya at the Magic Box, where the proprietress informs them of Willow's dark magick act and the fact that she too has returned to her demon ways. As such, Anya is able to track Willow into the woods, where the powerful witch has finally chased down Warren.

The murderer uses a combination of magick and technology to keep Willow at bay, but it ultimately proves useless as she catches up with him by binding his arms and legs in roots and branches. Willow conjures up Warren's ex-girlfriend to haunt him and then takes the bullet she removed from Buffy's body and has it slowly burrow into his chest. Buffy, Xander, and Anya arrive just in time to watch the torture end as Willow skins Warren alive. As his body bursts into flames, Willow turns to her friends and hauntingly says, "One down."

QUOTE OF THE WEEK:
Xander turns to humor in the face of tragedy:
"You've got to stop doing this. This dying thing is funny once, maybe twice . . ."

LOVE IN VEIN:
Willow's motivated solely by seeking revenge on Tara's death. Buffy is surprised to learn that Spike has left and asks if Clem knows when he'll be back. Xander is quietly devastated to learn that Anya has reverted to her old ways, and because of him.

POP-CULTURE IQ:
Xander likens Willow's magical overpowering of his car to the 1989 horror movie (he'll have a spiffy new adultlike car in season seven):
"Fine! Fine! Puppet Master wants to drive? Go right ahead!"

CONTINUITY:
The episode picks up minutes after "Seeing Red" left off. The demon that speaks to Willow in the opening clarifies that when she resurrected Buffy she raised "one killed by mystical forces," however, Tara was taken by natural order by human means. Andrew lamely suggests that he and Warren weren't going to just jet away and leave Jonathan behind after their failed armored car heist—Andrew was going to carry him. Warren goes into the same demon bar in which Spike played kitten poker back in "Life Serial." Rack's back—he and his magickal dealer's pad were introduced in "Wrecked." Warren is shocked to hear that no one in the demon community has heard of him or "the Trio," or his robots and freeze ray. Right before Willow kills Warren, she echoes the signature phrase of her evil doppelganger, Vampire Willow, by saying, "Bored now" ("The Wish" and "Doppelgangland").

> Clem mentions that he's been dying to see The Wedding Planner. It's the appropriate choice, considering that the film was directed by Adam Shankman, the choreographer for "Once More, with Feeling."

DRAMATIS PERSONAE:
Buffy explains to Dawn and Xander that she can't kill Warren because he's human and the human world has its own rules for dealing with people like that. Although sometimes those rules don't work, she and her friends can't control the universe. If they could, the magick wouldn't change Willow the way it does and they'd be able to bring Tara and their mom back.

Willow is called "the new power" by Rack, who also says, "anyone with intuition can feel it. She's going to blow this town apart." She has the ability to sense Warren's essence. When Xander reminds her that the magick's too strong and "there's no coming back from it," Willow informs him that she's not coming back.

Anya, being a demon again, can sense that something terrible has happened to Tara. Normally she would have to go to Willow to help her exact vengeance, but Willow wants to do it on her own.

FROM THE ORIGINAL TELEPLAY:
The African villager warns Spike off with the following words translated into English:
  "You can't go in there, it's very dangerous. . . . Stop! You'll die! Stop!"

Grave
Episode 6.22

WRITTEN BY: David Fury
DIRECTED BY: James A. Contner
SPECIAL GUEST STAR: Anthony Stewart Head as Rupert Giles
GUEST STARS: Danny Strong as Jonathan, Tom Lenk as Andrew
CO-STARS: Steven W. Bailey as Cave Demon, Brett Wagner as Trucker

THE PLOT THICKENS:
Giles keeps Willow at bay with magick borrowed from a very powerful coven in Devon. The coven alerted him to the problems in Sunnydale and he teleported there immediately to help. Giles and Buffy reunite, but Willow uses her mind to control Anya, and the demon releases the witch from her magickal binding.

Xander tries to lead Dawn, Jonathan, and Andrew to safety, but his lack of leadership skills exerts itself. Dawn contrasts his inaction with Spike's ability to act, which causes Xander to slip about the attempted rape. In the meantime, Spike continues to undergo his torturous tasks to get what he needs to make him into his former self.

The magick battle between Willow and Giles rages on, tearing apart the Magic Box. Willow ups the ante by sending a fireball to attack Jonathan and Andrew and whomever they may be with. Buffy is forced to leave Giles's side to save Dawn, Xander, and the others. The battle weakens Willow, and really takes its toll on Giles, but there's still enough for Willow to siphon an incredible amount of magick from him to recharge her powers.

Buffy beats the fireball to the cemetery and pushes Jonathan and Andrew out of the way as it hits. The impact sends Xander headfirst into a headstone and causes the earth to open and swallow Dawn and Buffy. Knowing an opportunity when they see one, Jonathan and Andrew hightail it for Mexico.

With Giles's borrowed power, Willow has access to more power than any mortal ever before. It gives her a direct link to all of humanity and she really feels their pain. Her new mission is to end that pain by ending the world, and she blows out of the Magic Box to do so.

Giles can see through Willow's eyes and tells Anya the witch's evil plan. The demon teleports into the deep hole that Buffy and Dawn are in to share the news while the revived Xander listens from above. Willow has gone to Kingman's Bluff to exhume the buried temple of the she-demon Prosperexa to bring about the end of the world. Giles has said that no magickal or supernatural force—including the Slayer—can stop her. Anya then returns to Giles, because his own future does not look promising either.

Buffy calls for Xander to send down a rope, but he doesn't reply. Willow senses that the Slayer will not give up and sends some demons made of the earth to Buffy to ensure that the Slayer dies in battle. With too many demons to handle, Buffy finally realizes that she can no longer shelter her sister from the world and the duo fights side by side to stay alive.

Willow directs her power at the effigy atop the temple to set about the end of the world, but Xander interrupts with his usual brand of humor. He tells her that he's not going to stop her, but if she's going to end the world then he, as her best friend since childhood, deserves to be the first to go. As the pure magick Giles hoped she would drain from him starts to affect her, the real Willow begins to resurface. Xander insists that he loves her no matter what and his words are enough to break down the dark magick and return her hair, eyes, and self to normal.

In the end Giles recovers under Anya's watchful eyes, Buffy and Dawn climb out of their "grave" to see the world together, and Xander and Willow begin the healing process. Meanwhile, Spike completes his tasks and gets a reward, though it's not the one he had expected: the demon restores Spike's soul.

QUOTE OF THE WEEK:
XANDER: "The first day of kindergarten you cried because you broke the yellow crayon and you were too afraid to tell anyone. You've come pretty far, ending the world, *not a terrific notion*, but the thing is, yeah. I love you. I loved crayon-breaking Willow and I love scary veiny Willow. So if I'm going out, it's here. If you wanna kill the world, well then, start with me. I've earned that."
WILLOW: "You think I won't."
XANDER: "It doesn't matter. I'll still love you."

> This episode was originally shown on UPN with "Two to Go" as the series's two-hour season finale.

LOVE IN VEIN:
In the end, it's Xander's love for his best friend that saves the world, finally making him the hero.

POP-CULTURE IQ:
Willow references the movie *Alice Doesn't Live Here Anymore*:
"Willow doesn't live here anymore."

Willow echoes the wicked witch from *The Wizard of Oz*:
> "Fly, my pretty. Fly."

Anya quotes cartoon mouse Speedy Gonzales:
> "Holy Frijole!"

Xander alludes to the Van Morrison song "Brown-Eyed Girl":
> "Hey, black-eyed girl."

Xander suggests an end befitting many Looney Tunes characters, most notably Wile E. Coyote:
> "Well, I was going to walk you off a cliff and hand you an anvil, but it seemed kind of cartoony."

CONTINUITY:
Willow refers to the fight she and Giles had in "All the Way," in which he called her a "rank arrogant amateur." Giles notices that Buffy cut her hair and that Anya has colored her hair and is now blond. Giles informs Buffy that the Council doesn't have a clue about what's going on, or "much of anything really." Buffy updates Giles on all that he's missed, including Willow's abuse of magick, Dawn being a total klepto, Xander leaving Anya at the altar, and Anya becoming a demon again. She also admits that she's working at the Doublemeat Palace and sleeping with Spike, and there was a period of time she thought the real world was a dream and she lived in an insane asylum. After spending two years trying to protect Dawn by shielding her from the world, Buffy realizes the better way is to show her the world.

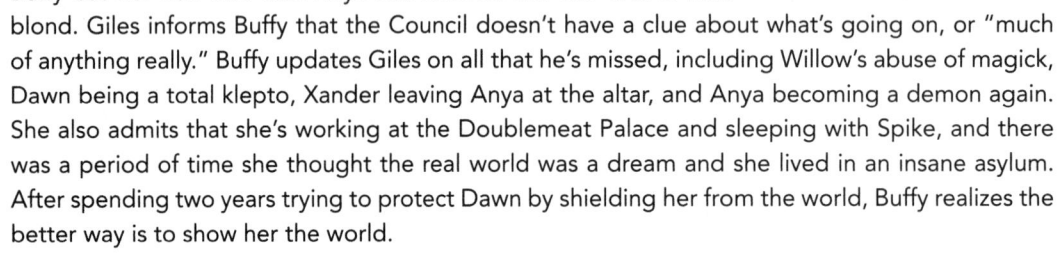

DRAMATIS PERSONAE:
Giles was contacted by a powerful coven in Devon that sensed a dangerous magickal force in Sunnydale that was fueled by grief. A seer in the coven told him about Tara. They then imbued him with their powers.

Anya says that mind control mojo doesn't work on vengeance demons, but Willow's extreme power proves her wrong.

Dawn insists that her sister can't really protect her from everything, especially the fact that people she loves keep dying.

> **ANDREW WHO?**
> Willow: "You probably think you're buying escape time for Jonathan and the other one."

FROM THE ORIGINAL TELEPLAY:
Giles describes the true essence of magick in a line cut due to length:
> "Which comes, in all its purity, from the Earth itself."

TOM LENK (ANDREW WELLS)

You've had all sorts of roles since you last appeared on *Buffy the Vampire Slayer*, from appearances in *Cabin in the Woods* and *Much Ado About Nothing* to a recurring role on *Witches of East End* and guest spots on series like *Transparent*, *Episodes*, and *How I Met Your Mother*. Which of those other roles would you hope *Buffy* fans would track down and watch, if they haven't seen it?

TOM: "It would have to be my role as Alex Moore in *Buyer and Cellar*, which is a one-man play that I have performed at regional theaters, so you can't actually track it down. Sad panda! It's a fictional piece inspired by Barbra Streisand's book, *My Passion for Design*, and the single actor plays all the various characters, including Babs herself. It's a nonstop, one hour and forty-five minute tour de force, no intermission, and it was the most fun and most challenging thing I have ever done. My favorite moment was crying tears out of my right eye as Barbra, and then immediately flip-flopping to the dry side of my face as the lead character, Alex. *So much fun!* Just reading Jonathan Tolins's wonderful play will make you *howl* out loud to yourself, so check it out!"

You have a theater background, including the role of Franz in the Broadway production of *Rock of Ages* and many others. You also do live comedy at Groundlings, Upright Citizens Brigade, and more, and your website is loaded with your comedy videos. What's your first love, or are they all a part of the same love for performance?

TOM: "I grew up doing community theater, and it's definitely where I fell in love with performing. The wonderful thing about film/TV is that it's about capturing a special moment on film to be shared over and over with people, and live performance is all about that special moment between you and the audience that can never be captured again. (Wow, am I a poet now? Hashtag blessed.) Both are satisfying in different ways, and I feel lucky to get to do both all the time."

Looking back, do you have a particular memory that stands out about auditioning for the role of Andrew?

TOM: "I remember practicing the lines in my car and [feeling like] I knew exactly what to do . . . yet at the same time I had *no idea* how I was going to do it. That probably makes no sense, but I think it was something that took me a while to rediscover again, years later—the art of auditioning, which is to go into an audition room trusting that you get to perform for someone . . . do a mini play just for them . . . and you've learned the words as best you can, but you have no idea how you're going to say it. Because in real life, people don't plan how they are going to say things, right? So I guess it's all about giving yourself permission to just let it happen, and if it's terrible, it's terrible. 'Overpreparing kills the magic,' right? What I remember most about that audition was that I had worked on it just enough and I was able to trust that I could surprise myself in the room with something I hadn't planned."

Did you have any idea after that first episode that Andrew would be back, or that he'd become a Big Bad?

TOM: "I got signed on to do ten episodes with Danny Strong and Adam Busch for that season, and everything after that was a sweet surprise!"

How often do you get recognized in public? Do you enjoy it, or do you want to hide?

TOM: "Frequently enough to inflate my ego ever so slightly, and not frequently enough to deflate it about the same amount? It's fun when people let you know that you made them laugh or they enjoyed your performance! Sometimes people aren't sure where they recognize me [from], so I give them the option of 'same high school [or] same gym'? And then I go to: 'I'm an actor, so you may have seen me in something,' but I do have a policy against listing my credits until you hear something you recognize, because that's what googling me after I walk away is for. Technology!"

Andrew has played a big role in Joss's official comic-book continuation. Have you read those stories, and, if so, what did you think?

TOM: "I checked out the first few. It was cool to see myself in comic-book form! I feel like they really captured my nose!"

Everyone says that working on a long-running TV series is a lot like high school, with circles of friends and then those people you wish you'd hung out with more. Who do you wish you'd hung out with more?

TOM: "It was more like middle school for me, as I was only there two years and I spent most of my time anxiously trying to get everyone to like me and praying that no one would ever toss the football to me. And by 'football' I mean large bottle of fake blood. That stuff is so sticky, you *don't* want to touch it. Looking back, I wish I had spent less time worrying if I was going to get killed off and spent more time appreciating every moment of being on such a historic TV show!"

What are you working on now, and what does the future hold for Tom Lenk?

TOM: "Well, now that I'm an 'influencer' in the world of FASHUN/COMEDY/CRAFTING via Instagram and the #LenkLewkForLess, I spend my days running my EMPYRE. The *Lenk Lewk* TV show is now in development and hopefully by the time this book is printed it's on your basic cable channel. Pray for me."

ADAM BUSCH (WARREN MEARS)

You've had all sorts of roles since you last appeared on *Buffy*, from *Point Pleasant* to *Men at Work*, and numerous guest spots. And, of course, you started your career with a role in *Léon: The Professional* and then as Noah in the landmark Nickelodeon series *The Mystery Files of Shelby Woo*. Not including your role as Warren on *Buffy*, what has been your favorite role? And which role would you hope *Buffy* fans would track down and watch, if they haven't seen it?

ADAM: "I've made a number of films with Stephen Elliott. He's one of my favorite authors and has become a very interesting filmmaker. When James Franco turned [Stephen's] novel *The Adderall Diaries* into a film, Stephen made his own film about that experience, very much like Bukowski's *Hollywood*. Authors who have had their novels turned into films appear in the film as themselves—Jerry Stahl, Susan Orlean . . . Denis Johnson didn't want to appear on camera but gave [Elliott] the rights to his poems and journals, so I got to play him. I like films that shed a light on things and don't pussyfoot around. Amber [Benson] and I made a film called *Drones*, and it was our lumpy love letter to the *Buffy* fandom and fan culture. We both grew up as fans of television, music, and politics, and can successfully see it from all angles. We tried to put that into *Drones*, and I would steer any *Buffy* fan with interest in that direction."

You've got a film coming up called *Rebel in the Rye*, about author J. D. Salinger. The film is written and directed by Danny Strong. How was it working with your old friend in his first turn as director?

ADAM: "My relationship with Danny Strong and Tom Lenk is something I'm grateful for and unnecessarily protective of. It's important to me. Their opinions have always held so much weight with me. They're both brilliant examples of a thing that Felicia Day said best: 'If you're honest about what makes you happy and work harder than anyone else at it, people will recognize that, they'll relate, and they'll find you.' They're so different and so talented. Working on Danny's projects is the most fun I've ever had as an actor, and they are the performances I'm most proud of. He truly brings out the best in me. How he sees me, how I appear in his eyes, is something I will continue to strive to match. He can just give me a look and I know what he wants. His capacity for understanding human behavior and the conviction of his perspective know no bounds. He continues to reflect back at us honest emotion and real struggle in everything he creates. I would follow Danny Strong anywhere. I would race him to the bottom."

Looking back now, what stands out to you about the process of being cast as Warren—about the audition or your first look at the script, or both?

ADAM: "Two things. I remember reading Warren for Joss and noticing peripherally that after I'd said a line or two he started nodding his head frantically up and down. I knew he had made up his mind and the rest of this reading was out of politeness. What I didn't know was whether it was good or bad. In those moments, anything is possible.

"Later, as Warren and the trio continued to make the transition from joke to threat, I couldn't tell if I was changing to suit the writers or if the writers were actively changing me as a person. That I could, when necessary, view any human monster as yet another victim of abandonment and fear. They were asking me to at the very least compartmentalize an unforgivable perspective long enough to focus on the struggle of anyone who feels they are not understood, not heard. Who feels they are acknowledged only when they are told to go away and to hush up. Danny and Tom understand that. It's another reason I'm such fans of them and of Joss. It's rare. We need more of it all over."

Did you have any idea after that first episode that Warren would be back, or that he'd come to play a pivotal role in the series?

ADAM: "I never knew until it happened. And sometimes afterward. That's partially on me because I was young and not interested in anything but the truth and Joss's perspective."

How often do you get recognized in public, and when you do get recognized, is it from *Buffy*, from *Men at Work*, from *Colony*? Do you enjoy it, or do you want to hide?

ADAM: "I can always tell what I'm being recognized from by the way the person's face falls once they remember. It's a unique experience that I don't know if many people can relate to. It's not only that they're immediately angry and disgusted at seeing this face they associate with the worst humanity has to offer, it's how comfortable and at ease they are expressing it to me. As if they alone are internalizing this experience. As if it was fair. I do wish I was better at it. I'm constantly searching for something to say or do to make it easier for the person. For both of us. I imagine it's the same for Amanda Knox. She could relate. We would have a lot to talk about."

So much time has passed. What are your favorite behind-the-scenes memories of your time on the show?

ADAM: "We shot for a bit on 9/11. I was flying back from New York City that morning and went right to the set. We only got through one angle of one scene before the news got around and we shut down. It was a bit where Warren plants something on Tara's sweater at school. It's the only time Amber and I appear on-screen together. 9/11."

Everyone says that working on a long-running TV series is a lot like high school, with circles of friends and then those people you wish you'd hung out with more. Who do you wish you'd hung out with more?

ADAM: "I always admired Tony Head, and it wasn't until he started making records again that we ever connected. Still, it wasn't until this year that I had a chance to spend a few days with him in England, and it just exceeded all expectations. I had recently rescued a pit bull, the first pet I've ever had. My folks never had any animals growing up, and I had no relationship with them to speak of. It was all I wanted to talk about. It turns out he and his wife are these intense and vocal animal advocates, and we just ranted for days about everything from Cesar Millan, Lee Strasberg, Proust, Chekov, *Little Britain*, and how it all relates to dogs. I could live there like that forever."

Throughout your life, you've also been a musician—writing songs, performing, and touring for years as a part of the band Common Rotation. Do you still pursue music?

ADAM: "I continue to produce records and work with Dan Bern and The Best Fest. Recently I've been fronting a rock-and-roll outfit, and honestly it's the most fun I've ever had in music. Coming from this folk world primarily, it's surprisingly liberating. It wasn't until I stopped listening to what friends said that I found my voice. Making money from music feels illegal, but I've got this new thing I've been trying out. When people offer me money, I take it."

Overall, how would you characterize the influence of your time on *Buffy* on your life?

ADAM: "It's the source of the most important relationships in my life."

What are you working on now, and what does the future hold for Adam Busch?

ADAM: "Grandpa vs. Prowler is hitting the road with Dead Sara. We'll be everywhere from New York City to Texas. I'll be touring the Midwest with Dan Bern after that. I place songs in TV and film and have had a lot of fun with that. I continue to work on *Colony* for USA. I've been the head of documentary programming for Slamdance for a number of years now, and there are few greater feelings in the world than telling a first-time filmmaker that yes, they have in fact made something. I like spending time with my dog. She's the best I have to offer."

DANNY STRONG (JONATHAN LEVENSON)

When you search "Danny Strong" on IMDb, the first thing that comes up is "Danny Strong—Writer." I suspect that seems normal now, but is that something you foresaw twenty years ago, when you made your first appearance on *Buffy*?

DANNY: "No, when I started doing *Buffy*, I hadn't started writing yet. It wasn't even on my radar as something that would eventually become my career. I took a number of writing courses in college, as I was interested in it, but when I graduated, I was solely focused on my acting career for several years."

You're the co-creator of the Fox TV hit *Empire*, and you've written, directed, and produced in TV and feature films some of the most successful films of the past few years, including writing the two-part *The Hunger Games: Mockingjay*. Your first writing credits include two major successes for HBO, *Recount* and *Game Change*, as well as *The Butler*, directed by your *Empire* co-creator Lee Daniels. So how does a working actor in Los Angeles go from *Buffy* and *Gilmore Girls* to writing major projects for HBO? Am I wrong in thinking producers tend to be dubious about actors who want to be screenwriters?

DANNY: "The good thing about writing is all that matters is what's on the page. Once someone starts reading a script, they don't care whose name is on it, they just hope it can hold their interest. Also, people in the development world know that actors have the potential to be very good writers if they have the skills for it. Who better to write a document for actors than an actor? So I never encountered any reluctance from people about being a writer because I was an actor. The script would either be good or not, and it didn't matter what else I had done with my life."

Despite your success as a writer, producer, and now director as well, you've continued to act in various series in recurring and guest parts, as in *Justified*, *Girls*, and *Mad Men*. Will you always continue to act, no matter how successful you become in your other jobs?

DANNY: "I love acting, and I do it from time to time when cool parts in cool projects come my way. I spent fifteen years pounding the pavement really hard trying to get any acting job I could possibly land so that I'd be able to pay my rent and qualify for health insurance, so it's really nice now to only act in projects that I want to be a part of. I have no plans to stop acting, but at the same time I'm not actively seeking acting work, as my own projects are my main focus. When neat stuff comes my way, I usually do it if I dig it."

We're a little *Gilmore Girls* obsessed in our house, and we were all so happy to see you appear in the revival. What was it like to step back into that show as if it had never stopped, and would you take part if there was ever a similar return for *Buffy*?

DANNY: "I loved being a part of the *Gilmore Girls* revival. I'm so proud to have been a character in that wonderful world and ensemble. It was a blast going back, particularly working with Liza [Weil], who I think is one of the coolest people I know. Alexis [Bledel] is such a lovely soul too, and so it was great to see them both again. Also, I'm a huge fan of Amy Sherman-Palladino and Dan Palladino; I'd go anywhere they ask me. As for a *Buffy* revival, just tell me when and where, and I'll bring the magic bone and jet pack!"

Your early acting career was full of recurring and guest roles on shows like *Saved by the Bell*, *Seinfeld*, *Clueless*, and *Boy Meets World*, as well as the film *Pleasantville*. When Jonathan first shows up in *Buffy*, he was another one of those parts, but in time he became a part of the world and story of the show that fans counted on to be there. To what do you attribute that evolution, and do you remember when you recognized that the character had become a real part of the fabric of the show?

DANNY: "The only thing I know is that Joss liked my work and enjoyed having the character on the show. I think he dug that I was the perennial victim. I also heard David Greenwalt was a fan too, so those are pretty great advocates to have in your corner. The first time I realized that the character was a real part of the fabric of the show was at the first Posting Board Party. I showed up not knowing if anyone would even recognize me, and then I was mobbed with people telling me Jonathan had a big following online. I was stunned and blown away. It was the first time I ever had so many people tell me they liked my work. It meant a lot to me, and I went home beaming."

Of all the roles you've played that *Buffy* fans may not be familiar with, which role would you hope they would track down and watch?

DANNY: "Great question! I have no idea! I've been fortunate enough to have worked on many great TV shows, and they've all been really fun characters for me to play, so I'm not really partial to any of them. There are a few I'd tell people to avoid, but I don't have a particular favorite."

You've recently written and directed *Rebel in the Rye*, a film about the life of J. D. Salinger, the reclusive author of *The Catcher in the Rye*. It's the first feature film you've directed, and it is having its world premiere at the Sundance Film Festival. How was that experience?

DANNY: "It was a wonderful experience and really challenging. The shoot was only twenty-six days, which is very short for a film of this size and ambition, so it was quite a hustle getting it done. I loved finally being in charge of a company. I feel like I've been vice president for ten years, so it was great to get to sit in the Oval Office."

Looking back now, what stands out to you about the process of being cast as Jonathan—about the audition or your first look at the script, or both?

DANNY: "I remember the audition like it was yesterday. I was auditioning for multiple one-line parts in the original pilot presentation for Joss, and I remember on one of the parts I made him laugh. I love getting a laugh (I was a stage actor for years), so the fact that I cracked him up with my one line felt great. He gave me one of those nods that said, "You nailed it." I remember reading the script thinking it was really cool and hip, but I had no idea I was reading the birth of TV history."

So much time has passed. What are your favorite behind-the-scenes memories of your time on the show?

DANNY: "I loved working with Adam Busch and Tom Lenk. So many of our scenes were with each other, so for a season we were constantly working together. They are both hilarious and such great guys. I also distinctly remember Charisma Carpenter spanking me as I walked by her. I told her to do it again, and her eyes lit up and she whacked my ass really hard. That wasn't just a *Buffy* highlight, but perhaps a top-five life highlight."

Everyone says that working on a long-running TV series is a lot like high school, with circles of friends and then those people you wish you'd hung out with more. Who do you wish you'd hung out with more?

DANNY: "Charisma Carpenter (see previous answer)."

What are you working on now, and what does the future hold for Danny Strong?

DANNY: "Right now I'm finishing *Rebel in the Rye*, writing a new pilot for Fox, working on multiple stage pieces, and I have a great recurring role on a Showtime show for next season [*Billions*]. My hope is to continue writing, directing, acting, and producing in film, TV, and theater."

DREW Z. GREENBERG (WRITER)

Putting you on the spot now. You're co-executive producer and a writer on *Agents of S.H.I.E.L.D.*, and before that you filled those same roles on *Arrow*. But when you were growing up . . . were you a Marvel kid or a DC kid?

DREW: "When I was growing up, I was a *Love Boat* kid. (Seriously, I wasn't a comic-book reader as a kid. I loved, loved, *loved* Saturday morning cartoons, so I got a healthy dose of the Super Friends and the Batman/Tarzan Adventure Hour, but that's about as close as it came for me. But that means I get to be neutral in that particular battle.)"

There's an element of "chosen family" that burns brightly in both *Arrow* and *Agents of S.H.I.E.L.D.*, and *Buffy* really raised the bar for that sort of character structure. How much of an influence do you think it has been on TV in general, and specifically on those two shows?

DREW: "I feel that *Buffy* was the next level up in terms of 'chosen family' stories, a tradition that had previously been redefined by 1970s workplace comedies. *Barney Miller*, *Mary Tyler Moore*, *M*A*S*H*, and their ilk—all those shows about oddballs finding their family on the job, something that had been much rarer in the previous era of warm and idealistic family sitcoms and single-character, square-jawed dramatic heroes. So I feel like *Buffy* was the inheritor of that genre, only Joss's genius move was making high school the workplace—Buffy and her friends had a job to do, and that job left them rather isolated with only each other to understand what they were going through . . . just like being a cop, a news producer, or a medic in the Korean War. By opening it up to teenagers, it allowed those workplace stories to be filled with the kind of pure, unfiltered emotion that high school students experience before the world teaches them to swallow all their feelings (in my case, with lots and lots of pizza and french fries, but we're all different). But because the kids forming this family had a huge job, the show took them seriously, even with their heartache, their angst, their insecurity. That family they formed was saving the world. And in that way, *Buffy* raised the bar for other genre shows to explore themes of what it means to be a chosen family even in the face of impending, apocalyptic doom—genuine emotion paired with genuine scares and thrills had a lot more precedent because of the world Joss created."

Most *Buffy* writers had at least a handful of produced episodes, if not runs on other series, before being hired onto the show. You'd had a single episode of *Queer as Folk* produced. Aside from obvious writing chops, I'm sure a lot of up-and-coming TV writers would like to know, what do you think inspired such confidence?

DREW: "It didn't feel like confidence at the time, I can tell you that. I was scared out of my mind. But one of the things I had going for me was that I'd taken three years to get my law degree first. So I always knew that once writing didn't work out, I could return home and start practicing law. (Something which, at the time, my mother reminded me. She has since come around.) A lot of people will tell you that if you really want to write, you can't fathom doing anything else. And for them, that reasoning makes sense. For me, knowing my world wouldn't end if I failed at writing allowed me to go all-out gonzo with it, and I'm sure it was that sense of security that helped me find some measure of success. (That and a really good pilot script—if I may say so myself.)"

Do you remember what it was like getting hired for the first time? How did that come about?

DREW: "Oh, I remember getting the call about *Buffy* very, very well. It still ranks as a watershed moment for me. My pilot spec had been making the rounds and was getting me some great meetings that season, including a meeting at Mutant Enemy, which led to my meeting with Joss and Marti Noxon. Everyone had assured me so many times that *Buffy* wasn't looking for any new writers that year, so I was still thinking of sitting down with Joss and Marti as a friendly general meeting even while I was walking into their offices. Getting the call that they'd made an offer was life changing. I called my parents, and I don't think they totally knew what a *Buffy* was, but they still seemed happy for me."

What is your favorite of the *Buffy* episodes you wrote, and why?

DREW: "I was partial to 'Smashed,' since it was my first *Buffy* episode and featured awesome plot developments I'd been waiting to see as a fan. And I was pretty fond of 'The Killer in Me,' because I liked the story and because it was the first chance I had to articulate what I liked about being gay—something that was not very commonly heard on TV up till that point. (And Joss and Marti heartily encouraged me in putting that discussion into the episode, and I always liked that too.)"

You've worked on a lot of other fantastic series. What single episode of one of those other series would you love the *Buffy* fans to hunt down and watch, and why?

DREW: "I always felt that *Warehouse 13* had a lot of *Buffy*'s DNA in it—we did humor, drama, whiz-bang sci-fi, horror, genuine emotion . . . oftentimes all in the same episode. I liked bringing some of that *Buffy* sensibility to an episode I wrote called 'For the Team,' in which two of our agents, Myka and Claudia, are forced to work with supposed bad guy Helena G. Wells (yes, H. G. Wells was a woman, long and delightful story), and all of our women got to be strong and smart and funny and they fought each other, then they saved each other, and I loved it. And who picks just one? Besides, I just assume all the real *Buffy* fans have already watched the *Agents of S.H.I.E.L.D.* season two episode 'Face My Enemy,' in which Clark Gregg and Ming-Na Wen get to crack wise, kick ass, break your heart, and also dance. I was pretty proud of that one too."

Some of the show's writers engaged regularly with fans and others didn't. How much do you still interact with fans of the many shows you've worked on, and what are your thoughts on the relationship between modern TV and its fans?

DREW: "Ha-ha, I think I'm skipping this one to avoid getting in trouble, heh."

I've heard so many people talk about *Buffy* changing their lives—in many cases *saving* their lives. How do you feel when you hear that sort of thing?

DREW: "What I find incredible is that every show reaches someone. I love it when people feel moved by something we did on *Buffy* or *Warehouse 13* or *Agents of S.H.I.E.L.D.* I understand that kind of reaction—I had the same kind of reaction to *Buffy* when I watched it at home before I worked on it. (And I reacted that way to *My So-Called Life* and *West Wing* and *Sports Night* and *Parenthood* and *St. Elsewhere*, so I feel you.) Something about what these characters are going through speaks to you and the struggle you're experiencing right now in your own life, and you take comfort in it. But what I love about TV is how far-reaching it is—you just know that somewhere out there, someone has dedicated the entirety of their fan energy to worshipping, like, *Trapper John, M.D.* Or *Dynasty II: The Colbys*. Television gets to so many people on so many different levels, and in ways some of us might overlook in our zeal for our own particular object of TV affection, and you never know what's going to impact people. Or how."

So much time has passed. What are your favorite behind-the-scenes memories of your time on the show?

DREW: "I have so many fond memories of working on *Buffy*. I loved the day Doug Petrie tried teaching me how to throw a football. I loved ordering pies with Jane [Espenson] and Rebecca [Rand Kirshner] and sitting on the floor in Jane's office to eat them. I loved the day Joss came back from working on the musical episode with scripts and a demo CD, and we all sat in a room reading till we got to a song, then he'd play the demo for us, then we'd keep reading. But more than anything, I loved what a hands-on education it was. Joss made sure that every *Buffy* writer stayed involved in the episode from the initial story break all the way through production and then through post-production. And that's not always the case on every show. So I got to learn how every department works to make an episode of TV happen, and that's knowledge I took with me to every show I've been on since. It's invaluable."

You're incredibly busy, always, but what do you have coming up that we don't know about yet?

DREW: "More *Agents of S.H.I.E.L.D.*! The show has some cool turns coming this season."

SEASON 7

Help
Episode 7.4

WRITTEN BY: Rebecca Rand Kirshner
DIRECTED BY: Rick Rosenthal
GUEST STARS: Azura Skye as Cassie, Zachary Bryan as Peter Nichols, Glen Morshower as Mr. Newton, Rick Gonzalez as Tomas, Kevin Christy as Josh, Sarah Hagan as Amanda, Beth Skipp as Lulu, Anthony Harrell as Matthew, Jarrett Lennon as Martin, DB Woodside as Principal Wood
CO-STARS: J. Barton as Mike Helgenburg, Daniel Dehring as Red Robed #1, AJ Wedding as Red Robed #2, Marci Lynn Ross as Dead Woman

THE PLOT THICKENS:
Buffy is still settling into her new job counseling Sunnydale students with their varied problems. For the most part, she deals with everyday issues—quiet girls, disenfranchised boys—but when a girl named Cassie admits that she's going to die next Friday, Buffy realizes that she's in way over her head.

Cassie clarifies that she doesn't intend to commit suicide, but she sometimes knows things that are going to happen, and one of the things she knows about is her coming death. Buffy immediately reports the situation to Principal Wood, who shares her concern but admits that there's only so much they can do. While they talk, Buffy spills some coffee on her shirt, which was another thing that Cassie knew was going to happen.

The problem now seems more in the area of the mystical, and Buffy assigns Dawn the task of befriending Cassie to see if she can help. She also sets the team to work on what could be after this precog girl. After reading Cassie's journal and dark poetry postings online, they come up with info on her alcoholic father.

The Slayer goes to deal with the drunken dad, but it doesn't look like that's the right path, especially when she finds Cassie waiting outside her dad's house thanking the Slayer for help but telling her not to bother. Buffy refuses to sit back and do nothing, while at the same time, a group of red-robed figures are preparing some kind of ritual at the school.

Dawn throws herself into the role of spy but quickly becomes close to Cassie. Dawn's prime suspect—a possibly lovelorn male friend of Cassie's—only confirms that Cassie isn't counting on having a future.

Buffy continues her search, pumping Spike for garbled—and useless—information. In the meantime, a jerk of a classmate distracts Dawn while Cassie is kidnapped and brought to the library by the group of red-robed students who want to use her to summon a demon. Buffy arrives in time to stop the sacrifice, but not the demon summoning. It attacks. She defends with an assist from Spike and manages to save Cassie. She even saves the girl again when a booby trap goes off as they leave. But the Slayer can't save Cassie from a heart defect, and the girl passes on, just as she knew she would.

Unsure how to deal with the real problems of life that her new job presents, Buffy returns to work, accepting the fact that she might not be able to help everyone.

QUOTE OF THE WEEK:
Willow lets Xander down gently when he discovers that she once wrote poetry about him:
"I'm over you, sweetie."

LOVE IN VEIN:
Willow visits Tara's grave for the first time. Cassie tells Spike that "someday she'll tell you."

POP-CULTURE IQ:
Xander refers to the slogan for Dwight D. Eisenhower's presidential campaign and the tagline of the National Dairy Council:
"From beneath you it devours. . . . It's not the friendliest jingle, is it? It's no 'I like Ike' or 'Milk, it does a body good.'"
Willow explains the finer points of the Internet to a guy clearly still looking at linoleum:
WILLOW: "Have you googled her?"
XANDER: "Willow! She's seventeen!"
WILLOW: "It's a search engine."

Willow reveals a little about her adolescence and the stories she used to make up about the teenage doctor played by Neil Patrick Harris in the TV series *Doogie Howser, M.D.*:

"Look, all I'm saying is this is normal teen stuff. You join chat rooms, you write poetry, you post Doogie Howser fan fic."

Cassie lists skating at the famous rink in New York as one of the things she would like to do before she dies:

"I'd love to ice-skate at Rockefeller Center."

Buffy mixes up her shellfish when referring to the band Blue Oyster Cult:

"I bet it's 'cause you forgot the boom box blaring some heavy metal thing like . . . Blue Clam Cult."

> *According to Tara's headstone, she was born October 16, 1980, and died May 7, 2002.*

CONTINUITY:

Dawn references Willow's disappearing act in "Same Time, Same Place," noting that their friend is not "part of the gang here" in the funeral home on patrol. Amanda, the girl who was sent to Buffy because of her shyness (and for beating the crap out of a guy for picking on her), will play a larger role in fighting the new Big Bad later in the season. Cassie tells Buffy that she will make a difference, but it's unclear just what she means. Buffy rebuffs Peter's clumsy advances, but soon—under the influence of a letterman's jacket—she won't care about age differences (or legality!).

DRAMATIS PERSONAE:

Buffy's office hours are from ten to four.

Willow worries that she will not be able to deal with the coming evil and is, frankly, scared of what she might do.

Dawn is taking a ceramics class at high school (following her excellent—and ironic—grasp of negative space in her junior high art class).

Principal Wood claims that he's from Beverly Hills.

> In keeping with Jewish tradition, Willow places stones on top of Tara's headstone to mark her visit.

FROM THE ORIGINAL TELEPLAY:
Anya mistakenly counsels a scorned woman instead of helping her seek vengeance in a scene cut due to length:

ANYA: "What a creepazoid. It's like he didn't just forget your birthday, but the day on which, in keeping with modern American tradition, one's life is celebrated. One's very self. He didn't celebrate your self."

(But later . . .)

ANYA: "But anyway, this boyfriend of yours—it sounds like maybe he was just trying to do what you wanted."

(And later still . . .)

LULU: "Thanks, you've been a big help."

She exits. Anya smiles. Until she realizes that she didn't wreak any vengeance. She looks up, but Lulu is gone.

ANYA: "Wait . . ."

Selfless
Episode 7.5

WRITTEN BY: Drew Goddard
DIRECTED BY: David Solomon
GUEST STARS: Abraham Benrubi as Olaf, Andy Umberger as D'Hoffryn, Kali Rocha as Halfrek, Joyce Guy as Professor Hawkins, Jennifer Shon as Rachel
CO-STARS: Taylor Sutherland as Villager #1, MaryBeth Scherr as Villager #2, Alessandro Mastrobuono as Villager #3, Daniel Spanton as Viking #1, John Timmons as Viking #2

THE PLOT THICKENS:
Xander continues to worry about Anya's well-being as a newly restored vengeance demon but takes her recent act of reversing the giant-worm curse as a good sign. Unfortunately the signs are all bad at a fraternity house at UC Sunnydale, where the bodies of about a dozen frat brothers lie with their hearts ripped out around a blood-soaked Anya.

Cut to Sjornjost, AD 880. Olaf the pre-troll returns from a rough day of pillaging to his woman, Anya—or actually, Aud. Although Olaf would rather talk of breeding, Aud steers the conversation to the fact that she doesn't really fit in with the townsfolk and then talks about the load-bearing serving wench, who seems to catch Olaf's eye. He denies it, of course, professing love for his rabbit-raising girl.

Meanwhile, it's time for Willow to go back to school, where she runs into Anya coming out of the frat house with blood literally on her hands. Not deterred by Anya's pathetic cover-up attempts, Willow goes to investigate and finds the carnage, along with a girl huddled in a closet. Through her babbling the recently dumped girl manages to tell Willow that she had made a wish that her ex and his friends would know what it felt like to have their hearts ripped out. Anya conjured the demon to do just that, but it's still around and Willow is forced to tap into a little dark magick to repel it.

Back in the past, Aud has had enough of her cheating Olaf and turned him into a troll. Her work got the attention of D'Hoffryn, with an offer to make her a vengeance demon named Anyanka.

Speaking of demons, Willow alerts Buffy to the new one on the loose. As the witch goes to confront Anya, the Slayer takes Xander in search of the spiderlike heart stealer. They find it, kill it, and return home, surprised to learn from Willow that Anya was the one who summoned it. Buffy realizes that the time has come. She must kill Anya.

Xander tries to hold her off, reminding her of all the other demons she's spared. But Buffy counters that this is different. This is what she has to do, and while it's never easy, it's necessary.

St. Petersburg, 1905. Anyanka has worked her demonic ways to get revenge *and* start a rather impressive Russian revolution. As she and Halfrek enjoy the carnage around them, Anyanka simply notes that "vengeance is what I am."

Xander catches up with Anya at the scene of the bloody crime just moments before Buffy arrives. Even though Xander won't accept the truth, both the Slayer and the demon know what must be done, and a fight ensues in which Anya is stabbed through the chest. She then flashes back to a year ago, when she sang a song of love and finally found her new identity as Mrs. Anya Christina Emmanuella Jenkins *Harris*.

But vengeance demons don't die that easily.

As the battle continues, D'Hoffryn arrives after being summoned by Willow. He asks what Anya wants to do. She reveals she wants to reverse the horrible spell, even though she knows that the exchange is the life of a vengeance demon. What Anya didn't count on was that D'Hoffryn takes Halfrek's life instead, going for the hurt instead of the kill.

Anya is made human once again, although she no longer knows who she is.

QUOTE OF THE WEEK:
Olaf tells Anya why he loves her:
"You speak your mind, and are annoying."

LOVE IN VEIN:
Spike is still speaking with a manifestation of Buffy, although the real Buffy cannot see the other one. Xander admits that he still loves Anya and doesn't understand how Buffy would want to kill her since the Slayer spent the better part of the last year "boning" a demon that was just as murderous. Eventually the conversation shifts to how Buffy did kill Angel when she had to in "Becoming, Part Two." Buffy is seen professing her love for and belief in Spike, but when the real Buffy shows up, Spike thinks he's imagining a Buffy who says what he wants to hear. The real Buffy only tells him to get out of the basement before it kills him.

POP-CULTURE IQ:
Spike makes a reference to Edgar Allan Poe's *The Cask of Amontillado*:
"Scream 'Montresor' all you like, pet."

D'Hoffryn notes that the bodies of the college boys looks slightly reminiscent of ads for the clothing store (plus the blood and gore, naturally):

"It's like somebody slaughtered an Abercrombie and Fitch catalog."

CONTINUITY:
Xander brings up his recent interaction with Anya in "Beneath You" and "Same Time, Same Place." Olaf the troll and former boyfriend was introduced in "Triangle." Anya reminds Willow of her flayage in "Villains." Willow retrieves the talisman D'Hoffryn gave her in "Something Blue" to call him up for help. Anya asks Buffy if she has any friends left that she hasn't tried to kill, making reference to "Normal Again." Anya flashes back to a scene not seen in "Once More, with Feeling," in which Xander mumbles in his sleep that he just wants a "happy . . . ending . . ." and the neighbors complain about a stain, wondering if the dry cleaner will be able to get the mustard out. (David Fury and Marti Noxon reprise their singing roles as "Mustard Guy" and "Ticket Lady.") Anya wears the same dress in the musical number that she wore in her non-wedding. Hallie wasn't killed when she was run through with a sword in "Older and Far Away." Xander and Buffy butt heads over how to handle this situation. An additional truth almost comes out when Buffy reminds Xander that he had come to her with a message from Willow to "Kick his [Angel's] ass." Needless to say, Willow's surprised by that little piece of information. D'Hoffryn's actions remind the gang (and viewers) that despite his levity at times—such as at the non-wedding—he is still evil, something Spike spent the better part of a year trying to remind them when he was fully chipped. When Anya notes that D'Hoffryn should have killed her, he repeats the now common phrase "From beneath you, it devours," warning that all good things come in time, as a potential major piece of foreshadowing.

> ALL ROADS LEAD TO LA . . .
> Andy Umberger (D'Hoffryn) played Ronald Meltzer in the first-season *Angel* episode "I Fall to Pieces."

DRAMATIS PERSONAE:
Willow, understandably, suffered a bit of a drop-off in her grades in the middle of her last semester but managed to turn that around and ace all her finals, like magick (well, similar to magick, but not really).

Anya, back when she was Aud (pronounced "Odd"), had quite a little bunny collection. She also thought nothing of freely giving away rabbits, exchanging them simply for goodwill and not goods and services. Even back when she was Aud, Anya was known for being most aggressive in her not fitting in with people and her tendency to speak her mind. As Anyanka, nothing really interested her besides her work as a vengeance demon. Anya, in song, claims that she likes to bowl and is good at math.

Basements are bad for **Spike**.

FROM THE ORIGINAL TELEPLAY:
When Willow summons D'Hoffryn, the script gives the following translation of the Latin she uses to call him up:

"Blessed be the name of D'Hoffryn. Let this space be now a gateway to the world of Arashmaharr."

When D'Hoffryn tells Anya she must pay a price for reversing the spell, Xander comes up with an alternative suggestion in a line cut due to length:

"Something that involves grueling, hard labor. At fair market value, taking into account your project's special needs."

Conversations with Dead People
Episode 7.7

Widely considered the high-water mark for season seven, "Conversations with Dead People" is also a fantastic reason to peek behind the curtain of the series's production. In a reported crunch for time, and with scheduling conflicts for some cast members, the writers hatched the idea to do an episode in which characters would be split up for their own solo adventures, each story line penned by a different writer, and all contributing to the titular theme. Buffy has an amiable graveyard conversation with a vamped-out classmate before dusting him; Dawn receives a message from her late mother's ghost; Spike walks a woman home from a bar and kills her in front of her own home; influenced by the spirit of Warren, Andrew murders Jonathan; and Willow is visited by a "ghost" who encourages her to take her own life, and who is eventually revealed to be "The First," a.k.a. The First Evil. Despite the quietness of the episode, it remains one of the series's most chilling and sets the stage for the climactic episodes to come.

WRITTEN BY: Jane Espenson and Drew Goddard
DIRECTED BY: Nick Marck
GUEST STARS: Danny Strong as Jonathan, Adam Busch as Warren, Tom Lenk as Andrew, Jonathan M. Woodward as Holden Webster, with Azura Skye as Cassie, Kristine Sutherland as Joyce Summers
CO-STARS: Stacey Scowley as Young Woman

THE PLOT THICKENS:
It's a minute after eight p.m. on November 12, 2002. Another typical Sunnydale night. Buffy's on patrol, Spike is drowning his sorrows at the Bronze, Willow's at the library, and Dawn's home alone. But isn't it usually the typical nights when something happens?

The first sign of trouble comes when Jonathan and Andrew return to town. Granted, they're usually a minor threat, but it only takes minutes before they're breaking into the new Sunnydale High on a mysterious mission to hopefully get themselves on the Slayer's good side. Too bad Jonathan doesn't realize that Andrew is speaking with a very deceased Warren as the two living members of the former trio dig up the Seal of Danzalthar in the school basement.

Willow also gets a late-night visit from one of the recently departed. Cassie, the girl Buffy tried to keep from a premature, predestined death makes an appearance at the campus library, claiming that Tara's sending messages through her. Willow needs to stop all magick for good or else she will put everyone in danger again.

In the meantime, Dawn is under attack in her own home. The spirit of her mom seems to be trying to reach her, but evil forces are conspiring against Joyce. As the house rumbles and nearly falls apart, Dawn resorts to magick to save her mom and try to make contact.

Things are a little more calm in the graveyard as Buffy comes across a new vamp in the form of an old acquaintance from high school. Holden Webster, former student of psychology, is a little thrilled by his new power and the fact that he and the Slayer are now mortal enemies. Between trading punches, his schooling kicks in and he manages to get Buffy to open up about things she won't even tell her friends.

As each of the vignettes spirals out of control, startling discoveries are made around Sunnydale. The being in the form of Cassie reveals its true identity as the one everyone's been talking about with the "From beneath you, it devours." Joyce appears to tell her younger daughter that when things are very bad, Buffy will not choose Dawn. Andrew stabs Jonathan over the Seal of Danzalthar and his blood spills across the symbol. And just as Buffy kills Holden, she learns that Spike was the vampire's recent sire . . . while Spike is busy feasting on a female victim's neck.

QUOTE OF THE WEEK:
Andrew confuses the translation of a now familiar phrase:
  "It eats you, starting with your bottom."

LOVE IN VEIN:
Buffy's high school ex-boyfriend Scott Hope told everyone that she was gay after they broke up. Ironically enough, Scott apparently came out of the closet last year. She tells Holden that her father was the reason for her parents' splitting up because he cheated—or at least, she thinks he cheated. Cassie tells Willow that the reason she's not allowed to see her girlfriend is because the witch killed people.

POP-CULTURE IQ:
Jonathan reminds Andrew of the ease with which he picked up the language of one of *Star Trek*'s most popular alien races. (And yes, there really is a Klingon dictionary.):
  "You learned the entire Klingon dictionary in two and a half weeks."

Buffy makes yet another reference to the 1982 film directed by Sam Raimi:

"Yeah, I really need emotional therapy from *Evil Dead*."

Andrew echoes a line from *Back to the Future* when comparing Jonathan to Michael J. Fox's character, Marty McFly:

"Think, McFly."

Once again, Warren refers to Jonathan as the character from *Indiana Jones and the Temple of Doom*:

"Short Round pulls off his end of the bargain, we'll both be gods."

Andrew refers to the Clive Barker film from 1987:

"I feel like we're in *Hellraiser*. . . . I hate Pinhead."

With the return of the geeks, *Star Wars* references once again abound:

JONATHAN: "Echo Two to Echo One." (*The Empire Strikes Back*)
WARREN: "C'mon! 'If you strike me down . . .'"
ANDREW: "'. . . I shall become more powerful than you can possibly imagine.'"
(*Star Wars: A New Hope*)
ANDREW: "That boy is our last hope."
WARREN: "No. There is another." (*The Empire Strikes Back*)

> **SIX DEGREES OF . . . LA**
> Jonathan M. Woodward (Holden) appeared in the fourth season finale of *Angel* as (X), a lab guy who shows Fred around the research department at Wolfram & Hart. She becomes his boss once the gang accepts the invitation to run the law firm, and his character carried over to season five of *Angel*.

CONTINUITY:

Jonathan and Andrew return after fleeing to Mexico in "Grave." Dawn is on the phone with her friend Kit from "Lessons." Cassie reappears after having died in "Help." Joyce appears lying dead on the sofa just as she had in "The Body." Dawn echoes her sister's words when Buffy found her mother there: "Mom . . . Mom . . . Mommy?" Andrew suggests that if their plan works, they could maybe join the Slayer's gang and even hang at her house, which does kind of happen, for him at least. Cassie tries to convince Willow that everything Giles told her about magick in "Lessons" and "Beneath You" is false. Spike is killing people again. Buffy chose Dawn when she threatened to let the world end if

Dawn was harmed in "The Gift." As Willow unmasks "Cassie's" true face and intent, everyone begins to learn they can't trust anything or each other.

> The episode title appears on-screen at the opening. The only other time this happened was "Once More, with Feeling." The title of the episode is a play on the bestseller *Conversations with God*, by Neale Donald Walsch.

DRAMATIS PERSONAE:

Buffy helped Holden move a light board when he was the lighting designer for their junior year production of *Pippin*. He dropped the board on her foot. Buffy tells Holden that she behaved like a monster during her "relationship" with Spike. She ultimately admits that many of her problems stem from the fact that she feels superior to everyone, simply because she is the Slayer. She is able to be completely open with Holden.

Jonathan finally realizes that high school wasn't really as horrible as he remembers. In fact, he now misses everyone from his past, whether they even knew him or not. He wants to know how they're all doing, because no matter what they may think of him (or not even think of him at all), he cares about them. That's why he came back to Sunnydale to stop whatever it is he is trying to stop.

FROM THE ORIGINAL TELEPLAY:

In the original teleplay Tara actually visited Willow in person. However, arrangements to have Amber Benson return for the episode were unsuccessful. Here's a brief piece of their original exchange.

TARA: "I'm sorry to wake you."

WILLOW: "Ha . . ."

TARA: "Ha—what?"

WILLOW: "Is that like a dream joke thing? You're sorry to wake me, but I'm clearly *not* awake and if I was awake and you really were here, would you be sorry to wake me? I mean, after all this time and—oh God, I'm babbling. I'm dream babbling and it's the best dream of my life and I'm wasting it and—"

TARA: "I just meant, I liked watching you sleep."

Also, although the new Big Bad has yet to be mentioned by name in dialogue, the script already refers to it as "The First."

> The date and time at the opening of the episode corresponds with the date and time the episode originally aired.

Showtime
Episode 7.11

WRITTEN BY: David Fury
DIRECTED BY: Michael Grossman
SPECIAL GUEST STAR: Anthony Stewart Head as Rupert Giles
GUEST STARS: Tom Lenk as Andrew, Iyari Limon as Kennedy, Clara Bryant as Molly, Indigo as Rona, Amanda Marie Fuller as Eve
CO-STARS: Camden Toy as Ubervamp, Lalaine as Chloe, Felicia Day as Vi

THE PLOT THICKENS:
A new Potential named Rona arrives in Sunnydale and is immediately under attack by a trio of Bringers. Buffy comes to Rona's aid and welcomes the girl to the Hellmouth. The rest of the gathered Potentials—Kennedy, Molly, Chloe, and Eve—along with the Scoobies try to settle in for a restless night's sleep.

When Buffy returns, Giles informs her that there is an oracle called Beljoxa's Eye that might be able to help them with information on The First, but Anya is reluctant to seek it out. The ex-demon eventually agrees to take Giles to a demon contact to open the gateway to the oracle's dark dimension. Meanwhile, The First continues to taunt its captive Spike with visions of the Slayer. The vampire cannot immediately tell the difference.

Willow receives a call from her old coven friends and learns that a Potential arrived in Sunnydale two days ago, which sends Buffy and Xander in a rush to find the girl. They arrive way too late, but are more surprised to find that the dead girl is one of the Potentials they've already found: Eve. At the same time, Eve is in the basement with the other Potentials, spreading gloom and doom.

Buffy hurries home and threatens The First in the form of Eve to leave, although there is little the Slayer can actually do. The First knows it has done its damage and leaves the Scoobies and the truly freaked Potentials with the threat that it will be sending the Turok-Han that evening.

Meanwhile, in another dimension, Giles and Anya learn why The First has chosen now of all times to make its move. When Willow and the Slayerettes resurrected Buffy the year before, they irrevocably altered the mystical forces surrounding the Chosen line, making it prime time for The First to strike.

As darkness approaches, the Potentials get more and more stressed about the coming evil. Buffy loads them with weapons as Willow reluctantly readies with the magick to create a barrier to keep the ubervamp out. The Bringers take positions around the house as the ubervamp arrives.

The Turok-Han easily smashes into the house and nearly overpowers Willow's barrier with its strength. Seeing no other option, Buffy instructs everyone to run and they battle their way past the Bringers and out into the night. Buffy splits from the rest of the team, hoping the ubervamp will follow her, but it goes off after the Potentials.

Xander leads the gang to a construction site, where they are attacked by the ubervamp. Buffy arrives moments later, causing Dawn to realize that this was set up so the Potentials could see Action Buffy take on the Big Baddy. The Slayer uses her power to fight off the ubervamp and decapitate it, turning the demon to dust. She then leaves an impressed group of Potentials to go and release Spike.

QUOTE OF THE WEEK:
  KENNEDY: "How's evil taste?"
  WILLOW: "A little chalky."

LOVE IN VEIN:
Kennedy continues to make subtle moves on Willow. Once again Anya is turned down after an offer of sex. Last time it was with Spike in "Sleeper." This time it's with her demon contact, Torg.

POP-CULTURE IQ:
Andrew compares the lack of excitement to his apparent reaction to the film *Star Wars Episode One: The Phantom Menace*:
  "I'm bored. *Episode One* bored."
Xander makes reference to Edgar Rice Burroughs's novel *The Land That Time Forgot*:
  "The vampire that time forgot?"
Buffy's threat to her captive dissolves under Andrew's appreciation for the work of Stephen King:
  BUFFY: "Did you see the movie *Misery*?"
  ANDREW: "Six times. But the book was scarier 'cause instead of crushing his foot with a sledgehammer, Kathy Bates chopped it off with . . ."
Andrew continues the James Bond discussion he had with Warren and Jonathan in "Life Serial":
  "License to kill . . . pretty cool. You know, Timothy Dalton never got his props. . . ."
It can only be assumed that Andrew is referring to "Six Degrees of Kevin Bacon," the game in which all actors can be linked to Kevin Bacon in six movie roles or less:
  "You wanna play Kevin Bacon?"

Andrew refers to the DC Comics team of heroes:

> "Where would the Justice League have been if they hadn't put their differences aside to stop the Imperium and its shape-shifting alien horde?"

Andrew makes with more Star Wars references:

> "Um . . . deflector shields up. . . . Deflector shields up!"

Buffy's battle with the ubervamp is reminiscent of the gladiator-like arena in the 1985 film *Mad Max Beyond Thunderdome*:

> **BUFFY:** "Welcome to Thunderdome."
> **ANDREW:** "Two men enter, one man leaves."

> Buffy greets Rona by saying, "Welcome to the Hellmouth," which is the title of the show's premiere episode.

CONTINUITY:
Giles has the coven in England working on locating potential Slayers. Anya learns that she and her friends are essentially the ones to blame for The First's awakening and committing murders because they revived the Slayer in "Bargaining." Willow is scared to use her magick, not only because of her past slip into the dark magicks, but because the last time she used a spell in reference to The First in "Bring on the Night," it turned it against her. Xander takes the gang to the future site of the new public library that's scheduled to open May of 2003, if he ever gets back to work (although he needn't worry about missing that deadline).

DRAMATIS PERSONAE:
Buffy, **Willow**, and **Xander** speak telepathically to set up their plan to take out the ubervamp. In the past Willow has been the one to initiate telepathy ("The Gift" and "Bargaining"), but this time Buffy makes the first thought.

Anya is still coming under attack from some members of the demon community. She spent a night with her demon contact, Torg, over three lifetimes ago, although she claims it wasn't so much a date as they both happened to be invited to the same massacre.

Kennedy has a half sister and apparently comes from money. Her childhood home had a couple of wings to it, although the family house in the Hamptons only had one wing. She has known how to use a crossbow since she was eight.

FROM THE ORIGINAL TELEPLAY:
The First, in the guise of Eve, leaves one last threat to the Potentials before it disappears:

"And Chloe, honey . . . you don't have to worry about getting called to be the Slayer before you're ready. You'll be dead before that happens. All o' you."

Storyteller
Episode 7.16

WRITTEN BY: Jane Espenson
DIRECTED BY: Marita Grabiak
GUEST STARS: Danny Strong as Jonathan, Adam Busch as Warren, Tom Lenk as Andrew, Iyari Limon as Kennedy, Sarah Hagan as Amanda, Indigo as Rona, DB Woodside as Principal Wood
CO-STARS: Alan Loayze as Stressed-Out Boy, Corin Amber Norton as Crying Girl, Sujata DeChoudhury as Shy Girl, TW Leshner as Feral Teen

THE PLOT THICKENS:
Today's tale opens in an elegant study where Andrew, dressed in an equally elegant smoking jacket, begins to tell us a story that he likes to call "Buffy, a Slayer of the Vampyrs." In reality Andrew is hogging the bathroom while he records the introduction to his documentary on Buffy and her friends.

Buffy is the only one who seems to mind the video documenting of their lives. In fact, most of the team agrees that it would be nice to have a record of events if they do manage to save the world from the apocalypse. And if they don't, well, then what would be the harm?

Andrew introduces the team one by one and gives a little background on the events in Sunnydale thus far, presenting a bit of a revisionist history on his part in the events. Though he envisions her as a hero, he kind of tunes out while the Slayer lectures the team again with news of her recent vision of ubervamps.

In the meantime, things are heating up at Hellmouth High. It's like all the problems of the past (and some new ones) are popping up all at the same time, causing the students and faculty to go quite insane. Even Wood briefly gets caught up in the evil when he and Buffy go to check out the Seal of Danzalthar.

Andrew uses the documentary as an opportunity to get a little background on the players and interviews Anya and Xander on their failed romance. This ultimately leads to a sexual reunion for the former fiancés that turns out to be more of a momentary thing.

Realizing the answer to combating the evil oozing from the now glowing Seal may rest in Andrew, Buffy interrogates him for information. He again goes into his stories—taking a brief sidetrack to dream about being a god—and drops a hint regarding an important piece of information. The knife he used to kill Jonathan has ancient writing on the handle, which is just the clue they need to lead Buffy and Willow to a solution to their problem.

Buffy takes Andrew to the high school along with Spike and Wood as backup. Things are looking pretty grim as the team battles the unfortunately possessed students to get to the basement. Buffy leaves Wood and Spike to guard the door as she and Andrew head for the Seal. As the two left behind keep the students away, Wood gets the opportunity to kill the vamp that killed his mom, but fails to take it in time.

Buffy is forced to fight a few more students to get to the Seal, where she finally reveals the plan to Andrew. Only his blood will reverse the power of the Seal. Afraid that he's going to die, Andrew starts to tell his stories once more, but reality eventually wins out. As Buffy holds him over the Seal, Andrew finally admits to being a murderer, and his tears of repentance are what actually stop the Seal from its evil glow. He returns home to his video camera, but shuts it off, not wanting to tell any more stories.

> The inscription on the dagger reads "The blood which I spill I consecrate to the oldest evil."

QUOTE OF THE WEEK:
Andrew opens the episode, à la *Masterpiece Theatre*:
"Oh, hello there gentle viewers! You caught me catching up on an old favorite. It's wonderful to get lost in a story, isn't it? Adventure and heroics and discovery, don't they just take you away?"

LOVE IN VEIN:
Andrew sees that Kennedy and Willow seem to be taking steps toward being comfortable around each other again. Later he kind of misses a heavy make-out session between the pair while he appreciates some of Xander's handiwork. It's hinted that Spike isn't the only one in the house that

Andrew seems to have a crush on. It was one year ago to the day that Xander and Anya were supposed to be wed. They both admit to still loving each other, and prove it by making love on Spike's cot in the basement. However, it is more of a "one more time" type of session than a "let's get back together" thing.

> The vampire in the Mutant Enemy logo sings Andrew's lines "We are as gods" in place of its usual "Grrr, arrgh!"

POP-CULTURE IQ:
Wood paraphrases Forrest Gump's mother's most famous quote, "Stupid is as stupid does":
"Evil is as evil does."
Andrew asks for a drink with a little kick:
"But it tickles and I'm all tense. Can't I have a cool and refreshing Zima?"

CONTINUITY:
Continuity abounds in this episode as Andrew stands by his "big board" and brings the audience up to date on the happenings thus far. He also recalls some rather "Andrew friendly" memories of his schemes with Warren and Jonathan, as well as *his* powerful magick that kept evil Willow at bay in "Two to Go." A handful of students blind themselves with the symbols of The First over their eyes like the Bringers have. As the students are being more and more affected by the Seal, Buffy sees one girl start to disappear like Marcie did in "Out of Mind, Out of Sight." The little unslaughtered pig from "Never Leave Me" makes a brief cameo.

DRAMATIS PERSONAE:
Andrew reveals that while he was in Mexico he had visions of some of the events to come (including the deaths of Slayers around the world, the Seal opening, and the ubervamp). He can speak Tawarick, the language inscribed on the dagger. Andrew finally admits to himself that he killed Jonathan because he listened to "Warren" and was happy to pretend that he thought it was actually his dead friend.

> Andrew's revised history of the events in "Two to Go" are composed of clips from that episode as well as entirely new material featuring Andrew and Jonathan.

FROM THE ORIGINAL TELEPLAY:

As Buffy and Wood look over the blueprints of the school, the principal notes that Amanda's concern about certain groups in "Potential" could be well founded.

> **WOOD:** "I think our biggest problem is here in the music room. I fear there could be open hostilities between swing choir and the marching band."
>
> **BUFFY:** "I don't know if we can keep a lid on this all by ourselves. We might need some kind of help."
>
> **WOOD:** "Like what? Police?"

Later they do reveal they needed help in more lines cut due to length:

> **BUFFY:** "We had to call in guards to keep the place from going up like a prison riot."
>
> **ANDREW:** "Oh my."
>
> **WOOD:** "The guards were still clearing kids out of there when we left."

Chosen
Episode 7.22

WRITTEN AND DIRECTED BY: Joss Whedon
SPECIAL GUEST STARS: Anthony Stewart Head as Rupert Giles, Eliza Dushku as Faith, Nathan Fillion as Caleb
GUEST STARS: David Boreanaz as Angel, Tom Lenk as Andrew, Iyari Limon as Kennedy, Sarah Hagan as Amanda, Indigo as Rona, DB Woodside as Principal Wood
CO-STARS: Felicia Day as Vi, Mary Wilcher as Shannon, Demetra Raven as Girl at Bat, Katie Gray as Indian Girl, Lisa Ann Cabasa as Injured Girl, Ally Matsumura as Japanese Girl, Kelli Wheeler as School Girl, Jenna Edwards as Trailer Girl, Julia Lang as Potential with Power #2

THE PLOT THICKENS:
The series finale picks up right where the previous episode left off. Satisfying all the fans of Buffy and Angel's romance, Buffy and Angel are kissing. Then Big Bad Caleb gets up and clocks Angel. The Slayer does battle with the evil preacher once more, this time putting an end to him for good by splitting him in two. Spike continues to watch as Angel gives Buffy some files and an amulet meant to be worn by someone "ensouled, but stronger than human . . . a champion." But Spike leaves before he finds out that Buffy is not going to let Angel be the one to wear it or stick around for the fight.

Buffy returns home and gets a swift kick from her sister for sending her away. The Slayer shares the new info with the gang and then goes down to see Spike. The vampire tells her he knows she's seen Angel, but is surprised to learn that she sent tall, dark, and forehead away. When he asks about the trinket Angel brought, she reiterates that it is supposed to be worn by a champion before she hands it over to him. With Faith taking up her bed, Buffy needs a place to stay and—after a slight miscommunication—Spike offers his cot to her.

In the middle of the night Buffy gets up to pace and gets a surprise visit from The First in the form of herself. It reminds her that into every generation a Slayer is born and that the Chosen One is alone. Spike wakes at the end of The First's ramblings and asks Buffy what's wrong. She replies that she just realized something she never realized before: they're going to win.

The next morning Buffy shares her new plan with her friends. The gang is shocked by its audacity, but Giles is the first to proclaim its brilliance, even though Willow is afraid that an awful lot of it depends on anther dalliance with the powerful magicks. Buffy shares the plan with the Potentials, telling them that the following morning she's opening the Seal of Danzalthar and going into the Hellmouth along with anyone who chooses to come.

Following a night of difficult discussions and unlikely pastimes, the team of Slayers, Potentials, and civilians enters Sunnydale High. As Kennedy goes to the principal's office to set things up for Willow, Faith takes Spike and the Potentials down to the Seal, preparing them to enter the Hellmouth. The plan is to take care of the ubervamps at their source, but if they get up into the school, three teams of Giles and Wood, Anya and Andrew, and Xander and Dawn will keep them from getting out into the world. Dawn refuses to actually say good-bye to her sister and the teams split, leaving Buffy, Xander, Willow, and Giles a moment alone wondering what to do tomorrow; shopping is the choice of the majority.

The Slayers and the Potentials cut their hands and open the Seal, entering the Hellmouth. It doesn't take long for the thousands of ubervamps to see them and attack. Above them, Willow works a spell on the scythe. Her body flows with white magick as she spreads the power of the Slayer from the weapon to all the Potentials in the Hellmouth and around the world. Kennedy then takes the scythe to Buffy and joins the battle.

The fight is vicious as dozens of ubervamps and a few of the new Slayers, including Amanda, meet their deaths. Some of the vamps get up into the school and, along with the Bringers, do battle with the upstairs team. Wood is wounded . . . and Anya is killed.

The First taunts Buffy as she falls with a seemingly mortal wound, but disappears when the Slayer rises again. The talisman around Spike's neck finally takes effect and a beam of destructive energy bursts up through the school. Sunlight comes shining in, filtering through the amulet to kill the ubervamps and destroy the Hellmouth.

Faith calls the retreat, but Buffy refuses to leave Spike. The gang gathers upstairs and hops a waiting school bus out of the deserted town while Buffy reluctantly says good-bye. As the sunlight destroys Spike, Buffy heads to the rooftops to chase the bus as the Hellmouth implodes, taking the town with it. Buffy manages to leap onto the bus and rides it out of town.

Outside the former town limits, the gang stops to take account of what's happened. Wood surprises Faith by not dying. Andrew tells Xander that Anya died a valiant death. But what everyone is wondering is what to do tomorrow now that the Hellmouth is gone and the Chosen One is no longer just one.

Buffy simply smiles.

QUOTE OF THE WEEK:
Giles echoes his concern for the world that he expressed at the end of the series opener "Welcome to the Hellmouth/The Harvest" (1.1 and 1.2), following a conversation with Buffy, Xander, and Willow that is also familiar:

"The Earth is definitely doomed."

LOVE IN VEIN:
Buffy tells Angel she needs him to prepare a second front in case she fails, but that's only one of the reasons she doesn't want him involved in the battle. Buffy makes it clear that Spike's not her

boyfriend, but he is in her heart (although she doesn't see "fat grandchildren" in a future with Spike, echoing Jenny Calendar's thwarted wish for her future in "Amends"). Buffy finally realizes that, in light of her failed relationships, there's nothing "wrong" with her, she's just not ready as a "whole person" to be in one yet. And, although she doesn't think far enough ahead to know when she'll be ready for another relationship, she does admit that Angel is in her thoughts. Spike is equally jealous and takes out his frustration on a punching bag with a crude drawing of the vampire who "wears lifts, you know." As Cassie predicted in "Conversations with Dead People," Buffy does tell Spike that she loves him. He knows it's not true—at least not in the way he wants it to be—but appreciates that she said it. Faith worries that Wood thought she was blowing him off when she blew him off after their tryst. The principal makes it clear that he's not up for her "defensive isolationist Slayer crap" and some guy out there may be pretty decent if she ever gave him the chance to surprise her, which he does. Willow tells Kennedy that the Potential will have to kill her if the magick takes over. Kennedy is with her the whole time, lending support. In the end Xander worries only about Anya.

POP-CULTURE IQ:
Angel notes that the translation regarding the amulet's power was kind of unclear and could have said it had the power of a bathroom cleaner:

"Has a purifying power . . . or a cleansing power—or possibly scrubbing bubbles . . ."

Buffy brings up *Dawson's Creek*, another series that saw its finale in 2003, since Angel acted the same way when she was with Riley:

"Are you gonna come by and get all Dawson on me every time I have a boyfriend?"

Giles and some of the gang take time out to play some Dungeons & Dragons as the apocalypse approaches:

"Could it possibly get uglier? I used to be a highly respected Watcher. Now I'm a wounded dwarf with the mystical strength of a doily."

Anya refers to Andrew as the leader/narrator of a D&D game:

"So that leaves me and the Dungeon Master in the North Hall."

Spike makes reference to the song by Alice Cooper:

"I think it's fair to say school's out for bloody summer."

The gang mourns the loss of Sunnydale:

DAWN: "We destroyed the mall? I fought on the wrong side."

XANDER: "All those shops gone . . . The Gap, Starbucks, Toys 'R' Us . . . who will remember those landmarks unless we tell the world of them?"

> **FACES OF THE FIRST**
> Throughout the season, The First took the following forms: Warren, Glory, Adam, Mayor Wilkins, Drusilla, The Master, Buffy, Cassie, Spike, Jonathan, Eve (Potential), Nikki Wood, Chloe (Potential), Betty (Caleb's victim), Caleb

CONTINUITY:
Seven seasons of history come into play throughout the episode, which takes up where the last one left off, mid-kiss. Angel notes that the information and the amulet did not come from a reliable source, namely Lilah. He received the information in the season finale of *Angel*, "Home." Oz smelled Willow's presence in "Lovers Walk"; Angel smells Spike on Buffy, just as Spike later smells Angel on Buffy. In "Conversations with Dead People," Cassie foretold that Buffy would "go someplace dark, underground" and that she "would make a difference." Buffy's realization that she's going to win comes about in the basement. The "basement" (well, actually the Hellmouth below the basement) of the high school finally does kill Spike. Giles mentions another Hellmouth in Cleveland, as was discussed in "The Wish" as the place Buffy ends up in the Doppelgangland world, instead of first coming to Sunnydale.

> In fitting tribute, the vampire in the Mutant Enemy logo turns directly to the audience when it says its "Grrr, arrgh!" for the last time in the series.

DRAMATIS PERSONAE:
Buffy is no longer the Chosen "One," which means she no longer has to bear that mantle of responsibility alone.

Willow turns white with power and Kennedy tells her she is a goddess. She can feel the Slayers wakening to their power all around the world.

Xander, after hearing that Anya died protecting Andrew, says, "That's my girl. Always doing the stupid thing."

Giles and **Buffy** have a moment of reconciliation when he tells her the plan is bloody brilliant and she responds that his opinion does matter.

Anya finds her strength to rally against the ubervamps and the Bringers by calling up her hatred for floppy . . . hoppy . . . *bunnies*.

Dawn refers to herself as Watcher Junior.

Spike feels his soul in the end and knows it's really there.

Andrew wonders why he didn't die.

FROM THE ORIGINAL TELEPLAY:
Dawn tells the Potentials a bedtime story:

DAWN: "And the Master grabbed Buffy from behind and bit her. She tried to move, but he was too strong. He fed on her blood and tossed her in the water, cackling insanely as the bubbles rose around her and she slowly drowned to death."

VI: "Do you have any *other* stories?"

DAWN: "She gets up again. It's very romantic. Guys, you gotta stop worrying. It's Buffy. She always saves the day."

Robin makes good on his promise to surprise Faith one day, in this case by not dying:
"Surprise."

And here's how it ends following Dawn's question, "What are we gonna do now?":
Buffy looks at them, looks back at the crater, and we are in full close-up as she considers the question, a small smile creeping onto her lips as she decides on her answer.
BLACK OUT.
END OF SHOW.

> By the time this episode aired, The WB had already announced that James Marsters, as Spike, would appear on *Angel* the following fall, thus allaying the fears of many devoted fans that Spike wouldn't survive. After all, as the two shows have often proven, death isn't necessarily the end of anything.

IT DIDN'T END IN SUNNYDALE

The Official Post-TV Seasons

Several years after the final episode of *Buffy* aired, Joss Whedon decided that maybe the show wasn't as over as the series finale had made it seem. Dark Horse Comics had done *Buffy* comics throughout the TV series run, but those were never considered to be "in continuity," or part of the official story. In 2007 all that changed. Joss teamed up with the folks at Dark Horse to create *Buffy the Vampire Slayer: Season Eight*—an official comic-book continuation of the television series, with Joss writing the first story arc and overseeing (or "executive producing") the whole endeavor. *Season Eight*, it turned out, was only the beginning, and the Dark Horse Buffyverse currently runs up through *Season Eleven*.

So . . . where did Joss and company take your favorite characters in this official continuity? We're very glad you asked. . . .

SEASON EIGHT

Picking up a year after the conclusion of the TV series, *Season Eight* presents a startlingly different status quo for Buffy and the now-scattered Scooby Gang. Taking full advantage of the comic-book form, Joss and artist Georges Jeanty reintroduce Buffy and Xander as the leaders of a global network of magick and technology, which they and their team use to combat the forces of darkness around the world. It's established that there are eighteen hundred Slayers in the world, roughly a third of whom work for Buffy, broken down into ten squads. Some of the squad leaders are very familiar to us, including Giles (UK), Andrew Wells (Italy), Vi (New York City), and Faith, among others. Willow has become extraordinarily powerful, thanks in part to the demon Saga Vasuki, who is revealed to be her lover.

A variety of villains present themselves, not least of which is the US government, which paints Buffy and her network as terrorists, and which enlists Sunnydale's original witch, Amy Madison, and Tara's killer, Warren Mears, to try to take them down. We also encounter an evil British Slayer who wants the top position, and a collective of Japanese vampires doing their best to undermine our favorite Chosen One. All these "Little Bads" are secretly working in service to *Season Eight*'s Big Bad, a masked mystery man called Twilight.

Numerous subplots weave in and out of the forty issues (and three one-shots) that compose the sprawling *Season Eight*. Buffy sleeps with a fellow Slayer. Harmony—the much-loved airhead who went from Sunnydale classmate to vampire receptionist at Wolfram & Hart—becomes a reality TV star. Dawn loses her virginity to a guy who curses her, causing her to become a giant, then a centaur, before she eventually realizes that it was Xander she loved all along—and Xander loves her back! Buffy time travels, encountering Fray, a future Slayer whom Joss Whedon introduced in her own miniseries. The core gang visits Oz in Tibet to learn how to hide the magickal nature of both Slayers and witches, due to the fact that Twilight has learned how to track them by their magick, a sort of occult GPS.

Throughout these adventures, the core group begins to splinter again, as they have in the past. Trust is destroyed. In the midst of that atmosphere, Buffy turns to Angel, and despite everything at risk, they give in to their love and longing for each other . . . only to have Angel reveal that *he* has been Twilight all along . . . or, rather, that Twilight (a sort of Utopian limbo where they can live together forever) has possessed him. Twilight claims to have only admirable motives—but for Buffy and Angel to have their happy ending in this new, beautiful universe, they'll have to allow the old one to be destroyed, along with everyone in it.

Angel manages to shake off Twilight's influence, and—thanks to a tip from Spike—he and Buffy track down the source of Twilight's power: a mystical seed that is also the source of all magick in the world. Giles plans to destroy it, and it seems everyone is on the same page until Twilight possesses Angel again. Under Twilight's control, Angel murders Giles. In grief and rage, Buffy destroys the seed, which defeats Twilight but also extinguishes all magick in the universe. Supernatural creatures (like vampires and Slayers) remain, but witches and sorcerers are left completely powerless.

Faith learns that Giles has left her his estate, with the expectation that she will step up and become the leader he always believed her to be. She brings Angel there and begins the process of trying to help him heal. Buffy, however, gets no such ending. Hated by Slayers and the now-powerless witches, she moves into Xander and Dawn's San Francisco apartment. When we last see her, she has returned to the person she was when we first met her . . . the Slayer, hunting monsters by night.

Season Eight was written by Joss Whedon, with certain issues by Scott Allie, Brad Meltzer, Jim Krueger, Jeph Loeb, Brian K. Vaughan, and a host of writers from the original television series, including Jane Espenson, Drew Goddard, Steven S. DeKnight, Drew Z. Greenberg, and Doug Petrie. The arc was drawn primarily by Georges Jeanty, with certain issues illustrated by Paul Lee, Cliff Richards, Karl Moline, and Eric Wight.

SEASON NINE

Buffy the Vampire Slayer: Season Nine consists of two ongoing series (and several miniseries). In addition to the flagship title, Dark Horse launched *Angel & Faith*.

Season Nine begins with Buffy patrolling San Francisco, but in addition to the changes already detailed, other things have changed as well. With the death of magick, vampirism itself has been altered. It had previously been established that vampires were humans possessed by a certain brand of vampire . . . but now those demons aren't able to fully inhabit the dead, resulting in abominations Xander starts to call "zompires."

Xander and Dawn have settled down together into a life that seems almost ordinary. Likewise, Willow and Spike make appearances, but the now-magickless Willow soon leaves on a quest to try to restore magick to the universe, and Spike departs as well (the less said about his—ahem—spaceship, the better). Buffy teams up with a cop named Robert Dowling, and eventually learns that Anaheed, one of her roommates, is a Slayer who's been assigned to keep an eye on her.

Buffy's enemies this time include a man named Severin, who has the ability to leach magick from Slayers and demons. Among her allies are familiar faces, including Illyria (from *Angel*) and the vengeance demon D'Hoffryn. But the greatest fallout from *Season Eight*'s destruction of magick is that Dawn—a being created entirely of mystical energy—has begun to fade from existence. If they can't find a way to restore magick, Dawn will die.

Though Willow manages to restore her own powers and returns, she is only able to slow Dawn's dissolution. Soon Buffy, Willow, and Xander end up at the Deeper Well (a prison for ancient demons), where they hope to gather up the dregs of magick . . . enough to save Dawn. Severin and renegade Slayer Simone have done the same. While Severin is unable to handle the magick there, Willow charges herself up enough to form a new seed (like that destroyed in *Season Eight*). The seed will take a thousand years to restore magick, but Illyria and Willow persuade Severin to lend his power to speed things along. The end result is a massive explosion that restores magick to the world, killing Severin, Illyria, and others.

Dawn is saved, but Willow reports that she senses something different about the magick in the world. When we cut to a new vampire rising from the dead, we learn that the age of the "zompire" is over—this vampire retains its intelligence. But it is different from the vampires we've seen in the series before. This one can bear the sunlight without burning and can transform itself into a bat.

In the pages of *Angel & Faith*, Faith is in London trying to help Angel become the person he once was, even as Angel is trying to gather the fragments of Giles's soul in an effort to resurrect him. Meanwhile, some of those he recruited during his time as Twilight (including Whistler) are hunting him, furious that he betrayed them. While Whistler engages in nefarious deeds, Angel and Faith continue their quest to restore Giles to life . . . and Angel accumulates pieces of Giles's soul inside himself, which begins to influence his behavior, making him more Giles-like. They're aided in their efforts by two of Giles's great-aunts, Lavinia and Sophronia, who use magick to remain young, as well as an old friend of Giles's named Alasdair Coames.

With help from Willow, Spike, Gunn, and Connor (the latter two from *Angel*), and after a confrontation with the demon Eyghon (to whom Giles sold his soul, as revealed in the *Buffy* episode "The Dark Age"), Angel and Faith and their sidekicks finally manage to gather together all the pieces of Giles's soul and bring him back to life . . . but there's a twist they didn't see coming: Giles returns with all his memories intact, but he's in the body of his twelve-year-old self.

Young Giles is not at all happy about his physical state, but he's even more upset that they've been so focused on trying to save him that they've neglected the larger fight—the evil machinations of Eyghon, Whistler, and their allies. With their focus renewed, Angel and Faith soon track down and vanquish the villains, after which Faith and Giles return to the United States. Angel stays behind in London, where he intends to go back to spending his nights fighting the forces of darkness and helping those in need.

Season Nine also includes three miniseries. *Willow: Wonderland* reveals the character's journey into a magickal dimension, where she encounters former friends and former enemies, regains her magick, and makes peace with the dark elements of her spirit that once turned her into Dark Willow. The vital part of *Spike: A Dark Place* is that it destroys Spike's "spaceship" and returns him to a more familiar status quo. *Love vs. Life*—written by Buffy TV writer/producer Jane Espenson—follows new characters Billy and Anaheed, and presents Billy as the first male character to make a connection to the Slayer mythology.

The core series had a number of writers, including Whedon, Scott Allie, Drew Z. Greenberg, and Jane Espenson, but the majority of the issues were penned by Andrew Chambliss. Artists included Buffy stalwarts Georges Jeanty, Karl Moline, and Cliff Richards. The *Angel & Faith* series was written entirely by Christos Gage, and nearly all the issues were drawn by Rebekah Isaacs.

SEASON TEN

Season Ten continues to be split into two core titles—*Buffy the Vampire Slayer* and *Angel & Faith*—as the characters deal with fallout from the previous season's finale. The new breed of vampires are more powerful than their predecessors and much harder to kill (and they can walk in daylight!). Buffy is adjusting to the presence of a twelve-year-old Giles, Dawn is dealing with her near-death experience, and Xander is being visited by what seems to be Anya's ghost. Harmony now leads a group made up of most of the world's vampires, and they enter into a mutual nonaggression pact with Buffy.

One result of the earlier story line was that the book of *Vampyr* left to Buffy in Giles's will had its pages turn blank. Now Buffy and her friends realize they can write new rules for magick on those pages—a huge opportunity and responsibility. They form an alliance with D'Hoffryn and others to safeguard the book and monitor the new and evolving rules of magick.

Characters change and grow and there are subplots aplenty, including one in which Andrew resurrects the soul of Jonathan Levenson (the third member of the trio that included the two of them and Warren Mears) . . . but the digital body created for Jonathan is only temporary, and dead Jonathan is enraged. Eventually, this leads to Jonathan becoming the first-ever male vengeance demon.

Buffy and Spike enter into a new relationship and then encounter Archaeus, the ancient vampire who sired the Master (meaning Spike and Angel are of his vampiric bloodline). Buffy and Spike team up with Angel and make peace with him over the past and the present, and together they defeat Archaeus . . . who escapes through something called the Restless Door, a portal into various hell dimensions. The Restless Door is being repaired by a collective of demons who begin to stage demonic invasions of Earth. The military wants Buffy's help to combat these invasions, but Buffy mistrusts them—even though some of her friends, Willow included, are working with them.

When, in the midst of battle, fleeing demons destroy the Restless Door, they open a portal that will destroy the world unless Dawn ("The Key") goes through and closes it from the other side. She does so, and Xander goes with her, beginning a long odyssey as the two of them attempt to make their way back to the Earth dimension and their friends attempt to find and aid them.

The Big Bad of the series turns out to be D'Hoffryn, who betrays his initial alliance with Buffy and takes the *Vampyr* book in an effort to give himself enormous power, hoping to make himself unstoppable. In the end, his own cadre of vengeance demons turns against him, and D'Hoffryn is disempowered and defeated. A new council is formed to take charge of the book and to oversee the magick in the world, including Buffy, Giles, Willow, Riley Finn . . . and Dracula, among others.

Season Ten also includes a short comics story called "Where Are They Now?" The story features Harmony and the fan-favorite, saggy-skinned demon Clem making a documentary that leads to Buffy, Giles, and violence, of course.

Meanwhile, in *Angel & Faith*, Faith is traveling, trying to figure out what she wants from her life and future. Angel has set himself up as the protector of a London neighborhood that has come to be known as Magic Town, where many residents have magickally mutated into supernatural creatures, including a former Slayer called Nadira, who has become a seer. Nadira claims that Magic Town is sentient and that she can communicate with it.

Angel's adventure leads to encounters with a half demon named Pearl, Amy Madison, and—much to his surprise—Winifred Burkle, whom he knows to be dead. (During *Season Nine*, the demon Illyria, who had inhabited Fred's body, was seemingly killed.) As it turns out, Fred and Illyria are now sharing the body—but Illyria believes that Angel wants to expunge her from Fred's body. Illyria wreaks havoc until Fred is able to take control of her own body, and of Illyria.

Faith's story takes her first to South America to rescue Riley Finn and his wife, Samantha, from a vampire tribe, and then to London's Magic Town to become head of security for a company researching the magick there. Faith's boss has a particular fascination with the Fred/Illyria problem. This leads to a team-up between Faith and Fred, who go undercover to a local school, many of whose students turn out to be vampires in service to our old friend Drusilla.

Like Spike and Angel and the Master, Drusilla is part of the bloodline of the ancient vampire Archaeus, who has returned and brought Drusilla into his scheme, which revolves around a girl named Mary. Archaeus seems to want to make a deal with the sentient awareness of Magic Town, and he tries to force the seer Nadira to broker a deal. But when the sentient awareness of Magic Town inhabits a statue and comes to life, it becomes a menace all its own, attacking anyone who comes near.

When Archaeus attempts to persuade the sentient Magic to join forces with him, mayhem ensues. Drusilla and an army of vampires face off against the magickal creatures and human residents of Magic Town, but it is only when Archaeus attacks Nadira—who had been a friend to the Magic—that it sees the truth and defends her. In the end, it is the sentient Magic that truly defeats Archaeus, before retreating back to a bodiless existence.

The *Buffy* portion of *Season Ten* was written by Christos Gage, who collaborated on many issues with Xander himself, actor Nicholas Brendon. Most of the run was illustrated by Rebekah Isaacs, with certain issues by Karl Moline, Megan Levens, and Cliff Richards. The *Angel & Faith* run in *Season Ten* was written by Victor Gischler (with one issue by Kel McDonald) and illustrated by Will Conrad and Cliff Richards (with one issue by Derlis Santacruz).

SEASON ELEVEN

As of this writing, publication of *Buffy the Vampire Slayer: Season Eleven* is ongoing, but the series is much shorter than previous seasons, running for only twelve issues. The companion series this time is simply titled *Angel*, but is also considered part of *Season Eleven*.

How much longer Buffy's official adventures will continue remains to be seen.

Only Joss knows for sure.

WHERE ARE THEY NOW?

SARAH MICHELLE GELLAR (BUFFY SUMMERS) has made numerous film and television appearances since the end of the series. Her most notable film appearances have been in the smash horror films *The Grudge* and *The Return* as well as indie movies such as *Southland Tales* and *Veronika Decides to Die*. After the birth of her first child with husband Freddie Prinze Jr., Sarah took a two-year hiatus from acting. Subsequently, she's focused more on television roles, starring in two short-lived but fan-favorite series, *Ringer* and *The Crazy Ones*. A recent effort to develop a new series based on her earlier film *Cruel Intentions* seems to have stalled as of this writing. Sarah has also provided her voice to a number of animated projects, most notably the second season of *Star Wars Rebels*. When not working or spending time with Freddie and their two children, Sarah works on a variety of charitable endeavors, including Project Angel Food and the Make-A-Wish Foundation.

ALYSON HANNIGAN (WILLOW ROSENBERG) has become one of the most successful of the series's alumni, thanks to her 206 episodes as Lily Aldrin on *How I Met Your Mother*. In the years immediately following *Buffy*, Alyson appeared as a guest star on a number of series, including two episodes of *That '70s Show* and three of *Veronica Mars*. She has also been a popular guest star on a variety of animated series, voicing roles on *The Simpsons*, *Robot Chicken*, *American Dad!*, and kids' series *Sofia the First*. Alyson made her West End stage debut in 2004 in a production of *When Harry Met Sally*, opposite Luke Perry. In 2009 she won the People's Choice Award for Favorite TV Comedy Actress for her role on *How I Met Your Mother*. Alyson married *Buffy* costar Alexis Denisof in 2003, and the couple have two daughters. Alyson and Alexis are the godparents of Joss Whedon's son, Arden.

NICHOLAS BRENDON (XANDER HARRIS) has made numerous film and television appearances post-*Buffy*, most notably in thirteen episodes of *Kitchen Confidential* and twenty-one of *Criminal Minds*. He appeared in multiple episodes of *Private Practice* and voiced a character on the animated series *American Dragon: Jake Long*. Nicholas co-wrote many issues of Dark Horse Comics's *Buffy the Vampire Slayer: Season Ten*.

CHARISMA CARPENTER (CORDELIA CHASE) followed up *Buffy* with a move to its sister series, *Angel*, where she appeared as Cordelia for ninety-two episodes. Charisma has worked consistently in a wide variety of projects, including the first two *Expendables* films with Sylvester Stallone and numerous made-for-television movies. Her television series roles post-*Buffy* include the short-lived *Miss Match*, eleven episodes of *Veronica Mars*, twenty of *The Lying Game*, and guest-starring roles in a litany of popular series, including *Charmed*, *CSI*, *Burn Notice*, *Supernatural*, *Blue Bloods*, *Sons of Anarchy*, *Scream Queens*, and *Chicago P.D.* Charisma had a son, Donovan, in 2003.

EMMA CAULFIELD (ANYA JENKINS) has continued to appear in film and television, including a starring role in the horror hit *Darkness Falls* and seven episodes of the long-running fantasy series *Once Upon a Time*. Emma's other television appearances include guest-starring roles on such series as *Private Practice*, *Prime Suspect*, *Leverage*, *Royal Pains*, and *Supergirl*, and a recurring role on the TeenNick series *Gigantic*. Emma has voiced a variety of different roles on the animated series *Robot Chicken* and was the producer and star of the popular web series *Bandwagon*. She cowrote the IDW Comics webcomic *Contropussy*. Emma and her husband, Mark Leslie Ford, welcomed their first child in 2016.

ELIZA DUSHKU (FAITH LEHANE) reportedly turned down a Faith spinoff for her starring role on the series *Tru Calling*. In the years since, she is perhaps also best known for her starring role in the horror film *Wrong Turn* and the Joss Whedon series *Dollhouse*. Eliza has appeared in numerous films, including *Bottle Shock* and *The Alphabet Killer*, and in guest-starring roles on series such as *That '70s Show*, *Ugly Betty*, *The Big Bang Theory*, *White Collar*, and five episodes of *Banshee*. Eliza has also provided her voice to animated series, including *Hulk and the Agents of S.M.A.S.H.*, *Spider-Man Unlimited*, *Torchwood: Web of Lies*, and *The Cleveland Show*, and five video games, most notably *Saints Row 2*, as well as voicing Catwoman in two animated films. Her most recent starring role is in the horror thriller *Eloise* (2017).

MICHELLE TRACHTENBERG (DAWN SUMMERS) moved from *Buffy* to major roles in the films *EuroTrip*, *Ice Princess* (in which she put her real-life figure-skating skills on display), and *17 Again*, among others. Michelle found a whole new fan following with her role as the conniving Georgina Sparks on the series *Gossip Girl*, and appeared in series such as *Weeds* and *Six Feet Under*, as well as guest-starring roles in a variety of shows, including *Criminal Minds*, *Sleepy Hollow*, *NCIS: Los Angeles*, and *Law & Order: Criminal Intent*. She was one of the stars of the short-lived medical drama *Mercy* and has starred in a variety of TV movies. Like many of her fellow *Buffy* alums, Michelle has voiced characters in animated series, including roles on *Robot Chicken* and *The Super Hero Squad Show*.

DAVID BOREANAZ (ANGEL) spun out of *Buffy the Vampire Slayer* to topline his own series, *Angel*, for five seasons, and went on to star alongside Emily Deschanel for twelve seasons of *Bones*. Beginning with season four, David was also a producer on the series and has directed at least one episode per year. He starred in the horror film *Valentine* and has appeared in a number of independent films over the years, including *The Mighty Macs* and *Officer Down*. He appeared in the music video for Dido's hit single "White Flag." In animation, David voiced the role of Hal Jordan/Green Lantern in *Justice League: The New Frontier* as well as characters on *American Dad!* and *Family Guy* (on which he played himself). David and his wife, Jaime, have two children, a son and a daughter. In 2011, he and his father—television meteorologist Dave Roberts—were awarded the Gold Medal of the Pennsylvania Association of Broadcasters, the only time a father and son have been honored with the award together.

SETH GREEN (OZ) made an indelible mark on the series but went on to far greater pop-culture impact as the co-creator, executive producer, and primary voice actor on two-time Emmy Award–winning *Robot Chicken*. Seth is also the voice of Chris Griffin on the long-running animated series *Family Guy* and Leonardo on *Teenage Mutant Ninja Turtles*, and has voiced characters on *Star Wars: The Clone Wars*, *Phineas and Ferb*, *Hulk and the Agents of S.M.A.S.H.*, and *Avengers Assemble*, among many others. In the years since *Buffy*, he has appeared in such films as *The Italian Job*, *Without a Paddle*, *Sexy Evil Genius*, and *The Best Man*. On television, he also starred in the series *Four Kings* and *Dads* and guest-starred in a wide variety of shows, including *Crazy Ex-Girlfriend*, *Broad City*, *Community*, *How I Met Your Mother*, *Grey's Anatomy*, *Heroes*, *My Name Is Earl*, and *Mom*. Seth has also voiced characters in numerous video games, most notably Joker Moreau in three *Mass Effect* games. Seth and his wife, Clare Grant, were married in 2010.

ALEXIS DENISOF (WESLEY WYNDAM-PRYCE) shifted from *Buffy* to *Angel*, where he continued to play Wesley until the series finale. Alexis has appeared in numerous films and TV series since, including a starring role in the series *Finding Carter*, seventeen episodes of *Grimm*, and ten episodes as obnoxious newsman Sandy Rivers in *How I Met Your Mother* (which, of course, starred Alexis's wife, Alyson Hannigan). His other TV appearances include guest-starring roles on *Private Practice* and Joss Whedon's *Dollhouse*, as well as a role on Bryan Singer's web series *H+*. Over the years, Alexis has become one of Joss Whedon's go-to performers, and his film work has included parts in Whedon's modern take on *Much Ado About Nothing* and *The Avengers* (as Thanos's sidekick, "The Other," a character he reprised in the film *Guardians of the Galaxy*). Like many of his fellow Whedon alumni, Alexis has done his share of animated voice-over work, including roles in *Justice League Unlimited*, *All-Star Superman*, and *Robot Chicken*. Alexis and Alyson married in 2003 and have two children.

IN MEMORIAM

The family involved in the creation of both *Buffy the Vampire Slayer* and *Angel* has lost several dear friends in the years since *Buffy* went off the air. Here, we pay tribute to three of them.

ROBIN SACHS (ETHAN RAYNE) (1951–2013)

"Robin and I spent a lot of time together. He was very funny, very witty, very dry. We had great fun, especially in the episode where he turns me into the Fyarl demon, and we're drinking and he slips me a mickey. I really enjoyed that. When we did conventions together, we were always put together because we were sort of a similar generation. I always felt that he had that slight sadness that expats sometimes have when they find themselves creating a life abroad. But he had a wicked sense of humor. I was very fond of him and very sad to say good-bye."
—Anthony Stewart Head

"Robin Sachs was one of the funniest people I've ever met. I'd see him all the time at *Buffy* conventions and his Q and A's were so hilarious I'd make sure I'd go see him work the room. A terrific guy and a great talent."
—Danny Strong

"Robin and I became friends one long convention weekend, and maintained that friendship until his passing. He was charming as hell, of course, but also a kind, intelligent, down-to-earth man who always put those around him at ease, which is itself a rare talent. The world needs more like him."
—Christopher Golden

"I remember Robin as very intelligent and bright. A sweet, gentle soul."
—Cynthia Bergstrom

ANDY HALLETT (LORNE, THE HOST—ON *ANGEL*) (1975–2009)

"Andy was a family friend and a luminous spirit. The role of Lorne was created not just for, but because of, him. He was nuts. It got the better of him, but he was so dear and delightful and absolutely unique. I've pawned phrases off him that I use every day. He should stop fucking around and come back."
—Joss Whedon

"Andy was a gentle, lovely soul. I first met him when he was Joss's home-based assistant. Later I was happy to learn that he was cast in the role he inspired—The Host on *Angel* (later renamed Lorne). About my favorite experience while consulting on *Angel* was writing the Las Vegas episode 'The House Always Wins.' I spent time with Andy in the recording studio as he laid down his vocal tracks for Lorne's Vegas act. I'd never seen him happier. It was a dream come true for him, and he never stopped thanking me for helping to make it happen."
—David Fury

"Andy was a doll. I had him in the first film I directed, *Chance*, and he was so much fun. He had the biggest heart and really cared about fans and loved his friends and family so deeply. His death was a tragedy. A terrible, terrible loss."
—Amber Benson

"Andy Hallett had a beautiful soul. A true artist in every sense of the word."
—Danny Strong

"Andy was one of those people who shines the brightest in any room. A great loss."
—Jane Espenson

"I remember dancing with Andy at one of our wrap parties. We had so much fun together. He was a great guy. Much love and light to him."
—Cynthia Bergstrom

JOHN VULICH (SPECIAL MAKEUP FX SUPERVISOR) (1961–2016)

"John was a dear friend and wonderful collaborator. During our association on *Buffy*, John was always supportive and kind, and I cannot stress how much he will be missed by an entire generation of artists he inspired."
—Todd McIntosh

FINAL THOUGHTS FROM THE CREATOR OF *BUFFY*

Joss Whedon

Twenty years after the TV series debuted, and twenty-five years after the movie, *Buffy* is firmly in the rearview mirror for you . . . or is it? New seasons continue from Dark Horse Comics, talk of reboots or continuations keeps popping up, and new generations of fans are being born every day. Is *Buffy* really in the past for you, or does it continue along with you in some way, like an ex who never quite stops giving you "that look"?

JOSS: "I don't think you ever stop creating your work in your head. Whether you're fixing it or furthering it. But it's not front-burner stuff. I want to do something new. Well, newish."

From the outsider's perspective, it seems like Joss Whedon can do pretty much whatever he wants these days. It helps to have written and directed two of the biggest box-office hits of all time. You go back and forth between these huge films and writing smaller films for other directors, and of course trying to save the universe by creating political ads during the 2016 presidential campaign. So if it's true that you can do whatever you want—or near enough—how do you balance out those wants?

JOSS: "I find the project that has to be next. Not easy to do, but I did. It's a movie unlike anything I've written . . . except that it is, in some ways, the *Buffy* story. I think everything I do will have an aspect of that."

Many of the writers and actors from this show have stories about fans who have come up to them to share stories about *Buffy* changing their lives—or quite literally saving their lives. I'm sure you've heard it a million times. What does that mean to you, and did you ever imagine the series could have that kind of impact?

JOSS: "I hoped the series would subtly worm its way into people's psyches, and they would never know how it helped them. Turns out 'subtle' is not in my repertoire. When somebody says it affected them—or, more increasingly these days, their mom—it is every single time a shock and a delight. There's literally nothing an artist dreams of more, besides money. Money is always first. Ooh, delicious money. What was the question?"

***Buffy* trailblazed on TV and in pop culture, becoming a symbol of female empowerment. It seems a no-brainer now, but at the time, a TV series with a female lead—in which her male colleagues fell in line and treated her like their leader—was revolutionary. Was setting that example in your mind at all, or was it a happy by-product of your creative process?**

JOSS: "It was a deliberate act, but I didn't think of it as particularly revolutionary. It was how I saw the world, and I didn't think I could be the only one. I wasn't."

I think it's safe to assume that most Joss Whedon fans have seen *Buffy*, *Angel*, *Firefly*, *Dollhouse*, *Dr. Horrible's Sing-Along Blog*, and the Avengers films, but perhaps aren't as familiar with some of your other work. For instance, I didn't realize *In Your Eyes* existed until I just watched the trailer on IMDb, and now I've got to seek it out. If you had to name one project that's dear to you for your fans to seek out, from your early days of TV writing to animated films to comics to the smaller films you've done, what would it be and why?

JOSS: "*Toy Story*, obviously. . . . *Speed* is still fun. I thought *Parenthood* (the first version, with Ed Begley [Jr.]) was underrated. And my comics *Astonishing X-Men* and *Sugarshock* in particular."

So much time has passed. What are your favorite behind-the-scenes memories of your time making *Buffy*? I know there must be a thousand, but it would be wonderful if you'd offer us a few that perhaps you haven't talked much about that stay in your mind after all this time.

JOSS: "Shooting 'Once More, with Feeling' was a delight. Every day was a different song. Everyone was giving everything they had and [were] enjoying it, which after six seasons is pretty goddamn impressive. We knew it was bigger.

"And at the end of the series, after my last shot as director, I made myself climb onto the roof of the warehouse we shot in and take a moment. I never do that. But I stood up there and looked down on the Sunnydale street we'd built and told myself, 'Hey, I did this.' Didn't suck."

Everyone says that working on a long-running TV series is a lot like high school, with circles of friends and then those people you wish you'd hung out with more. Who do you wish you'd hung out with more while working on *Buffy*?

JOSS: "Oh, I got plenty of everyone, thank you. I just wish I could see them more now."

Despite that you wrote the musical episode of *Buffy* and *Dr. Horrible's Sing-Along Blog*, I suspect many fans don't realize how much music you've actually written, including the much-loved theme from *Firefly*, "The Ballad of Serenity." You've also written music for your films *Much Ado About Nothing* and *In Your Eyes*, a song for Amber Benson's indie film *Chance*, as well as—in your Disney days—a tune for *The Lion King II: Simba's Pride*. How important is music in your life, how did you start writing, and do you see yourself expanding your musical efforts in the future?

JOSS: "I hope to work in every genre of music—I think it's the highest art form. All of my dialogue is deliberately musical. That flow is crucial to how it fits in the mouth—and makes all of my work one insanely long aria, now that I think of it. . . ."

So we're back to Joss Whedon being able to do anything he wants. You've got a World War II horror film coming up. We're sure to know more by the time this book comes out, but what can you tell us about that, and what else do you have planned for 2017 and beyond?

JOSS: "There's not going to be anything beyond 2017. Didn't you watch the election?"

"Restless"
A Path to Premonitions

TELEPLAY WRITTEN AND DIRECTED BY JOSS WHEDON
ADDITIONAL COMMENTARY BY PAUL RUDITIS

Dreams have likely been studied and analyzed since the beginning of time. We share stories of our dreams with friends, loved ones, and therapists, looking for hidden meaning and secret desires while wondering what, if anything, they may have to do with our futures and waking lives. Dreams in *Buffy the Vampire Slayer* explore themes related to the characters and often have some kind of prophetic significance—none more so than the dreams in "Restless."

The journeys taken by Willow, Xander, Giles, and Buffy in "Restless" can be studied in many ways, taking up pages and pages of text exploring the dream imagery, its cultural significance, or its character development. For in-depth insight into what Joss Whedon was thinking as he wrote and directed this episode, there is no better source than the season four DVD with his commentary detailing the motifs he wanted to explore. The episode itself is a unique piece of television, but when looked at as part of the whole, it becomes clear that "Restless" lays the groundwork for everything to come in seasons five, six, and seven.

The dreams in the story delve into the characters' psyches and give just a glimpse of the journeys that will be explored throughout the rest of the series. Whether intentional or not, almost every page of the script includes some piece of foreshadowing of future episodes. What follows is an analysis of the pages from the shooting script (updated to include dialogue from the aired episode) and how the themes and images therein will play out over the rest of the series—an analysis written with the fortunate gift of hindsight, having seen the series through to its end. Varying from the painfully obvious to the more extreme stretches of coincidence, we will explore "Restless" as a prophecy of the show itself.

BUFFY THE VAMPIRE SLAYER

"RESTLESS"

TEASER

Previously on *Buffy*, the gang drifted apart throughout season four while Buffy became more involved with Riley and the Initiative. The part-man, part-demon, part-machine Adam worked, with Spike as his accomplice, to divide the Scoobies. In the end Willow, Xander, Giles, and Buffy magically joined together their strengths—Willow's spirit, Xander's heart, Giles's mind, and Buffy's body—so Buffy could take on Adam. The following comes as a result of that spell. . . .

1 INT. BUFFY'S FOYER/DINING ROOM—NIGHT

Buffy is at the door saying good-bye to Riley. Willow and Giles are in the dining room, Giles standing near enough to make conversation, not near enough to intrude.

> BUFFY
> Are you sure you'll be all right. Cause I could be there in the morning—

> RILEY
> It's just a debriefing. They're not gonna make me disappear, and they're not pinning anything on me. I got Graham and a lot of the guys testifying I'm the reason they're alive. I might actually get out of this with an honorable discharge.

> GILES
> In return for your silence, no doubt.

> RILEY
> Oh yeah. Having the inside scoop on the administration's own Bay of Mutated Pigs is definitely an advantage.

> WILLOW
> It's like you're blackmailing the government!
>   (off Riley's look)
> In a patriotic way . . .

                    RILEY
                (to Buffy)
          I'll call you when it's over.

They kiss.

Xander and Joyce emerge from the kitchen. Xander has a bowl of popcorn, Joyce a tray of drinks and snacks.

                    XANDER
          Dinner is served! My very own recipe.

                    WILLOW
          You pushed the button on the microwave that
          says "popcorn"?

                    XANDER
          Actually, I pushed "defrost." But Joyce was
          there in the clinch.

                    RILEY
          You guys have fun tonight.
                (to Joyce)
          It was very nice meeting you.

                    JOYCE
          It was nice meeting you . . . finally.

He smiles at Buffy, closes the door.

                    JOYCE (CONT'D)
                (to Buffy)
          Did you notice how pointedly I said "finally"?

                    BUFFY
          No . . .

They move into

2. INT. BUFFY'S LIVING ROOM—CONTINUING—NIGHT

                    XANDER
          Let the vidfest begin!

                    GILES
                (to Joyce)
You sure you won't join us?

                    JOYCE
                (setting down the tray)
No, you guys have your fun. I'm tired . . .
I can't believe you're not exhausted—have you
even slept since . . .

                    GILES
Still feel a little bit wired.

                    WILLOW
Yeah, that spell, that was powerful.

                    BUFFY
I don't think I could sleep.

                    XANDER
Well, we got plenty of vid. And I'm putting in
a preemptive bid for Apocalypse Now. Heh?

                    WILLOW
Did you get anything less Heart-of-Darknessy?

As they talk, they settle. Buffy and Willow on the couch with
blankets, Giles in an armchair, Xander on the floor with pillows,
near the TV. Joyce leaves them and heads up the stairs.

                    XANDER (O.C.)
Apocalypse Now is a gay romp! It's the feel-
good movie of whatever year it was!

                    BUFFY (O.C.)
                (sternly)
What else.

                    XANDER (O.C.)
Don't worry, I got plenty of chick-and-
British-guy flicks too. These puppies should
last us all night.

```
ANGLE: THE TV

The FBI warning is on it. We move in, and up to a clock reading
9:46.

DISSOLVE TO:

9:53
REVERSE ANGLE: THE GANG

Fast asleep, to a man. Buffy snores prodigiously.

                                                    BLACK OUT.

                        END OF TEASER
```

ACT ONE

3 INT. BUFFY'S LIVING ROOM—NIGHT

We see our four passed-out heroes. Camera moves slowly in on WILLOW, to her sleeping face, and we

DISSOLVE TO:

> Willow's dream focuses on her development from shy high school geek to strong, independent woman. Although one might assume the dream deals with the "secret" of her sexuality, it is really about her fear that she will one day be revealed as the geek she was in high school. Though she will always have some inherent insecurity, the events at the end of season six will put aside those concerns for good.

4. INT. TARA'S DORM ROOM—DAY

Though you can't tell if it's day or night—the curtains are drawn and the room is lit only by the ambient glow of the Christmas lights. They are all we see at first, hanging out of focus as the camera finds Tara's face, in profile. She speaks almost in whisper, smiling thoughtfully. Lying on her stomach, on the bed.

> TARA
> I think it's strange . . . I mean I think I should worry, that we haven't found her name.

CLOSE ON: WILLOW

She is looking down at something, intent on it—we don't know what it is, nor her relation to Tara in the room. She glances up briefly.

> WILLOW
> Who? Miss Kitty?

ANGLE: THE KITTEN

In the corner, in extreme slo-mo (120 frames per), attacks a red ball of string, framed before a gold pillow.

ANGLE: TARA

Also watches the kitten.

> TARA
> You'd think she'd let us know her name by now.

>   WILLOW
>   She will. She's not all grown yet.

Season five will introduce Buffy's sister, Dawn, who is "not all grown up yet" either. Like Miss Kitty, Dawn does not let anyone know her true name, and the fact that she is The Key will be kept a secret at first, even from her.

>   TARA
>   You're not worried?

>   WILLOW
>   I never worry here. I'm safe here.

Although the dream reference to safety has more to do with Willow's proximity to Tara, it's interesting to note that Tara's bedroom will turn out to be entirely unsafe at the end of season five when Glory begins her final assault on the gang in that location.

>   TARA
>   You don't know everything about me . . .

This will prove true in "Family," in which Willow does learn more about Tara's secrets, including the fact that Tara mistakenly believes she is a demon. We had a hint of this secret in "Goodbye Iowa," when Tara purposely messed up a spell she and Willow were casting to locate demons.

>   WILLOW
>   Have you told me your real name?

>   TARA
>   (smiles)
>   Oh, you know that . . .

ANGLE: A CALLIGRAPHY BRUSH

As Willow dips it into a well of ink. We see Willow's face as she moves the brush to where she is writing, very intent.

>   TARA (CONT'D)
>   They will find out, you know. About you.

>   WILLOW
>   I don't have time to think about that. You
>   know, I have all this homework to finish.

And for the first time, we see the room in tableau: Tara lies naked under the covers, her back exposed and covered in fine writing; Willow dips her pen and continues the text to the small of Tara's back.

> The sensual image of Willow writing on Tara's back will be remembered in stark contrast to the scene where Willow's body is covered in writing in "Villains." In that episode Willow absorbs the Magic Box's books on dark magick to avenge the death of her love.

      TARA
Are you gonna finish in time for class?

      WILLOW
I can be late.

      TARA
But you've never taken drama before. You might miss something important.

> Willow starts taking drama at the opening of season five. This is important growth for her character, as she was horrified of being onstage in "The Puppet Show" and "Nightmares."

      WILLOW
I don't want to leave here.

      TARA
Why not?

Willow moves to the window.

      WILLOW
It's so bright . . .

> Again, this takes us to the end of season five. In "Tough Love" Glory tears away the wall to Tara's dorm room, letting in the bright light. It is also the point where Tara reveals Dawn to be The Key by comparing her to light.

ANGLE: THE WINDOW

As Willow pulls the curtain aside to reveal that outside is all DESERT.

> The desert will play a key role in the future of the series on several occasions. Most notably, it is the place Giles will take Buffy when they are trying to contact the spirit of the First Slayer. However, expanding on the dream's relationship with the end of season five, it is also where the gang flees to after Glory discovers that Dawn is The Key.

Light cuts Willow's face, races up Tara's back as she looks back toward the window as well.

>   WILLOW (CONT'D)
>   And there's something out there . . .

ANGLE: IN THE DESERT

Something moves, briefly, out of focus. A human shape, in grey and dirty rags, moving like an animal.

5 INT. UNIVERSITY HALL—DAY

Willow walks along, lost in thought. Passes Oz and Xander, who have been talking.

> **Continuity Note:** Oz left Sunnydale in "Wild at Heart," though he did return briefly in "New Moon Rising."

>   OZ
>   Hey.

>   WILLOW
>   Hi, guys.

>   OZ
>   Heard you're taking drama.

>   WILLOW
>   Uh-huh.

>   OZ
>   Tough course.

>   WILLOW
>   You took it?

>   OZ
>   Oh, I've been here forever.

She comes to a bank of lockers that are incongruously placed in the wall, starts her combination.

                    XANDER
          So, whatchya been doing? Doing spells?
                    (to Oz)
          She does spells with Tara.

                    OZ
          I heard about that.

The school BELL rings. Willow becomes a little unnerved by it.

                    WILLOW
          I'm gonna be late.

She gives up on her combination, hurries away. We hold on Xander and Oz, watching her go.

                    XANDER
                    (sheepish)
          Sometimes I think about two women doing a
          spell . . . and then I do a spell by myself.

6 INT. BACKSTAGE—DAY

Willow enters into a whirl of activity—the place is crammed with students in costume, obviously getting ready for an imminent production. To one side, at the back of the stage, is a bright, lemon-yellow backdrop, a painted sunrise.

   The "painted sunrise" seems a fairly clear foreshadowing of Dawn.

On the opposite side, at the front of the stage, is an enormous red curtain, which separates them from the audience. A girl dressed as a 20s FLAPPER is sticking her head through the middle to peek at the audience. Pinspots highlight portions of the stage, colored lights occasionally sweeping across the throng. It's disorienting, particularly to Willow, who wades in tentatively, looking for some kind of guidance.

The first person she recognizes is HARMONY, who is dressed as a milkmaid, hair in braids.

                    HARMONY
          Isn't this exciting? Our first production!

She hugs Willow with gleeful camaraderie.

                        HARMONY (CONT'D)
            I can't wait till our scene! I love you! Don't
            step on my cues.

                        WILLOW
            Production?

The flapper pulls her head back from the curtain—it's BUFFY. Full
outfit, short black bob and everything.

Like Harmony (and everyone else here save Will), she's almost TOO
excited, almost like a commercial for being here.

                        BUFFY
            Oh my God the place is packed. Everybody's
            here.
                    (to Will, excited)
            Your whole family is in the front row—and they
            look really angry!

                        WILLOW
            There's a production?

                        HARMONY
            Somebody's got stage fright . . .

                        WILLOW
            Isn't this the first class?

                        RILEY
            Well you showed up late or you'd have a better
            part! I'm cowboy guy!

He is, in fact, sporting a dude-ish cowboy getup just as doofy as
his grin.

                        BUFFY
                    (to Will)
            Your costume is perfect.
                    (conspiratorially)
            Nobody's gonna know the truth. You know, about you.

Although Joss Whedon notes that this dream is about Willow's past geekiness, and it may also seem to be about her sexuality to some extent, there is also another truth she will keep secret as the series evolves. Throughout season six, Willow will delve deeper and deeper into dark magick, beginning with the spell to revive Buffy. She does manage to keep the truth on that issue from her friends until it becomes almost too late.

>
> WILLOW
> Costume?
>
> BUFFY
> You're already in character. I should have done that.

Staying for a moment with the theme of Willow hiding her magick, she is "already in character" in that her powers are already growing, though none of her friends is aware just how much.

>
> WILLOW
> But how come there's a—I mean, I was given to understand that a drama class would have a, you know, drama class. We haven't even rehearsed—
>
> HARMONY
> Well maybe some people haven't . . .
>
> RILEY
> (aside, to Harmony)
> I showed up on time so I got to be cowboy guy.
>
> WILLOW
> I just think it's really early to be putting on a play. I don't even know what—
> (panics)
> This isn't <u>Madame Butterfly</u>, is it? Because I have a whole problem with opera.

Continuity Note: Willow refers back to her dream from the episode "Nightmares," in which she was thrown onstage to perform in an opera she didn't know.

Giles rushes in, clearly in charge of this production. Claps his hands and addresses the troupe.

>
> GILES
> All right, everyone, pay attention. In just a few moments that curtain is going to open on our very first production. Everyone that

>   Willow has ever met is out in that audience,
>   including all of us. That means we have to
>   be perfect. Stay in character, remember your
>   lines, and energy energy energy. Especially in
>   the musical numbers.

"The musical numbers" seems a definite reference to the upcoming musical episode, "Once More, with Feeling," in which the energy in those musical numbers leads people to spontaneously combust. Interesting too is the fact that of all the major characters in that episode, Willow is the one who sings the least (though that had more to do with an actor request than plot development).

As he speaks, and Willow grows more and more unnerved, she notices

ANGLE: THE FIGURE FROM THE DESERT

Moving silently and quickly beyond the edge of the crowd. We see it only in glimpses, but slightly better than we did before. We won't catch all of this now, but: It's a woman. She appears to be in soiled rags, not unlike a mummy's. Black hair in coarse dreds—through neglect, not fashion. Face painted in colored clay. Long, almost clawlike nails.

We'll call her THE PRIMITIVE.

She carries a long, jagged blade. (Incredibly different from the blade carried by the villain in episode 22 of ANGEL, really I can't stress this enough.)

> Continuity Note: The script refers to the Angel season finale, "To Shanshu in LA," which aired immediately following this episode.

>   WILLOW
>   (whispers)
>   Did you guys see—
>
>   GILES
>   Remember, acting isn't about behaving. It's
>   about hiding. The audience wants to find you,
>   they want to strip you naked and eat you alive
>   so HIDE.

This last line of dialogue is just teeming with potential reference to the future. Aside from referencing Willow "hiding" her magick abuse, it also suggests the scene in which she finally reveals herself when she, quite literally, rips Warren's skin (or hide) off and kills him in "Villains." The line takes on an even more literal meaning when applied to the episode "Same Time, Same Place": Willow is paralyzed by the Gnarl, and her own hide is stripped away piece by piece as she is eaten alive, while her powers hide her from her friends because she is too ashamed to see them.

Harmony has gone VAMP and is trying to bite Giles, craning at various angles to get a better purchase on his neck. He swats at her as at a buzzing insect as he continues:

> GILES (CONT'D)
> Stop that. Costumes. Sets. The things that you . . . you know, things, you hold them and you touch them . . . you use them.
>
> HARMONY
> Props?
>
> GILES
> No . . .
>
> RILEY
> Props.
>
> GILES
> Yes. It's all about subterfuge.
> (to Harmony)
> That's very annoying.
> (to the company)
> Now get out there, lie like dogs and have a wonderful time. If we can stay in focus, keep our heads and if Willow can stop stepping on everyone's cues I know this will be the best production of <u>Death of a Salesman</u> we've ever done.
> (to Harmony)
> Stop it.
> (to the company)
> Good luck, everyone. Break a leg.

He bustles off and everyone begins talking at once: the nervous excitement of just-before-curtain. Willow looks around her, completely cut off from the energy—a fact that is highlighted when all the SOUND DIES OUT, though everyone continues chattering.

Willow makes her way slowly to the edge of the stage. She looks around, nervous about seeing the figure in rags again. She looks in the wings and sees:

ANGLE: THE CHEESE MAN

A skittish, balding, bespectacled little fellow in an old woolen suit. A voice not unlike Peter Lorre's. He says softly, conspiratorially:

> CHEESE MAN
> I've made a little space for the cheese slices . . .

TILT DOWN to see a row of American cheese slices on a small wooden table. Tilt back up as the Cheese Man smiles, hungry for approval.

Willow looks back at the bustling (still silent) crowd, moves slowly toward the edge of the red curtain. There are in fact two curtains, both red, about two feet apart. Willow hesitates a moment, then moves slowly between them, the camera following her, curtains billowing past lens on either side as she is enveloped.

7 BETWEEN THE CURTAINS

She journeys a while in this intimate space—it seems to go on a long while. Finally she finds Tara standing, waiting for her. They speak, voices low.

> TARA
> Things aren't going very well.

> WILLOW
> Well, NO. This drama class is just, I think they're really not doing things in the proper way, and now I'm in a play and my whole family's out there and why is there a cowboy in <u>Death of a Salesman</u> anyway?

> TARA
> You don't understand yet, do you.

> WILLOW
> Is there something following me?

                              TARA
          Yes.

                             WILLOW
          Well what should I do? The play's gonna start
          soon and I don't even know my lines!

                              TARA
          The play's already started. That's not the
          point.

Again, if we choose to look at this dream in terms of Willow's future magick abuse, one could infer that the reference to the fact that "the play's already started" is a comment on the powerful spell Willow cast to combine the gang's essences. In the future both Tara and Giles will warn her that she's doing too much dabbling.

8 ANGLE: ON STAGE

We see the play in progress. We are wide, taking in the proscenium. It is lit old style, from below. To the right is a plush divan, the only set dressing. On it is draped Buffy, smoking from a cigarette holder with languid boredom.

Harmony stands in the middle of the stage holding her milk pails on an old-fashioned cross-beam-yoke-type-thing, look I can't remember what they're called, I'm not like Joe Dictionary, okay?

Riley enters, from the left. Speaks, as they all do, in a big ol' stage voice.

                             RILEY
          Why hello, little lady. Can I hold those milk
          pails for you?

                            HARMONY
          Why thank you, but they are not very heavy.
          Why have you come to our lonely small town,
          which has no post office and very few exports?

                             RILEY
          I've come looking for a man.
                    (ominously, to the audience)
          A sales-man.

9 ANGLE: WITHIN THE CURTAINS

Tara and Willow continue to speak.

        TARA
  Everyone's starting to wonder about you . . .
  the real you. If they find out, they'll punish
  you. I can't help you with that.

Following Willow's time as Dark Willow, she does worry that Giles and the coven of witches in England, as well as her friends in Sunnydale, will punish her for her actions.

        WILLOW
  What should I . . . What's after me? Is it
  something I forgot to do? Was I supposed to—

        TARA
  Shhh . . .

She looks around, worried. Willow does also. Things seem to be moving around them, indistinct whispers buzzing by their ears.

10 ANGLE: ON STAGE

This time we are close on Buffy and Riley as Buffy spews a rapid-fire, venomous monologue to the unfeeling cowboy man.

In the background, Harmony is sitting on the divan in tears. A man (high school actor boy) in a black suit lies dead on the stage. Somehow, all of this is in focus.

        BUFFY
  What else could I expect from a bunch of low-
  rent, no-account hoodlums like you—hoodlums!
  Yes. I mean you and your friends, your whole
  sex, throw 'em all in the sea for all I care,
  throw 'em in and wait for the bubbles. Men,
  with your groping and spitting, all groin no
  brain three billion of ya passin' around the
  same worn-out urge. Men. With your . . . sales.

Though it was likely unintentional on Joss Whedon's part, the *Death of a Salesman* play in the dream is an interesting parallel to the events of the final season. The ultimate evil of The First appears in the guise of dead bodies, like the one lying on the stage, when a preacher with a western drawl, Caleb, comes to the "one-Starbucks town" looking for a

slayer. Buffy's vitriolic speech against men comes across as the female version of Caleb's misogynistic comments toward women. And finally, there's the fact that Willow is unsure of what part she plays in the fight against The First until the very end of the season.

11 ANGLE: INSIDE THE CURTAIN

Willow looks around, concerned at Tara's absence. The whispers continue around her. . . .

                        WILLOW
      Tara . . . Okay, this really isn't—

The sentence is not out before a blade SHOOTS through the curtain right in front of Willow's face. It is the ancient, blood-crusted blade of the Primitive.

Willow jerks back with a startled scream as the blade is withdrawn, plunged again just as close. She turns to flee the way she came—but the blade shoots out in front of her again. This time it pulls down, tears the curtain as an arm reaches in, swiping the blade at Willow.

Fingernails rip down another part of the curtain and the second arm claws at Willow, tries to grasp her, Willow backs away but the knife slices through her flailing hand, a deep gash on her palm as she stumbles, collapses into herself, crying out, waiting to be cut, to be carved.

A hand GRABS her, and she screams again—taking a good moment before she realizes it's not the Primitive.

She looks up to see Buffy, back in normal Buffy garb (and hair), reaching through one of the slashes in the curtain.

                        BUFFY
      Willow!

                        WILLOW
      Buffy, oh, God . . .

                        BUFFY
      Come on.

Willow rises shakily, steps through the curtain, Buffy holding on to her hand. Buffy looks around, tensed for action. They are standing in front of the curtain, but as they creep forward we see they are now in

12 INT. HIGH SCHOOL CLASSROOM—DUSK

The classroom is empty, lit by the last orange shafts of day. The curtain stands at the back, so Buffy and Willow move slowly to the front, ever alert, speaking in whispers.

> BUFFY
> Stay low.

Moving between desks. Buffy leads. She is all business, eyes front—almost brusque in her Slayerness.

> BUFFY (CONT'D)
> What did it look like?

> WILLOW
> I don't know. I don't know why it's after me.

> BUFFY
> You must have done something . . .

> WILLOW
> No! I never do anything! I'm very seldom naughty. I just came to class, and then the play was starting . . .

Willow's comments about being "very seldom naughty" will prove quite untrue by the end of season six, when her actions will be downright evil.

They've reached the front of the class. Buffy turns to Willow, really regards her for the first time.

> BUFFY
> Play's long over. Why are you still in costume?

> WILLOW
> Okay, still having to explain wherein this is just my outfit.

> BUFFY
> Willow, everybody already knows. Take it off.

                              WILLOW
                    No . . . No, I need it . . .

                              BUFFY
                    Oh, for God's sake just take it OFF.

And so saying, she grabs at an out-of-frame Willow, shoving her
to the front of the class and ripping the outfit from her. Buffy
stands, Will's outfit in hand, looking the girl over.

                              BUFFY (CONT'D)
                    That's better.

REVERSE ON: WILLOW

As we saw her once, a long time ago. Long, slightly duller red
hair. Plain grey frock that embodies the softer side of you know
what. (Uh, Sears, just in case you don't.) A hapless, almost sick
expression of embarrassment. She stands by the teacher's desk,
looking at herself.

> **Continuity Note:** The "Sears" line refers to a comment made by Cordelia about Willow's outfit in "Welcome to the Hellmouth."
>
> At this point it is revealed that Willow's fear is of being her old self. Interestingly, when she does turn evil due to her abuse of magick, Jonathan—one of her old (geekier) friends from high school—is the first to comment in "Two to Go" that she "packed her own lunches and wore floods and she was always . . . just Willow." She too will note that the old Willow is gone.

3 REVERSE ON: THE CLASSROOM

The curtain is gone from the back of the class. Buffy stands at the
front, looking at camera with disinterested contempt.

                              BUFFY (CONT'D)
                    It's much more realistic.

She sits behind a desk and we see the class is in fact filled.
Among the students, all of whom eye us with contempt, are Xander,
Harmony, Anya, Oz, and Tara. Oz and Tara lean in close to each
other, as though they've been whispering for some time.

                              HARMONY
                    See? Is everybody very clear on this now?

                    ANYA
                  (laughing)
        Oh my God! It's like a tragedy!

                    OZ
                  (to Tara)
        I tried to warn you . . .

Tara smirks, leans back in to Oz.

                    ANYA
        It's exactly like a Greek tragedy. There
        should only be Greeks.

In Greek tragedy, it is often "hubris," or excessive pride, that brings down a hero. At the end of season six, Willow becomes incredibly boastful of her abilities and is eventually taken down when she arrogantly tries to end her own pain and everyone else's.

Willow tries to stand up straight, tries to get on with class. She is holding a sheaf of loose-leaf papers.

                    WILLOW
                  (reciting)
        My book report. This summer, I read <u>The Lion,
        the Witch and the Wardrobe</u> . . .

                    XANDER
                  (to the ceiling)
        Oh, who CARES . . . ?

                    WILLOW
        This book has many themes. One of the first—

It LEAPS into frame, knocking Willow to the ground. No one even reacts (of course) as Willow thrashes, fighting for her life against the Primitive. It hasn't its knife this time, just struggles to hold the panicked girl down.

                    WILLOW (CONT'D)
        Help! Help me!

ANGLE: THE CLASS

Does nothing.

CLOSE ON: WILLOW

As a gnarled and filthy hand closes around her throat. The head is lowered to hers—we see its mouth open, dirty brown teeth as its mouth closes over Willow's—then we hear a great RUSH OF AIR as the life is sucked out of Willow, her eyes widen and her skin goes sallow, gaunt, the life force sucked out of her—

13 INT. BUFFY'S LIVING ROOM—NIGHT

—and she lies, unwakening, gasping for air, choking, dying in her sleep.

                                                    BLACK OUT.

                    END OF ACT ONE

ACT TWO

14 INT. BUFFY'S LIVING ROOM—NIGHT

We are still on Willow, gasping, convulsing slightly. Pan over to find Xander sleeping. He jerks his head awake.

> Xander's dream is fairly straightforward in that his concern is basically about never getting out of his parents' basement and, more importantly, out of his old life and the trap of his parents' unhappy lives. He takes his first step toward this reality when he does move into his own apartment in "The Replacement." He will continue to struggle with his fear of becoming his parents up through the episode "Hell's Bells," but will finally grow more secure in himself by the seventh season.

                    XANDER
          I'm awake! I'm good. Did I miss anything?

WIDEN to reveal Buffy and Giles are wide awake, Buffy munching on popcorn as they watch what's on TV.

                    GILES
          Nothing much at all, really.

                    BUFFY
          Bunch of massacring.

Xander turns his attention to the TV.

ANGLE: ON THE TV

Is the movie. Vietnam flick. It consists of a haggard SOLDIER marching in front of a rear-screen-projection jungle.

> Continuity Note: Xander took on the personality of his soldier costume in "Halloween," and some of the knowledge of military tactics stayed with him.

                    SOLDIER
          We've got to keep going, men! We've got to
          take that hill.
                    (keeps walking)
          Damn this war!
                    (walks)
          Men? Oh my God, what's happened to my MEN!!!

                    GILES
          I have to say, I really feel Apocalypse Now is
          overrated.

                    XANDER
               (staring, puzzled, at the screen)
          No, no . . . it gets better . . . I remember
          that it gets better . . .

                    BUFFY
          You want some corn?

                    XANDER
          Butter flavor?

                    BUFFY
          New car smell.

                    XANDER
          Cool.

He reaches for the bowl as she holds it out. His posture puts him
right by Willow—he looks at her gasping.

                    XANDER (CONT'D)
          What's her deal?

                    BUFFY
          Big faker.

Xander takes a handful, eats as he watches the flick.

                    GILES
          Oh, I'm beginning to understand this now. It's
          all about the journey, isn't it?

                    XANDER
          Well, thanks for making me have to pee.

He gets up, heads upstairs.

                    BUFFY
          You don't need any help, right?

The concept of needing Buffy's help is a recurring theme in Xander's life. He struggles against it from early in the series, and Anya will even sing, "When things get rough he just hides behind his Buffy" in "Once More, with Feeling." As he continues to grow more mature, Buffy will come to depend on him more, particularly with regard to her sister.

                      XANDER
    I got a system.

Camera FOLLOWS him up the staircase.

15 INT. BUFFY'S HOUSE—UPSTAIRS—CONTINUING—NIGHT

Xander crests the stairs, is heading for the bathroom when he hears something, turns to look.

Behind him is Joyce's bedroom. It's dark, and it's from that dark that Joyce emerges, wearing a burnished red silk robe. Her hair is carelessly tousled, her expression warm, a little sleepy. She looks, well, kinda sexy.

                      JOYCE
    Hey.

                      XANDER
    Hey, Joyce. Mrs. Summers.

He moves toward her—he will continue to do so, slowly, throughout their exchange.

                  XANDER (CONT'D)
    We're not making too much noise down there,
    are we?

                      JOYCE
    Oh, no. Anyway, they all left a while ago.

                      XANDER
    Oh. I should probably catch up.

                  JOYCE (SMILES)
    I've heard that before.

She leans in the doorway, the opening of her gown sliding up her leg. Xander notices this, and it gives him pause—but both he and Joyce are very calm. Comfortable.

                    XANDER
          I move pretty fast. You know, a man's always
          after . . .

                    JOYCE
          Conquest?

                    XANDER
          I'm a conquistador.

                    JOYCE
          What about comfort?

                    XANDER
          I'm a comfortador, also.

                    JOYCE
          I do know the difference. I've learned about
          boys.

                    XANDER
          That's cool about you.

                    JOYCE
          It's very late. Would you like to rest for a
          while?

As she says it, the camera drifts off her, into the room, resting
on the moonlit bed. The covers are tossed open, rumpled and
inviting.

                    XANDER
          Um, yeah. I'd like you. I'm just going to the
          bathroom first.

A moment before he breaks eye contact with her—he's still drawn to
her—then he steps back, heads down the hall to the bathroom.

LOW ANGLE PUSH IN ON JOYCE, affectionately watching him go.

                    JOYCE
          Don't get lost . . .

16 INT. BUFFY'S HOUSE—BATHROOM—CONTINUING—NIGHT

He enters, shuts the door. Stands over the toilet, unzips his (out of frame) fly. A moment, and he turns toward camera.

REVERSE ANGLE: OVER XANDER

The bathroom turns out to be a large room in the Initiative.

A group of some fifteen scientists and soldiers are standing politely, watching Xander as though he were a museum exhibit.

A moment more.

> XANDER
> Okay, I'm gonna find another bathroom.

He says, zipping his fly back up. Camera leads him back into

17 INT. BUFFY'S HOUSE—UPSTAIRS—CONTINUING—NIGHT

Where he crosses the (now empty) hall and steps into Buffy's room, which turns out to be

18 INT. XANDER'S BASEMENT—CONTINUING

Only a couple of lights are on. Xander shuts the door behind him, starts across the room. About halfway, he stops. Hears something. Looks around. Nothing.

> XANDER
> (calling out)
> I didn't order any vampires . . .

He moves to the stairs, starts up. Stops.

ANGLE: THE DOOR

Something moves behind it. Scratches at it.

Xander stares, clearly frightened.

The doorknob turns—but the door is locked. The knob rattles as the person behind it begins to get frustrated.

> XANDER (CONT'D)
> That's not the way out . . .

The person BANGS on the door. Once. Twice.

                        XANDER (CONT'D)
    That's not the way out . . .

And very carefully, so his feet don't creak the stairs, Xander backs off the staircase. He heads back to the door he came in by, throws it open and splits.

19 EXT. PLAYGROUND—DAY

Steadicamming toward the playground. Swings, carousel, sandbox. Buffy sits in the sandbox, idly digging sand with a little plastic shovel. Giles and Spike (who is dressed in a tweedy suit kind of like Giles's) sit on the swings.

> Buffy's digging in the sandbox brings up two future scenes. The first is when she is forced to dig herself out of her grave, and the second is one of the final scenes of the series, when Sunnydale is sucked into the desert ground. In the final view of the town it looks like it has been swallowed up in a really big sandbox.

Xander joins the group, still a little thrown by his basement experience.

                        XANDER
    Hey. There you are.

                        BUFFY
    You sure it's us you were looking for?

She smiles secretively at Giles, who returns it. Xander is aware he's missed something.

                        SPIKE
    Giles here is gonna teach me to be a watcher.
    Says I got the stuff.

                        GILES
    Spike's like a son to me . . .

> This is the only scene that Joss Whedon notes in his commentary as being something they were able to pay off later in the series, although the themes explored in the dreams obviously allowed them to follow up on many other elements. This particular part of the dream comes back in "Tabula Rasa," in which the gang loses their memories and Spike—dressed in the same tweed suit—believes himself to be Giles's son.

The concept of Spike becoming a Watcher—while far-fetched—does also play out in a way when he regains his soul and tries even harder to work for the side of good in the coming seasons and on *Angel*.

>   XANDER
>   Well, that's good. I was into that for a
>   while, but I got other stuff going on.

He indicates the nearby road, and we see:

20 ANGLE: THE ICE CREAM TRUCK

Where Xander is handing out ice cream to a few kids.

21 XANDER

In the park, watches himself in the truck. Says to the others:

>   XANDER
>   Gotta have something. Gotta be always moving
>   forward.
>
>   BUFFY
>   Like a shark.
>
>   XANDER
>   A shark with feet. And much less . . . fins.
>
>   SPIKE
>   AND on land.

This too is a reference to the future episode "Tabula Rasa," in which Spike is on the run from a loan shark demon who actually looks like a shark and walks on land.

>   GILES
>   Very good . . .

Xander looks down at Buffy in her sandbox. Worried.

>   XANDER
>   Buffy, are you sure you want to play there?
>   Pretty big sandbox.

ANGLE: BUFFY

Is in the same position and the same clothes, but now she is sitting in the actual desert.

> BUFFY
> I'm okay. It's not coming for me yet.

Xander is still in the park—so is Buffy, for the rest of the scene.

> XANDER
> I just mean . . . You can't protect yourself from . . . some stuff.

> BUFFY
> I'm way ahead of you, big brother.

> XANDER
> Brother?

As their relationship grows, particularly in the seventh season, Xander will have even more of a brotherly presence in Buffy's life. In a way, she will appoint him as Dawn's big brother, as he is constantly looking out for the girl and effectively given guardianship of her in "End of Days."

She looks at him, for the first time her air of superiority drains away. They hold a serious look for a moment.

Giles and Spike are swinging higher, enjoying themselves.

> GILES
> Come on, put your back into it! A watcher scoffs at gravity!

Xander looks at Buffy.

From the ice cream truck, Xander looks at Xander. From his POV, we see the tableau of the four of them, Xander and Buffy not moving, Giles and Spike swinging as high as they dare.

22 INT. ICE CREAM TRUCK—DAY

A moment more of watching them, and Xander starts to the front of the truck. Anya sits in the passenger seat. The truck is ALREADY MOVING, the suburban streets going slowly by in the windows in what is pretty clearly REAR-SCREEN PROJECTION.

Xander gets into the driver's seat.

ANYA
Do you know where you're going?

XANDER
North. To the mountains. The highest peak, the one they call "100 percent scary plummeting death." The test of a man.

ANYA
Do you know where you're going?

XANDER
No.

ANYA
I've been thinking about getting back into vengeance.

And Anya will get back into being a vengeance demon following Xander's abandoning her at their wedding in "Hell's Bells." She won't stay a demon for even a full year, however, because her heart is no longer in it.

XANDER
Is that right?

ANYA
Well, you know I miss it, I'm so at loose ends since I quit and I think this is gonna be a very big year for vengeance.

XANDER
I don't know . . .

ANYA
I've been keeping close tabs on cultural trends—a lot of men being unfaithful—very exciting things happening in the scorned women market. I don't wanna be left out.

XANDER
Yeah, but, isn't vengeance kind of . . . depressing?

ANYA
(petulant)
You don't want me to have a hobby.

>   XANDER
>   Not a vengeance hobby, no. It's dangerous.
>   People can't just do anything they want.
>   Society has rules, and borders, and an end
>   zone. It doesn't matter if . . .

Through the end of this, he's become aware of some giggling in the back of the truck. He looks back to see:

ANGLE: WILLOW AND TARA

Are standing in the back, dressed kinda trampy. Very close to each other, whispering and looking at Xander.

>   XANDER (CONT'D)
>   Do you mind? I am talking to my demon.

The idea of Anya going back into vengeance and the fact that she is "his demon" is, again, a concept that will be explored through seasons five and six. He will sing about his concern for "marrying a demon" in "Once More, with Feeling" and further explore the fear when he meets her demon-friend Halfrek in "Doublemeat Palace."

>   WILLOW
>   Sorry.

>   TARA
>   We just think you're really interesting.

They giggle a bit.

>   XANDER
>   (bravado)
>   Oh, I'm goin' places.

>   WILLOW
>   I'm way ahead of you.

>   XANDER
>   Is that right?

>   WILLOW
>   Watch this.

She and Tara move closer—

ANGLE: XANDER

We hold on Xander, pushing in incredibly slowly, while the girls show him something. Whatever that may be, we hold on him for quite a long time, and he remains impressively calm.

The girls, having (however marginally) separated, smile at Xander.

                    TARA
    Do you wanna come in the back with us?

They look to the further, darker back of the truck. Xander looks interested, then slightly perplexed. He looks over at Anya. She is still looking out at the road as she says:

                    ANYA
    Oh, go on.

> In this dream Anya has no problem with Xander joining Willow and Tara; however, her real fears of losing Xander to Willow will be addressed in "Triangle."

                    XANDER
    I don't have to . . .

                    ANYA
    I'll be fine. I think I've figured out how to
    steer by gesturing emphatically.

She does, waving the truck from drifting off the road, as Xander heads for the back of the truck.

23 REAR OF ICE CREAM TRUCK

ANGLE: XANDER is framed in the open back window of the ice cream truck. The rear-projected town drifts by as he pauses, then he heads to the back of the truck. He has to squeeze between a few crates and sundries. He keeps going. As he gets further back, he has to climb on top of things. The space gets smaller, gets darker He's still moving back—now he's squeezing through a space the size of an air vent.

Finally the space widens, and he finds himself tumbling out and landing on the floor, the floor of:

INT. XANDER'S BASEMENT—NIGHT

He looks around him. A little pissed. No girls. He checks around the room . . .

PUSH IN ON: THE UPSTAIRS DOOR

As something big SLAMS against it.

Camera dutches on Xander as he looks up, truly frightened.

Trying for bravado, he cries:

                      XANDER
    I know what's up there!

More pounding. Xander heads for the other door again, slowly, looking back.

ANGLE: THE STAIRCASE

As the door SLAMS open and a thick black shadow is thrown against the wall.

Now Xander's terrified. He turns to go—and bumps right into the CHEESE MAN.

Xander starts back. The Cheese Man holds up a plate of American cheese.

                    CHEESE MAN
    These will not protect you . . .

We hear footsteps on the stairs. The shadow moves.

Xander moves as well, past the Cheese Man and out the damn door.

24 INT. SCHOOL HALL—DAY

Or possibly night. Or possibly—why is everything so GREEN? Flat, green light fills the entire place, not that Xander notices. He is too busy moving through the crowd (it's fairly busy in here), looking ahead, looking behind him.

ANGLE: BEHIND HIM

Hidden by the crowd, but visible in glimpses, the PRIMITIVE is following him.

Xander pushes ahead until he sees Giles, moves to him.

>   XANDER
>   Giles!
>
>   GILES
>   Xander! What are you doing here?
>
>   XANDER
>   What's after me?
>
>   GILES
>   It's because of what we did. I know that.
>
>   XANDER
>   What we did?
>
>   GILES
>   The others have all gone ahead. Now listen
>   carefully. Your life may depend on what I am
>   about to tell you. You need to get to—

And at this moment, as Giles continues to speak, he is suddenly DUBBED INTO FRENCH. We can see him talking, but we can't understand a word any more than Xander can, unless we speak French, in which case la-di-da aren't we intellectual, I'm not Joe DICTIONARY, all RIGHT?

Continuity Note: Willow spoke French in Buffy's first dream in "Surprise."

>   GILES (CONT'D)
>   (French dubbing over:)
>   —the house where we're all sleeping. All your
>   friends are there having a wonderful time
>   and getting on with their lives. The creature
>   can't hurt you there.
>
>   XANDER
>   What? Go where? I don't understand.
>
>   GILES
>   (still dubbed)
>   Oh for God's sake, this is no time for your
>   idiotic games!

Anya rushes to them, worried. And dubbed.

                        ANYA
                 (with the dubbing)
    Xander! You have to come with us now!
    Everybody's waiting for you!

Although this line is intended to be about Xander's fear of being left behind, it's also interesting when viewed as referring to all the guests at his wedding waiting for him to arrive, particularly since Giles is one of the people not at the wedding, and therefore not waiting for him.

                        GILES
                     (dubly)
    That's what I've been trying to tell him.

                        XANDER
    Honey, I don't—I can't hear you . . .

Anya grabs his arm, starts dragging him.

                        ANYA
                     (dubbage)
    It's not important. I'll take you there.

                        XANDER
    Well, wait. Where are we going?

She just pulls, and Giles grabs an arm and pulls as well. Then a student starts helping. Then an Initiative soldier, Xander looking around confused, resisting as more and more students and soldiers grab hold of him, they hold him and turn him upside down, the camera also spinning upside down, he is calling out:

                    XANDER (CONT'D)
    Hey! Let go! Hey!

—as they hold his legs, his head and arms dragging on the ground, him calling for help that won't come.

25 INT. KURTZ'S SLEEPING QUARTERS—NIGHT

It's very dark. A fire burning in the background provides the only real illumination. A man lies on a cot in an alcove, almost entirely in blackness. Xander is led in by an Initiative soldier with a rifle. He makes Xander get on his knees before the alcove, then retires into the background.

If any of this seems familiar, it's because you've watched <u>Apocalypse Now</u> way too many times. If you haven't, you should—as much as possible, this scene should resemble the first meeting between Willard and Kurtz.

And though he will remain in darkness for a portion of the scene, and only be revealed in glimpses, it will be clear to some the moment he speaks that our "Kurtz" is PRINCIPAL SNYDER. He doesn't move, just lies there, his voice finally coming from the darkness:

>   SNYDER
>   Where you from, Harris?
>
>   XANDER
>   Well, the basement, mostly.
>
>   SNYDER
>   Were you born there?
>
>   XANDER
>   Possibly.

Snyder sits up, face still mostly in darkness.

>   SNYDER
>   I walked by your guidance counselor's office
>   one time, a bunch of you were sitting there,
>   waiting to be . . . shepherded, to be guided.
>   You and the other problems, glassy-eyed,
>   slack-jawed, I remember it smelled like dead
>   flowers. Like decay, and it hit me, yes, that's
>   what it is; the hope of our nation's future is
>   a bunch of mulch.

In the seventh season Buffy will be hired as a counselor at the new Sunnydale High.

>   XANDER
>   You know, I never got the chance to tell you
>   how glad I was you were eaten by a snake.

Continuity Note: This occurred in "Graduation Day, Part Two."

Snyder takes a shallow wooden bowl, dribbles water on the dome of his head as he continues.

                    SNYDER
        Where are you heading?

                    XANDER
        Well, I'm supposed to meet Tara and Willow . . .
        and possibly Buffy's mom . . .

                    SNYDER
        Do you know why they sent you here?

                    XANDER
        Not "sent" so much as "manhandled," but . . .
        no.

                    SNYDER
        Your time is running out.

                    XANDER
        No, I'm in my prime. This is prime time.

Snyder runs his hand over his head, slowly. Still looking down.

                    SNYDER
        Are you a soldier?

                    XANDER
        I'm a comfortador.

For the first time, Snyder really brings his face into the light, eyeing the boy with distant contempt.

                    SNYDER
        You're neither. You're a whipping boy, raised
        by mongrels, and set on a sacrificial stone.

Though Xander will not be "sacrificed," of the gang he will have the most personal sacrifice when he loses an eye to the cause in "Dirty Girls."

                    XANDER
        I'm getting a cramp . . .

He hears something. Looks around, then rises, slowly, backs away to find himself in

26 EXT. GILES' COURTYARD—NIGHT

He looks around, and we see:

ANGLE: THE ENTRANCE

The Primitive is just coming around the corner, walking on her knuckles like an ape.

Xander watches a moment more, then we hear a panther's ROAR, and Xander—

(NOTE: This is the beginning of a rather epic steadicam shot)—bails.

He moves into:

27 INT. GILES' APARTMENT—CONTINUING

Where Giles, Buffy and Anya are all looking at a passed-out and slightly convulsing Willow.

> GILES
> It's even more serious than I thought.

> BUFFY
> I can fight anything, right?

This is a question that will continue to be raised throughout seasons five, six, and seven as Buffy tries to learn more about her abilities. She will finally realize the extent of her powers when she knows she can beat The First in "Chosen."

> ANYA
> Maybe we should slap her.

Xander doesn't stop, keeps going, looking behind him, into Giles' hall, turns the corner into Buffy's hall, students ignoring him as he starts to walk even faster, very worried, he's almost at Buffy and Willow's room when the Primitive leaps into the hall from Giles' hall, Xander ducks into

INT. BUFFY AND WILLOW'S DORM ROOM—CONTINUING

                    XANDER
          Buffy?

But no one is there, he's increasingly freaked, throws open
Willow's closet door and bolts in, the CAMERA FOLLOWS HIM as he
works further into the closet, it turns left, a narrow wooden
corridor, Xander moves swiftly through it, still throwing looks
back, the corridor winds a bit and finally opens out onto (you
guessed it)

28 INT. XANDER'S BASEMENT—CONTINUING

You did guess it, didn't you?

(The steadicam shot ends.) Xander looks around—this is the worst.
And the POUNDING on the door upstairs has gotten louder. Xander
is compelled to move toward it, to the bottom of the stairs, to
look up.

                    XANDER
                  (whispers)
          That's not the way out . . .

ANGLE: THE DOOR: BURSTS open, a silhouetted figure of a burly man
standing at the entrance.

                    MAN
          What the Hell is wrong with you? You won't
          come upstairs?

                    XANDER
          I'm sorry . . .

                    MAN
          What are you, ashamed of us? Your mother's
          crying her guts out!

                    XANDER
          You don't understand . . .

The figure stomps down the stairs toward him.

                    MAN
          No, YOU don't understand! Line ends here, with
          us! You're not gonna change that. You haven't
          got the HEART.

Xander's dream father is more physically imposing than his real father turns out to be, as evidenced in "Hell's Bells." However, it's interesting to see how Xander imagines his father to be in his mind.

The comment that the "line ends here, with us" is another possible reference to Xander's abandonment of Anya at the altar. In doing so, Xander also loses the opportunity to continue the Harris line by raising a family. The false future he will see in "Hell's Bells" indicates that the idea of raising children who might grow to be like the rest of the family is, in fact, one of his greatest fears.

```
ANGLE: XANDER

Has backed against the wall, is not even looking at the approaching
figure. On the last word a hand suddenly PLUNGES into XANDER's
chest. Xander looks up into the eyes of the Primitive.

ANGLE: XANDER'S CHEST

As his heart is ripped out of it.

29 INT. BUFFY'S LIVING ROOM—NIGHT

Xander convulses like he's been shocked, but does not wake up. The
camera holds on him a moment, then tilts up and moves deliberately
toward Giles.

                                                        BLACK OUT.

                        END OF ACT TWO
```

ACT THREE

30 INT. GILES' APARTMENT—NIGHT

ANGLE: A POCKET WATCH

Swings before us, catching the light. We hear voices, far off and echoey:

> Giles's dream exemplifies the conflict between his playing the father figure to Buffy and his wanting to go off to have a life of his own. This conflict will first be mentioned to Willow in "Buffy vs. Dracula" when he tells her that he is moving to England. Of course, he does not actually move until the sixth season.

                    GILES
You have to stop thinking. Let it wash over you.

                    BUFFY
                    (amused)
You don't think it's a little old-fashioned?

                    GILES
This is the way women and men have behaved since the beginning, before time.

> This scene is indicative of the renewed training that Buffy will ask to undergo with Giles at the end of "Buffy vs. Dracula." It is her request that will keep him in Sunnydale, and postpone his trip to England until the sixth season. Later, in "Get It Done," Buffy will go against the way the Shadow Men, who created the First Slayer, behaved back in "the beginning."

ANGLE: GILES AND BUFFY

We are as far from them as we can be, they are a tableau within the apartment, all the furniture gone save the chair Buffy sits in, primly, erect, Giles standing before her with the watch held before her, swinging. She wears a little sundress, he his woolly suit.

                    GILES (V.O.)
Now look into the light.

> The concept of going "into the light" is a familiar one from recollections of near-death experiences. This line could possibly foreshadow Buffy's death, which finally does allow Giles to go home. However, her resurrection brings him back, at least temporarily.

CLOSE ON: BUFFY

As the light gambols about her eyes, and she laughs, playfully—

ANGLE: GILES' ARM

As Buffy grabs it, pulls him along . . .

31 EXT. GRAVEYARD/FAIR—NIGHT

Buffy pulls him along, trying to get him to hurry. In her sundress, with her insistent attitude, she resembles nothing so much as a child. Giles' dress is casual, hip but not undadlike. The familial image is reinforced by the presence of OLIVIA, who is both pregnant and pushing an empty stroller.

                    BUFFY
          Come on! Come on!

They are walking through a graveyard, to be sure, but there is a bit of the state fair to it as well. Many standing crypts and caskets line the lane. Families occasionally pass them by, certain crypts have been set up as ring toss games and the like. It's not obtrusive (i.e. Not A Generic Scary Carnival Nightmare With Wide Angle Shots Of Carousel Horses Type Thing), there's just a comfortable level of incongruity.

Buffy continues to pull, Giles good-naturedly to resist.

                    BUFFY (CONT'D)
          We're gonna miss all the good stuff!

                    OLIVIA
          Does she always want to train this badly?

Continuity Note: Olivia was introduced as Giles's "lady friend" in "Hush."

Here we have an example of Buffy using her desire to train to pull Giles away from Olivia and his future life of leisure.

                    GILES
          It appears she never heard the fable about
          patience.

                            OLIVIA
                  Which one is that?

                            GILES
                            (tries to think)
                  You know, with the fox, and the . . . less
                  patient fox.

Buffy's impatience will become an issue in the final episodes of season seven, when she wants to rush headlong into the lair of The First against the protests of her friends and the Potential Slayers. Of course, she winds up going there on her own and is rewarded by finding the Scythe that is ultimately the key to their survival.

                            BUFFY
                  Ooh! Here! Can I! Can I!

                            GILES
                  Yes, go ahead.

She lets go his hand, moves to a stand (of crypt-like stone) that has balls set up, three to a pile, and a dummy mock-up of a vampire that pops up and moves around at the back.

Buffy takes a ball, waits.

The dummy pops up and a tinny, recorded voice cries:

                            VOICE
                  I'm a vampire!

Buffy throws a ball, it goes wide.

                            GILES
                  Buffy, you have a sacred birthright to protect
                  mankind. Don't stick out your elbow.

She tries again, nails it. Looks to Giles for approval. He looks peevish.

                            GILES (CONT'D)
                  I haven't got any treats . . .

Buffy turns to the vendor, who hands her a cotton candy. She digs into it.

                    OLIVIA
          For God's sake, Rupert, go easy on the girl.

                    GILES
          This is my business. Blood of the lamb and all
          that.
                    (to Buffy)
          Now, you're gonna get that all over your face.

Buffy turns—and her face is caked with mud. She looks wild and primeval, breathing hard through her nose. (NOTE: This close-up will be filmed separately, when Buffy is all muddy in act four.)

                    GILES (CONT'D)
                    (shocked, whispers)
          I know you . . .

ANGLE: THE CRYPT at the end of the lane. Spike is leaning out of it, waving frantically at them.

                    SPIKE
                    (stage whisper)
          Come on! You're gonna miss everything!

32 INT. SPIKE'S CRYPT—NIGHT

Giles enters, Olivia (who is already there) trying to fold the stroller without much success. (Buffy is no longer present.)

                    GILES
          Don't push me about, you know, I have a great
          deal to do.

He is speaking to Spike, who stands before a group of tourists taking pictures, posing and making faces.

                    SPIKE
          I've hired myself out as an attraction.

                    GILES
          Sideshow freak?

While there is technically nothing "freakish" about Spike being a vampire in Sunnydale, he will become more sideshow-worthy when he becomes one of only two known vampires to have a soul. . . .

301

                         SPIKE
              At least it's showbiz . . .

   . . . and moves to LA

Olivia has failed to fold the stroller. She is sitting on the floor, crying, the misbent thing in her lap.

Giles looks at her, unsure how to help, torn—he must go.

Asks Spike for advice:

                         GILES
              What am I supposed to do with all of this?

                         SPIKE
              Gotta make up your mind, Rupes. What are you
              wasting time for? Haven't you figured it all out
              yet with your enormous squishy frontal lobes?

                         GILES
                    (starting to walk)
              I still think Buffy should have killed you.

This too will become a bit of a recurring theme, leading to conflict between Giles and Buffy, especially when he takes part in Wood's plan to kill Spike in "Lies My Parents Told Me."

He moves down through the crypt, not sure where he's heading. Passes the Cheese Man, who has slices of cheese on his head, including two with holes ripped out over his eyes.

                       CHEESE MAN
              I wear the cheese. It does not wear me.

Giles stares at him a moment, then continues.

                         GILES
              Honestly, you meet the most appalling sort of
              people . . .

He continues walking and exits the crypt, camera leading him into:

33 INT. THE BRONZE—CONTINUING

It's busy, people bustling about in the usual fashion. Giles starts making his way through the crowd to the front.

```
ANGLE: XANDER AND WILLOW

Are sitting on the couch in Giles' living room—except of course
it's in the middle of the club, near the stage. They look worried,
going through the books on Giles' coffee table.

Camera moves up to find Giles coming from behind them. He reaches
the living room setup, sits in a chair.

                    GILES
          I'm sorry I'm so late. There's a great deal
          going on, all at once.
```

Giles will show up almost too late at the end of the sixth season when he returns to find that his young charges have gotten into dire trouble without him.

```
                    WILLOW
                  (peevish)
          Don't we know it. Only at death's door over
          here . . . Look at Xander!

Xander opens his jacket to reveal a big wet bloodstain in the
middle of his (ripped) T-shirt.

                    XANDER
          Got the sucking chest wound swinging . . . I
          promised Anya I'd be there for her big night.
          Now I'll probably be pushing up daisies in
          the sense of being in the ground underneath
          them and fertilizing the soil with my
          decomposition.
```

Xander fails to make it to Anya's "big afternoon" when he does not show up for their wedding. He also isn't there for her death in "Chosen," nor does he even find her body before it is sucked down into the ground with the rest of Sunnydale.

```
Giles looks up at the stage and sees:

ANGLE: ANYA

Her big night appears to be a stand-up routine. She stands at the
mic in the spotlight, reading a joke (from a sheet of loose-leaf)
that she seems to have no real understanding of.
```

ANYA
Okay. A man walks into the office of a doctor. He is wearing on his head, a . . . there's a duck. Is that right?

UNSEEN PATRON (V.O.)
You suck!

ANYA
Quiet. You'll miss the humorous conclusion.

Giles turns back to the others.

GILES
She seems to be doing quite well.

WILLOW
Do you even know this is your fault?

GILES
We have to think about the facts, Willow. I'm very busy. Have a gig myself, you know.

WILLOW
Something is trying to kill us. It's like some primal . . . some animal force.

GILES
That used to be us.

XANDER
Don't get linear on me now, man . . .

ANGLE: ANYA

ANYA
And the duck tells the doctor, "there's a man that's attached to my ass."

Huge laughter from the crowd. Anya beams.

ANYA (CONT'D)
See, it was the duck and not the man that spoke.

Applause. She heads offstage.

                              WILLOW
          Rupert, if we don't know what we're fighting, I
          don't think we have a chance.

He gets up as she is speaking and heads onto the stage. Straps on
his acoustic guitar and, to great applause, sings:

> Giles's singing the exposition is another piece of foreshadowing for the musical episode, "Once More, with Feeling." In that episode the important hidden truths are revealed through song, and the gang reaches the finale in the Bronze.

                              GILES
                             (sings)
          It's strange. It's not like anything we've
          faced before, yet it seems familiar somehow.
          Of course! The spell we cast with Buffy must
          have released some primal evil, that's come
          back seeking . . . I'm not sure what. Willow,
          look through the Chronicles. Some reference
          to a warrior beast . . . Xander, help Willow
          and try not to bleed on my couch. We've got
          to warn Buffy. I tried her this morning but I
          only got her machine. Oh, wait . . .

> Another form of machine—namely the Buffybot—will take over in "Bargaining, Part One" when the real Buffy is unreachable following her death.

But the mic goes dead. All the noise stops but for a feedback hit.
Disappointed AWWs from the crowd. Willow and Xander barely look up
from their books.

Giles takes off his guitar, looks down at the mic cord. He tugs at
it, then gets on his hands and knees, following it, pulling himself
along behind a stack of speakers and equipment.

The cord becomes tangled in another, and more, soon Giles is
following a maze of entwined cable, still on his hands and knees,
no one visible, just all this equipment around him, and all this
. . . cable . . .

ANGLE: THE CABLE

As Giles' POCKET WATCH falls out of his pocket onto it.
Giles stops. Weary dread on his face.

                        GILES (CONT'D)
                Well, that was obvious.

WIDER ANGLE: The Primitive is perched on a speaker right behind him. We see her silhouetted by an indoor LIGHTNING

FLASH. Blade in hand.

Giles doesn't move as she creeps down behind him.

                        GILES (CONT'D)
                        (quietly terrified)
                I know who you are. And I can defeat you. With
                my intellect. Cripple you with my thoughts.

ANGLE: THE TOP OF HIS HEAD

As she prepares to cut it open.

                        GILES (CONT'D)
                Of course you underestimate me. You couldn't
                know . . .

EXTREME CLOSE ON: GILES' FACE

as blood begins to wash down it from out of frame.

                        GILES (CONT'D)
                You never had a watcher . . .

This is the first specific clue that they are dealing with the First Slayer. Although the First Slayer will play a more important role in Buffy's dream, it is here we learn that she did not have a Watcher. We will come to find in "Get It Done" that she did have a sort of Watchers Council, in the form of Shadow Men who charged her with protecting the world against evil.

FADE OUT:

34 INT. BUFFY'S LIVING ROOM—NIGHT

Giles takes in a gasping breath. His eyes do not open.

                                                    BLACK OUT.

                        END OF ACT THREE

ACT FOUR

35 INT. BUFFY'S LIVING ROOM—NIGHT

Hey, it's Buffy's turn! Therefore, close on her as we hear:

> Buffy's dream exemplifies her confusion over her destiny and her role as the Slayer. In this sequence we learn it is the essence of the First Slayer attacking the gang in their dreams because they went against the role of the Slayer as a lone entity. Buffy fights against this idea—as she has done before—knowing that she is more powerful with her friends. Even though she defies the First Slayer's words, Buffy will continue to wonder about her powers and her destiny through to the end of the series.

>> ANYA (O.S.)
>> (fierce whisper)
>> Buffy, wake up!

36 INT. BUFFY AND WILLOW'S DORM ROOM—MORNING

Buffy wakes up in her dorm bed, looking over at:

ANGLE: ANYA across the room in Willow's. She clutches at the covers, pulling them up to her chin in her fright.

>> ANYA
>> Buffy, you have to wake up! Right away!

>> BUFFY
>> I'm not really in charge of these things . . .

> Buffy claims that she is not in charge of waking herself up, which will prove true when she dies and has to rely on her friends to "wake her up."

>> ANYA
>> Please wake up oh please!

>> BUFFY
>> (turning onto her back)
>> I need my beauty sleep, okay, so stop—

ANGLE: BUFFY'S POV

Right above her, hanging from the ceiling, face right near hers, is the Primitive. It ROARS in her face—

37 INT. BUFFY'S BEDROOM—MORNING

Buffy WAKES suddenly—it was only a bad dream . . . WIDEN to see she's in her bedroom at home. She has made a mess of the sheets in her nightmare.

REVERSE ANGLE: BUFFY

Looks at the mess of a bed from the doorway.

We find TARA standing next to her. Tara is completely poised, quiet—clearly on top of whatever's going on here.

> BUFFY
> Faith and I just made that bed . . .

> TARA
> For who?

A dream sequence in "This Year's Girl" saw Buffy and Faith making the bed. During the dream Faith comments that "little sis" is coming, but Buffy has much to do before that happens.

> BUFFY
> I thought you were here to tell me. The guys aren't here, are they? We were gonna hang out, watch movies.

It is fitting that Tara serves as Buffy's dream guide, as she is the one person Buffy will turn to in the sixth season when she feels disconnected from the world and her friends.

> TARA
> You lost them.

> BUFFY
> No, I . . . I think they need me to find them.

She looks at the clock by the bed:

ANGLE: THE CLOCK reads 7:30

Buffy looks worried about the time.

> BUFFY (CONT'D)
> It's so late . . .

> TARA
> Oh, that clock's completely wrong.

In the dream sequence in "Graduation Day, Part Two," Faith mentioned that Little Miss Muffet was "counting down to seven three oh." Though there has been much speculation over the meaning of this phrase, it is generally accepted as the number of days from that original dream to Buffy's death in "The Gift." Tara's comment regarding the clock being "completely wrong" could not only mean that the waiting time has been cut in half, but also that the death coming at the end of that time will not be Buffy's final rest.

```
She produces a deck of tarot cards, tries to hand it to Buffy.
```

Continuity Note: Tara hands Buffy the Manus card from the tarot deck. It is the card Willow used in their joining spell to represent Buffy's essence.

```
                    TARA (CONT'D)
          Here.

                    BUFFY
          I'm never gonna use those.

Tara moves closer, whispers in Buffy's ear:

                    TARA
          You think you know. What's to come, what you
          are . . . You really have no idea.
```

Thus we have the theme of Buffy's dream, as well as her journey from this point through the end of the series. Throughout season five she will try to discover the true nature of her Slayer power. In season six she will worry that her return from death has made her a demon. It is in season seven that Buffy will finally accept what she is and how the Slayer's powers truly came about. Dracula will start her on this journey when he states that their power is both rooted in darkness in "Buffy vs. Dracula."

```
ANGLE: THE BEDROOM

The bed is made now. It's very still.

                    BUFFY
          I gotta find the others.

                    TARA
          Be back before dawn . . .
```

Though the early-morning imagery has been hinting at this, here would be the first mention of Buffy's sister-to-be by name.

```
Buffy leaves.
```

A38 INT. UNIVERSITY HALL—DAY

Buffy walks through the hall, searching for her friends. She stops a passing student.

                        BUFFY
    Have you seen my friends anywhere?
            (looking around)
    They wouldn't just disappear; they're my very
    good friends.

The language in this section of dialogue does not fit Buffy's normal speech pattern. However, it does match the way the Buffybot will speak.

The student just walks away. Buffy continues on, a bit peeved at the no response. A few feet on she stops, looking over at the wall. She moves to it and we see that a small hole has been broken through, showing a glimpse of the dark, cramped space behind.

Inside that space is Joyce.

                   BUFFY (CONT'D)
  Mom?

                   JOYCE
  Oh, hi, honey.

                   BUFFY
  Mom, why are you living in the walls?

                   JOYCE
  Oh, sweetie, no, I'm fine here. Don't worry
  about me.

                   BUFFY
  It looks dirty.

                   JOYCE
  Well, it seems that way to you . . . I made
  some lemonade, and I'm learning to play
  mah-jong. You go find your friends.

                   BUFFY
  I think they're in trouble-danger . . .

Joyce laughs.

                              JOYCE
            Sorry dear. Sorry. A mouse is playing with my
            knees.

                              BUFFY
            I really don't think you should live in there.

                              JOYCE
            Well, you could probably break through the
            wall . . .

In Joss Whedon's commentary he admits that he hadn't intended to foreshadow Joyce's death in this exchange, but in hindsight it seems very much like she is entombed. Joyce mentions that Buffy could probably "break through the wall," but in real life Buffy will discover that she is powerless to get her mom out of her tomb. Looking at the scene as Buffy joining her mother in death would also foreshadow the Slayer's own passing. Like she does in this scene, Buffy will leave her mother behind in "Heaven" when she "breaks through the wall" herself to find the friends that bring her back from the dead.

But Buffy has caught a glimpse of:

ANGLE: XANDER—Rounding a corner.

Buffy moves after him.

38 INT. INITIATIVE—DAY

We are quite wide in the bright white space. Riley and another man sit at opposite ends of the glass conference table. The other man some will recognize as ADAM, but he is entirely human. Riley wears his Sunday suit, Adam something similar.

Buffy approaches slowly, from a distance.

                              RILEY
            Hey there, killer.

Buffy will have a difficult time in the coming seasons distinguishing her Slayer self from that of a "killer." In the first episode of season five, "Buffy vs. Dracula," Dracula will echo Riley by calling her that same name. Later, in "Intervention," the First Slayer would seem to support the idea when she appears in the form of a guide telling Buffy that death is her gift. This is something she will come to accept in "The Gift," although Giles tries to convince her otherwise. Of course, the interpretation of death being her gift will change by the end of that episode.

                    BUFFY
          Riley! You're back!

                    RILEY
          I never left.

But he will leave, and then come back.

                    BUFFY
          How did the debriefing go?

                    RILEY
          I told you not to worry about that! It went
          great. They made me Surgeon General.

                    BUFFY
          Why didn't you come and tell me? We could have
          celebrated.

                    RILEY
          Oh, we're drawing up a plan for world
          domination. The key element? Coffeemakers that
          think.

This could be a reference to The Key and how it is a necessary element for Glory's domination . . . or just a coincidence.

                    BUFFY
          World domination. Is that a good?

                    RILEY
          Baby, we're the government. It's what we do.

                    ADAM
          She's uncomfortable with certain concepts.
          It's understandable.
                         (to Buffy)
          Aggression is a natural human tendency. Though
          you and me come by it another way.

                    BUFFY
          We're not demons.

Like her struggle with being a "killer," Buffy will also worry about being a "demon" throughout season six when she comes back "wrong." The fact that Spike can hurt her even though he has the chip in his head furthers this concern.

                    ADAM
          Is that a fact?

                    RILEY
          Buffy, we've got important work here. A lot of
          filing, and giving things names.

                    BUFFY
                       (to Adam)
          What was yours?

                    ADAM
          Before Adam? Not a man among us can remember.

A voice sounds on the intercom:

                    VOICE
          The demons have escaped. Please run for your
          lives.

Demons will escape at the end of seasons five (when the dimensions blend together) and seven (when the Hellmouth opens), though Buffy will be there to stop them both times.

The lights go dimmer as Buffy looks at Riley, panicked. The men are all business.

                    ADAM
          This could be trouble.

                    RILEY
          We'd better make a fort.

                    ADAM
          I'll get some pillows.

He exits as Buffy stands there, too frightened to speak up.

We see a passel of demons approaching from behind, out of focus.

                    BUFFY
          No wait . . . I have weapons . . .

She reaches into her bag.

INSERT: HER BAG

is filled with mud. She sinks her hand into it, pulls it back. Drops to her knees in a panic, reaching into the bag and finding nothing but mud.

She looks at it on her hands. Brings them to her face. Slowly, she starts covering her face in it, putting on more and more.

The demons are long gone. She looks up at Riley, face now looking just a little like it was when Giles saw it. Animal. Riley backs away, a scolding look on his face.

> RILEY
> If that's the way you want it baby, I guess you're on your own.

As the dream indicates, Buffy and Riley will continue to have trouble connecting because they are too different. He will eventually leave her for real in "Into the Woods."

Buffy watches him go. The light on her changes again, daylight streaming in from the side.

Once again there is a reference to Buffy "going into the light."

She stands, heads toward it.

ANGLE: BUFFY'S FEET

As she walks, we see sand on the ground. Finally she's walking only on sand.

ANGLE: HER FACE

Is no longer muddy. The wall behind her gives way to rock, and finally we are

42 EXT. DESERT—DAY

Buffy walks past the Initiative wall and into the bright white desert, the flat, sandy vista spreading out forever. Camera arms up to find that Buffy stands atop a lone large sand dune.

Buffy will visit the desert again when she goes on a spiritual journey in "Intervention" and in search of the Shadow Men in "Get It Done."

She looks around, worried.

                              BUFFY
                            (whispers)
                 I'm never gonna find them here . . .

ANGLE: TARA

Appears opposite Buffy on the dune, walking toward her. She is dressed
in Indian garb, midriff and skirt. Again, preternaturally calm.

                              TARA
                 Of course not. That's the reason you came.

She stands a ways apart, the two of them regarding each other.

                              BUFFY
                 You're not in my dream.

                              TARA
                            (agreeing)
                 I was borrowed. Someone has to speak for her.

Though this foreshadowing certainly wasn't intentional, when The First tries to convince Willow that Tara wants to talk in "Conversations with Dead People," it "borrows" the image of another to speak for it.

                              BUFFY
                 Let her speak for herself. That's what's done
                 in polite circles.

As she says this, the Primitive appears right behind her.

Buffy is aware of her, but does nothing.

The Primitive circles her, slowly, sniffing her, assessing her.
Buffy is rigid, the Primitive all angles and motion, finally ending
up in front of Buffy.

This is not the last time Buffy will interact with an image of the First Slayer. The so-called Primitive will appear in future episodes, including "Intervention" and "Get It Done."

As this is happening, we cut between the two slayers as though they
are conversing, though it is Tara who speaks for the Primitive.

                          BUFFY (CONT'D)
                         (to the Primitive)
                 Why do you follow me?

                    TARA
          I don't.

                    BUFFY
          Where are my friends?

                    TARA
          You're asking the wrong questions.

                    BUFFY
                (calm anger)
          Make her speak.

                    TARA
          I have no speech. No name. I live in
          the action of death. The blood-cry, the
          penetrating wound. I am destruction. Absolute.
          Alone.

                    BUFFY (REALIZING)
          The Slayer.

                    TARA
          The first.

The Primitive stands erect at that, facing Buffy with defiant pride.

Buffy looks down, at her hand. Sees:

INSERT: The deck of tarot cards that Tara had tried to hand her. The top card is actually a bird's-eye view of the four friends asleep in Buffy's living room (CGI insert).

                    BUFFY
          I'm not alone.

The Primitive growls, snaps her teeth at Buffy.

                    TARA
          The Slayer doesn't walk in the world.

                    BUFFY
          I walk. I talk. I shop, I sneeze, I'm gonna be a
          fireman when the floods roll back. There's trees in
          the desert since you moved out, and I don't sleep
          on a bed of bones. Now give me back my friends.

The Primitive struggles to contain her rage, finally spitting forth:

> PRIMITIVE
> No . . . friends . . . just the kill . . . we are . . . alone.

As she says this last, the Cheese Man leans into frame, dangling a couple of slices invitingly.

> BUFFY
> That's it. I'm waking up.

> As with so many times before, Buffy does not play by other people's rules. She will make this same type of decision when she refuses the Shadow Men's "gift" in "Get It Done." This concept of breaking the rules will be most prophetic when she uses Willow's powers in combination with the Scythe to divide the power of the Slayer among all the Potential Slayers in the world so that she is truly no longer alone.

The Primitive LEAPS into frame, knocking Buffy back out of it. And they fight, briefly, the Primitive strong with primal rage, Buffy more sophisticated, the martial artist.

After a quick exchange Buffy comes up at the edge of the dune, saying:

> BUFFY (CONT'D)
> It's over.

The Primitive dives at her, tackling her and they both roll down the dune and we hard cut to:

43 INT. BUFFY'S LIVING ROOM—NIGHT

Buffy wakes up. Everything is the same as it was, except Buffy is lying in the middle of the floor. She raises herself, looks over at the gang—they are still sleeping.

Buffy is about to speak when the Primitive drops into frame right in her face and stabs her, bringing the knife down again and again . . .

She stops. Buffy looks pretty bored. There is no blood on her.

> BUFFY
> Are you quite finished?

She gets up, moves back to where she was sleeping. The Primitive stands, bewildered.

>   BUFFY (CONT'D)
>   You just have to get over the whole primal
>   power thing. You're not the source of me.

She sits, makes herself comfy.

>   BUFFY (CONT'D)
>   Also, in terms of hair care, you really want
>   to say "what kind of impression am I making in
>   the workplace?" 'Cause that particular look—

And in midsentence:

SMASH CUT TO:

A44 INT. BUFFY'S LIVING ROOM—NIGHT

She wakes, for real—gasping with the intensity of it. Looks about as the other four go through the same thing.

They look at each other, overwhelmed.

44 INT. BUFFY'S FOYER/DINING ROOM—NIGHT

Buffy and the others sit around the table, Buffy nearest the foyer, Xander with his back to the kitchen. They all look a little tired . . . and wired.

>   WILLOW
>   The First Slayer . . . wow.

>   XANDER
>   Not big with the socialization.

>   WILLOW
>   Or the floss . . .

>   GILES
>   Somehow, our joining with Buffy and invoking
>   the essence of the Slayer's power was an
>   affront to the source of that power.

> BUFFY
> You know, you coulda brought that up before we did it.

> GILES
> I did! I said there could be dire consequences.

> BUFFY
> Yeah, but you say that about everything.

Joyce enters from upstairs.

> JOYCE
> I'm guessing I missed some fun.

> WILLOW
> The spirit of the First Slayer tried to kill us in our dreams.

> JOYCE
> Oh. You want some hot chocolate?

A chorus of:

> ALL
> Yes please—that sounds nice—thanks, yeah . . .

> JOYCE
> Xander?

Xander turns to her and, suddenly remembering his dream, becomes quite uncomfortable.

> XANDER
> Yes? What, Joyce—dyeh, Buffy's mom?

> JOYCE
> Will you be my kitchen buddy again? Help me carry?

> XANDER
> Yes. Sure. Buffy's mom.

She exits. Giles looks at Buffy, who seems pensive.

                        GILES
            You all right?

                        BUFFY
            Yeah, I just . . . I think I might jump in the
            shower.

                        GILES
            You do seem a bit . . .

                        BUFFY
            Yeah. I guess . . . The First Slayer. I
            never really thought about . . . it was just
            intense. I guess you guys got a taste of that,
            huh?

                        XANDER
            Yeah, from now on, you keep your slayer
            friends out of my dreams, is that clear?

                        WILLOW
            She's not good for the sleeping.

Buffy rises, saying as she heads upstairs:

                        BUFFY
            Yeah, well at least you all didn't dream about
            that guy with the cheese . . .

She exits, leaving the others looking slowly up, at each other, very perturbed.

                        BUFFY (O.C.)
            Don't know where the Hell that came from . . .

45 INT. BUFFY'S UPSTAIRS HALL—CONTINUING

Buffy reaches the top of the stairs, heads for the bathroom. Stops, goes toward her room.

46 INT. BUFFY'S BEDROOM—CONTINUING

Buffy enters, stands in the doorway. The lights are off, but she can see okay.

ANGLE: THE BED

Quiet and neat.

Buffy regards it, regards the room. We hear:

                    TARA (V.O.)
    You think you know. What's to come, what you
    are . . . You haven't even begun.

Buffy stands a moment longer, looking into the dark.

She leaves. For a beat, we hold on the empty room.

                                          BLACK OUT.

                  END OF SHOW

ABOUT THE AUTHOR

Christopher Golden is the *New York Times* bestselling author of *Snowblind*, *Tin Men*, *Ararat*, and many other novels. He co-created (with Mike Mignola) two cult favorite comic-book series, *Baltimore* and *Joe Golem: Occult Detective*. As editor, his anthologies include *The New Dead*, *Seize the Night*, and *Dark Cities*. Once upon a time, he wrote a great many novels, comics, video games, and nonfiction books in the worlds of *Buffy the Vampire Slayer* and *Angel* and loved every minute of it. Please visit him at christophergolden.com.